Kerstin Fink

Knowledge Potential Measurement and Un

WIRTSCHAFTSINFORMATIK

Kerstin Fink

Knowledge Potential Measurement and Uncertainty

Deutscher Universitäts-Verlag

Bibliografische Information Der Deutschen Bibliothek
Die Deutsche Bibliothek verzeichnet diese Publikation in der Deutschen Nationalbibliografie; detaillierte bibliografische Daten sind im Internet über <http://dnb.ddb.de> abrufbar.

Habilitationsschrift Universität Innsbruck, 2003

1. Auflage Juli 2004

Lektorat: Ute Wrasmann / Anita Wilke

Der Deutsche Universitäts-Verlag ist ein Unternehmen von Springer Science+Business Media.
www.duv.de

Umschlaggestaltung: Regine Zimmer, Dipl.-Designerin, Frankfurt/Main
Gedruckt auf säurefreiem und chlorfrei gebleichtem Papier

ISBN-13: 978-3-8244-2183-1 e-ISBN-13: 978-3-322-81240-7
DOI: 10.1007/ 978-3-322-81240-7

Acknowledgements

Many people have helped to make this book possible. The contributions and creative ideas of Professor Friedrich Roithmayr, Chair of the Department of Information Systems at the Leopold-Franzens University of Innsbruck, were continuing sources of insight and intellectual guidance. His advice and encouragement were of special importance. I also give special acknowledgement to Professor Helmut Beran, Chair of the Department of Systems Research and Statistics at the Johannes Kepler University of Linz, for his extensive information and discussions on measurement. Special thanks go to Professor Dieter Ehrenberg, Chair of the Department of Information Systems at the University of Leipzig, for his valuable suggestions and contributions to this book.

I relied on facilities of Stanford University and my thanks go to all of the people who supported me at Stanford. Furthermore, I relied on the facilities of the University of New Orleans, Louisiana, where I conducted my case studies of CTL, DataSolve, and Resurgence™. I appreciate the interest and cooperation of the interviewed managers and knowledge workers of those companies. CenterAustria at the University of New Orleans gave me support and coordination help, and I express special thanks to Professor Gordon H. Mueller and to Gertraud Griessner for their overall assistance in this project. I also thank Bank Austria, Sony Austria, and SAP Austria for their support.

I deeply appreciate the support of University Research Professor Charles D. Hadley, Chair of the Department Political Science at the University of New Orleans, for his penetrating commentary on the manuscript and for his many suggestions for revision and restatement to improve the content. I also thank all of my friends and colleagues who helped me accomplish this book. Finally, I acknowledge a debt of gratitude to my parents for their continued encouragement and support.

Kerstin Fink

Contents

List of Illustrations

List of Tables

Abbreviations

AFS	Assurance & Financial Services
AI	Artificial Intelligence
AICPA	American Institute of Certified Public Accountants
APQC	American Productivity and Quality Center
BPM	Business Process Management
BSC	Balanced Scorecard
BZCs	Customers with zero or negative value to the business
C(M(t))	Conceptualisation of a Mental Model
C(t)	Conceptual Model of the System
CALL	Center for Army Lessons Learned
CE	Capital Employed
CEO	Chief Executive Officer
cf	certainty factor
CIO	Chief Information Officer
CIV	Calculated Intangible Value
CKO	Chief Knowledge Officer
COO	Chief Operating Officer
CRM	Customer Relationship Management
CVA	Combined Value Added
DAGs	Directed Acyclic Graphs
DCF, dcf_{ic}	Discounted Cash Flow
DIC	Direct Intellectual Capital
E	Energy
EAI	Enterprise Application Integration
ECM	Enterprise Content Management
EVA	Economic Value Added
GCRMTC	Gulf Coast Region Maritime Technology Center
h	Planck constant ($6.63 * 10^{-34}$ Js)
HC	Human Capital
I&CS	Information and Communication Systems
IAM	Intangible Asset Monitor

IC	Intellectual Capital
IN	Input
IVA	Intellectual Value Added
IVR	Intellectual Value Ratio
JIT	Just-in-Time
Js	Joule seconds
KCRM	Knowledge-enabled Customer Relationship Management
KE	Knowledge-Engineer
KM	Knowledge Management
KMS	Knowledge Management Systems
KP	Knowledge Potential
KW	Knowledge Worker
m	mass
$m^{(K)}$	knowledge mass
M(t)	User's Mental Model of the Target System
MCM	Market Capitalization Methods
MGCs	Most Growable Customers
MIT	Massachusetts Institute of Technology
MVA	Market Value Added or Monetary Value Added (McPherson)
MVCs	Most Valuable Customers
NOPAT	Net Operating Profit After Tax
NLP	Natural Language Processing
NPV	Net Present Value
OECD	Organisation for Economic Co-operation and Development
OLAP	On-Line Analytical Processing
OUT	Output
p	momentum
$p^{(K)}$	knowledge momentum
PV	Present Value
R&D	Research and Development
ROA	Return on Assets
ROI	Return on Investment
SC	Scorecard

sc	structural capital
SOCP	Ship Operations Cooperative Program
STVA	Structural Capital to the Value Added
$S_{p,i}$	Uncertainty for knowledge momentum
$S_{x,i}$	Uncertainty for knowledge position
t	time or target system
TF	Technology Factor
TQM	Total Quality Management
v	velocity
$v^{(K)}$	knowledge velocity
VA	Value Added
VACA	Value Added Capital
VAHU	Value Added Human Capital
VAIC™	Value Added Intellectual Capital
v_m	Stock market value
VTA, v_{TA}	Values of Tangible Assets
x	position
$x^{(K)}$	knowledge position
z	Standard Score

1 Research Framework

"To know is not to prove, nor to explain.
It is to accede to vision. But if we are
to have vision, we must learn to
participate in the object of vision.
The apprenticeship is hard."

(Antoine de Saint-Exupéry)

1.1 Research Problem

The management of knowledge has become a major research field in different disciplines in the last ten years [see for example DeCh00; Malh00; Neef98; Prus97; Rugg97; Whit02]. However, in recent years, not only *knowledge management*, but also primarily the *measurement of knowledge* [see for example HoBe01; Skyr98; Tiwa00] is developing into a new research field. Skyrme [Skyr98] sees the measurement and management of knowledge-based assets as one of the most important issues for knowledge organizations. As a result, new methods, new methodologies, and new tools have to be developed to measure the knowledge of organizations and of the knowledge workers. Skyrme employs the slogan "What is not measured, is not managed" [Skyr98, p. 5].

A range of quantitative measures - mainly money-based - is available to measure the value of a firm and its intellectual capital. The focus is primarily in the measurement of stocks or flows. Business measurements are the bases for decision making. Defining and measuring the value of a company are key strategic concerns in contemporary companies. In the knowledge-economy [Stew97], the value of the company's knowledge and its measurements are the key drivers for success. In the knowledge-based economy, the management and the measurement of intangible assets has become one of the most important issues. Historically, business focused on the measurement of tangible assets such as the return on investment, cash flow, and the cost of sales. In the recent years, the focus shifted towards measuring intangible assets such as customer satisfaction and the knowledge of the company personnel. In light of this transition, companies are trying to combine both financial and nonfinancial measurements to achieve optimal organizational well-being. Even at the beginning of the 21st century, knowledge management and measurement remains a "black box". There are many books, conferences, and articles dealing with knowledge in a broad sense, but the frameworks, methods or methodologies for measuring the knowledge of an individual and the knowledge value of a company remain few.

The Organisation for Economic Co-operation and Development (OECD) has introduced a new research agenda [OECD00] with the objective to improve the understanding of knowledge and to transform the term knowledge-economy from a slogan. In 1996, the OECD introduced the term knowledge-based economy [OECD96], while Drucker used the expression “The new society of organizations” [Druc92] or Steward talked of the “knowledge economy” [Stew97]. In 2000, the OECD identified a new research agenda about the management of knowledge and learning. Since knowledge is a human resource which is very “slippery” and always linked to the experience of a person who is the holder of knowledge, its management must be based on new strategic issues. The expert system movement of the 1980s already has shown how difficult it is to create rules that cover even narrow knowledge domains and how even more difficult it is to update and modify the knowledge structure. In organizations, knowledge often is linked to power, therefore the management of knowledge sometimes can be seen as a threat. The OECD research agenda [OECD00, p. 99] states that case studies of knowledge management at the firm or at organization levels are needed to set up benchmark criteria.

A second new OECD research area concentrates on the measurement of the knowledge and learning [OECD00]. Knowledge measurement systems can help policy makers identify where outcomes fall short of expectations. In the near future, it will be more important to calculate the amount of knowledge in specific sectors and the rate at which knowledge is produced with much more accuracy. The OECD describes the issues for the new research agenda on measurement as follows [OECD00, pp. 100-101]:

> *"Investigations has begun in several Directorates of the OECD into areas such as networks and clusters, which facilitate innovation, collaboration and the collective development of knowledge; ...the development of frameworks for measuring company level intellectual capital. ... Some of the challenges for the OECD will be to describe informal processes of the production of knowledge and learning that can explain performance. For example, can indicators of*

tacit knowledge be established? ... How can we measure the performance of learning organisations?"

The importance of measurement systems for knowledge also is pointed out by Pearson in *The Knowledge Management Yearbook 2000-2001* [Pear00]. To ensure that a company is successful, business, technology, and human elements must be integrated and balanced. A similar view is proposed by Koulopoulos and Frappaolo [KoFr00, pp. 418] who introduce a knowledge audit with the objectives of uncovering the definition of knowledge in an organization and of identifying the existing management practices such as hierarchies, communication structures or reporting processes.

Furthermore, there is an aspect of uncertainty associated with knowledge management and measurement. If we look at our daily reasoning processes, most of our decisions are based on uncertain premises, meaning that most of our action relies on guesses; we weight situations based on the conflicting evidence. In general, we have to accept the fact that uncertainty is a fact of life. Nature shows us that uncertainty exists from quantum to cosmological scales. For example, the weather forecast is a science in its own rights, but it is limited due to uncertainty. No matter how much computation and algorithms are used for modeling the weather forecast, it is too complex for specific statements. Complex systems, such as the ecosystem, the economy, society, and climate border chaos and order where the Nature is very creative. In the knowledge management environment complexity and uncertainty are combined forces influencing the system and making it difficult to predict an outcome. Uncertainty is responsible for the fact that the more a system gets complex, the less precise statements can be made.

Kilmann [Kilm01] is introducing the *"quantum organization"* as a new paradigm to manage organizational transformation in a world which is highly interconnected and where success depends whether the participants progress towards self-aware consciousness. This means, that the process of transformation in organizations requires that individuals develop a self-aware consciousness. The transformation for organizations has to be seen in the light of the shift from the old paradigm which Kilmann [Kilm01, pp. 17] calls "Cartesian-Newtonian Paradigm", to the new paradigm, the *"Quantum-Relativistic Paradigm"*. The traditional old paradigm[1] separates people from an outside, objective material universe. This worldview is influenced by the separation of consciousness and matter. The physical world exists on its own, and it is unaffected by human beings. This means, that the human mind has no effect on the nature of the physical reality. The old paradigm is underlying a deterministic certainty in the sense that objects are inert and only moved by external forces. Objects can be compared with a billiard ball for which position and momentum can be determined simultaneously and precisely.

The changing paradigm is influenced by the relevance of quantum mechanical thinking. The key question for Kilmann is why is it possible to apply quantum-based principles to medium-sized objects such as people and organizations [Kilm01, pp. 41]. One reason for choosing the "Quantum-Relativistic Paradigm" is to look at the self-motion of particles and people. For Kilmann both particles and people can be seen as monads because they are free to choose their direction and motion by themselves and because they do not need external forces to move them. Nuclear particles are similar to human beings. They have the freedom to go anywhere and even to transform themselves into a variety of other forms. This process causes uncertainty in the sense of the Uncertainty Principle of Heisenberg [Grib99]. In quantum physics, position and momentum uncertainty are the archetypal example discovered by Werner Heisenberg. This principle means that no entity can have both precisely determined momentum and precisely determined position at the same time. Photons and people are at self-motion. A second explanation for the new paradigm is the nature of the human brain which is subdivided into two halves, the left and the right hemispheres. While the left brain is associated with more logical thinking, the right brain is responsible for processes that enable a person to recognize whole images. Zohar discusses the nature of the human being from a *quantum thinking* perspective [Zoha97, p. 21]:

---

[1] In 1962, Thomas Kuhn wrote *The Structure of Scientific Revolution*, and fathered, defined and popularized the concept of "paradigm shift". Kuhn argues that scientific advancement is not evolutionary, but rather it is a series of peaceful interludes punctuated by intellectually violent revolutions. Kuhn argued that a scientific revolution is a noncumulative developmental episode in which an older paradigm is replaced in whole or in part by an incompatible new one. But the new paradigm cannot build on the preceding one. A Paradigm Shift must be thought of as a change from one way of thinking to another. It just does not happen, but it is driven by agents of change [Enzy92].

> *"The essence of quantum thinking is that it is the thinking of precedes categories, structures, and accepted patterns of thought, or mind-sets. It is with quantum thinking that we create our categories, change our structures, and transform our patterns of thought. Quantum thinking is vital to creative thinking and leadership in organizations. It is the key to any genuine organizational transformation. It is the key to shifting our paradigm. Quantum thinking can link between the brain's creativity, organizational transformation and leadership, and the ideas found in the new science."*

In quantum thinking the left and right brain are exchanging information, thus neurons are oscillating across the functions. The major characteristic of the new paradigm is that human beings as well as nuclear particles are self-motion monads. This means, there always will be an uncertainty if one tries to locate both position and momentum. In the old paradigm, organizations trained, recruited, and rewarded its employees according to a deterministic view; there was no interconnection between the organization and its employees. People were seen as inert molar objects controlled by external forces. In order to transform an organization into a new form, the knowledge and experience of the individuals are at the center of considerations. Kilmann describes the change from the old to new paradigm as follows [Kilm01, p. 48]:

> *"When people and their organizations are the subject of study, the Cartesian-Newtonian Paradigm simply cannot handle the uncertainty of movement to their next position or state of being – including each person's next perception, thought, and behavior. Therefore, human evolution and organizational transformation involve much more than a single push from an external source of energy. Besides being self-motion monads with a mind of their own, people can know several nonordinary states of consciousness; self-aware people can assimilate and disseminate the accumulated knowledge contained within the one universal consciousness. As people become even more self-aware and conscious, both hemispheres of their mental organ will play an increasingly crucial role in self-motion, self-development, and thus quantum thinking."*

Ray and Rinzler also discuss the paradigm shift from the Newtonian worldview to the new paradigm in their book *The New Paradigm in Business* [RaRi93]. The Newtonian view is determined by a mechanistic science in which organizations follow a bureaucratic or mechanistic organizational view. The Newtonian organization often is very controlled, and it has an administrative and hierarchical system. Employees perform their task and just do their daily job. The orders and assignments come from top management, and decisions were made based on data. In the business today, everybody is connected with everybody else and business is done through networking, creativity, and intuition [RaRi93, p. 5]. This new way of working also demands a different kind of organizational structure and a new view of dealing with employees. In the new paradigm, the knowledge of employees, the skills and experiences of experts gained over a long period of learning and communicating with other people stand at the center of consideration. The basic assumption of the new paradigm is that the problem solving process of an individual is directed by his inner knowledge and experience. Kilmann uses the term "quantum organization" [Kilm01, pp. 67] as opposed to Newtonian organization. The term "quantum organization" is used synonymous with networked organization or knowledge-creating organization. A "Quantum organization" is characterized by a set of seven categories [Kilm01, pp. 69]:

1. *The Inclusion of Consciousness in Self-Designing Systems.* This means that each employee has knowledge, skills, and experience to influence the design of the organizational system. It is a proactive approach which also includes the knowledge of stakeholders such as customers, competitors, suppliers and other partners. Each individual is contributing creativity and knowledge-in-action to solve problems.
2. *Organizations as Conscious Participants Actively Involved in Self-Designing Processes.* This dimension of quantum organizations implies that each employee tries to design value-added processes throughout the organization. Participants should reflect on their processes and built new knowledge which is applied to add value to the organization.
3. *Cross-Boundary Processes as Explicitly Addressed and Infused with Information.* In a quantum organization, its members are encouraged to exchange knowledge with other partners across the organizational boundary.
4. *The Conscious Self-Management of a Flexibly Designed Organization.* In contrast to the Newtonian organization, the subunits in the quantum organization are responsible for the self-management of all different kinds of tasks such as hiring,

training, recruiting, educating and learning. The knowledge workers are individuals who have the freedom to self-design and self-manage daily work in order to develop creative solutions to customer problems.

5. *The Internal Commitment of Active Participants.* In a quantum organization, employees are committed to discover new knowledge and to build new knowledge and to refresh the existing experiences in educational programs. The knowledge worker is responsible for seeking new opportunities for constant improvement of his own knowledge and, by this, improvement for the whole organization.
6. *The Empowered Relations Among Active Participants.* The high-level professionals in a quantum organization exchange their skills and experiences with other knowledge workers within or even outside the organization. A cross-boundary connection and communication with other participants helps to foster and exchange knowledge across national boundaries and to gain and improve the existing knowledge base.
7. *The Eternal Self-Transformation of Flexibly Designed Organizations.* Finally, a quantum organization has to nourish the trust, commitment and creativity gained in the past and transform it into present and future activities. The transformation only will be successful if the knowledge of joint ventures, mergers and acquisitions, and global networks will be used for a creative problem solving process. The useful knowledge gain will build an organization that can rely on the experience and skills of its knowledge workers.

If organizations are transforming into the new paradigm, they need a corresponding quantum infrastructure [Kilm01, p. 80] which enables their employees to use self-awareness and self-motion skills, for teambuilding, structure, strategy, process, and culture. The experts with their skills have to have a cultural environment which is not built on a standard operating system like the Newtonian organization, but rather one built on a system of complex problem solving which often requires not only the expertise of one professional but also the sharing of knowledge with diverse experts through networking and communication.

The term "quantum organization" used by Kilmann is used synonymously for the term referred to today as a **"knowledge organization"**. The basic assumption is that society is in transition from an old paradigm to a new paradigm governed by the knowledge and skills of the knowledge workers. According to Sveiby [Svei97; http://www.sveiby.com/articles/KOS1.html#TheKnowledgeOrganisation, Date 2003-02-15] the business logic of a knowledge organization depends on the key experts with their experiences, skills, and their relationship to the customers to solve customer problems. In knowledge organizations, the key employees are not seen as a cost factor but rather as a valuable asset and, furthermore, as a revenue creator. Knowledge flows between partners such as the customers or other shareholders who are central to knowledge organization. Roithmayr and Fink describe the term knowledge organization with the following characteristics [RoFi97, p. 504; RoFi98]:

- Competence for solving complex customer problems with a high quality standard;
- Customer orientation;
- Knowledge potential of its experts (knowledge worker);
- Networking ability with other partners; and
- High velocity (speed) in the implementation of the problem solutions.

For North [Nort98, pp. 25], a knowledge organization must have the ability to transfer its knowledge to the market and to use its knowledge optimally in order to guarantee the company success. Starbuck [Star97, pp. 147] uses the term "knowledge intensive firm" which is a firm that sees knowledge as the most important input over other inputs such as capital or labor. In knowledge intensive firms such as research and development (R&D) departments or consulting firms, the selling of the knowledge of experts to other businesses is crucial for the success of the company. For North [Nort98, p. 28], knowledge intensive companies offer individual customer solutions which are difficult to imitate and to substitute. For knowledge organizations the acquisition and transfer of knowledge is a learning process characterized by the speed of learning and by the application of knowledge to the development of individual solution for customer problems. So, through knowledge management, organizations are enabled to create, identify, and renew the company's knowledge base and to deliver innovative products and services to the customer. Knowledge management is a process of systematically managed and leveraged knowledge in an organization. For Mockler and Dologite [MoDo02, p. 14] knowledge management

> *"refers to the process of identifying and generating, systematically gathering, organizing and providing access to, and putting to use anything and everything which might be useful to know when performing some specified*

> *business activity. The knowledge management process is designed to increase profitability and competitive advantage in the marketplace."*

In a global and interconnected society, it is more difficult for companies to know where the best and most valuable knowledge is, thus it becomes more difficult to know what the knowledge is. The Chief Executive Officer (CEO) of Nestlé, Rupert Gasser, has used the phrase: "If Nestlé only knew what Nestlé knows"[2].

The key players in a knowledge organization are the experts with their skills and experiences. The term expert is used synonymous with the term **knowledge worker** or professional. A knowledge worker is defined as a person who has the ability to solve complex customer problems quickly (or, in quantum mechanics terms, with high velocity) by using the experiences and skills gained in a long learning process [Fink00a, pp. 130.]. For Amar [Amar02, p. 3 and p. 5], knowledge organizations "require skills derived from freethinking and unbounded actions of those working for them. They grow on skills that bring uniqueness, newness, and creativity. ... Since innovation is the most important input, and human intellect the most important capital, management of these organizations has to focus on how to put the two together in their operating system". Amar points out that experts in knowledge organizations work together not only to achieve the goals of the organizations, but also to achieve the fulfilment of their own goals by using the organization as a vehicle to achieve them. Managers in organizations have to recognize that the uniqueness and creativity of each knowledge worker will lead to customer satisfaction and to the success of the company. Knowledge workers are characterized by a high individuality and by the denial of formal and bureaucratic structures. Therefore, managers of knowledge workers must first understand the skills, experiences, individual needs, and motivations of a knowledge worker, and they must find an optimal working place for them in the organization. This means, that knowledge work is primarily intellectual work. The assignment of a job to an expert in a knowledge organization, therefore, should be guided by the degree of the intellectual work and creativity of the position. The major competitive advantage of a knowledge organization is the pool of knowledge workers who find creative

---

[2] This statement was made by CEO Ing. Rupert Gasser during the Nestlé Award Ceremony at the University of Innsbruck in 2001.

and quick problem solutions [Amar02, p. 235], hence seven identified characteristics should be taken into consideration [Amar02, pp. 66]:

- To connect the doer's work with the system outcome, end products, or services, and/or with incoming factors, inputs, services, or raw materials;
- To have professional and social interaction within and outside the organization provided by or through the knowledge work;
- To perform a variety of knowledge tasks and skills;
- To know how important and how visible the knowledge worker's part is in the organization's scheme of things, project, product, or service to the outcome;
- To believe others have a high regard for this work;
- To employ state-of-the-art technology in performance of this work;
- To provide opportunities for new learning and personal growth.

After this overview of the definition of the terms "knowledge organization" and "knowledge worker", the key question is what does the term **knowledge** mean? The relationship between data, information and knowledge is widely recognized in literature [Earl96, pp. 3]. Tiwana [Tiwa00, pp. 59] defines *data* as "a set of particular and objective facts about an event or simply the structured record of a transaction". According to the *Dictionary of Computer Terms* [DoCo92, p. 90], data is defined as "factual information. *Data* is the plural of the word *datum,* which means 'a single fact'". Heinrich and Roithmayr [HeHR04, p. 166] also use a similar view of the term data. The difficulty lies in making sense out of these single pieces of statements to support decisions. An example is a grocery store cashier who adds data to the store's database every time an item is sold, but the database does not give any information about the purpose of the buy. Connected with the term "data" is the use of quantitative rather than qualitative methods. Data are stored in the technology system of an organization. Data are just raw material, and they do not include any interpretation or judgement. Data are the basis for the creation of information.

The term *information* is defined by Laudon and Laudon [LaLa00, p. 7] as "data that have been shaped into a form that is meaningful and useful to human beings". For Davenport and Prusak, the word information is associated with a sender and a receiver, thus "the word 'inform' originally meant, 'to give shape to' and information is meant to shape the person who gets it" [DaPr98, p. 3]. The receiver is the person who adds meaning to the information from the sender. Data are transformed into information at the moment when the raw material supports a decision or problem solving process. In this case information is used to obtain an objective [ReKr96, p. 4].

The most difficult term to define *knowledge,* especially since it has a wide range of definitions in the knowledge management and measurement literature. Many authors follow the definition of knowledge given by Davenport and Prusak [DaPr98, p. 5]:

> *"Knowledge is a fluid mix a framed experience, values, contextual information, and expert insight that provides a framework for evaluating and incorporating new experiences and information. It originates and is applied in the mind of knowers."*

This definition tries to capture almost all characteristics of the term knowledge. Knowledge is close to action and is referred to as knowledge-in-action[3]. Synonymous with the word knowledge are tacit knowledge used by Nonaka and Takeuchi [KrIN00; NoTa95] or implicit knowledge used by Polanyi [Pola97, pp. 135]. The term tacit knowledge is subjective and content specific; it is the experience based on the knowledge that cannot be expressed in words, sentences, or formula. Tacit knowledge is stored in the heads of people. Explicit knowledge in contrast, is codified knowledge, and it can be transmitted in systematic and formal ways such as documents, manuals or databases. The term knowledge can be defined as the tacit or implicit knowledge that an innovative and creative person possesses and their ability to turn the learned skills or experience into a knowledge-in-action [Fink00a, pp. 31]. It is the task of the **knowledge-engineer** (see Chapter 5.2) to measure the knowledge-in-action of the experts and to get as much information of the tacit knowledge as possible. A knowledge-engineer has the responsibility to leverage the knowledge embedded in every knowledge worker. The knowledge-engineer's job is to establish an atmosphere of knowledge sharing for measurement purposes. Furthermore, a knowledge-engineer must have social skills to act as someone to be trusted, to care about training programs, and to have interviewer abilities.

[3] For a detailed discussion of the term knowledge, especially the action-orientation of the word, look at Chapter 5.3.1.

1.2 Research Field and Research Question

Figure "Research Area" portrays the matrix for possible research fields according to the importance of the expert knowledge to the knowledge organization and according to the level of knowledge uncertainty associated with the tacit knowledge of the experts. The combination of the two axes creates four research areas: (1) a high level of knowledge uncertainty and a low knowledge importance; (2) a low level of knowledge uncertainty and a low knowledge importance; (3) a low level of knowledge uncertainty and a high knowledge importance; and (4) finally a high level of knowledge uncertainty and a high level of knowledge importance.

Area 1 in the matrix represents an area of low interest in the measurement of knowledge in an organization because the knowledge is not as important to the management, and, furthermore, it is characterized by a high uncertainty. The effort to measure knowledge uncertainty is not justified because of the low level of importance of this kind of expert knowledge is to the organization.

Area 2 demands no knowledge measurement at all because both categories - importance and knowledge uncertainty - are low. An example of this kind of knowledge is that it is already known by the company and it is of almost no future importance to build new knowledge and share it with other partners. A broad audience knows the knowledge is not special to the organization. This area contains the explicit and codified knowledge of an organization.

Area 3 in the matrix shows a kind of knowledge that has a certain category, thus it already is measured because the importance of the experts knowledge is considered very high. This area covers the result of the measurement process and subsequent action program. The organization already has invested time and money to measure the skills and tacit knowledge of the knowledge workers, and it has started an action program to improve the existing knowledge and in order to add value to the organization.

The fourth matrix area *(Area 4)* describes the main research area. The research focuses on the measurement process of the highly uncertain knowledge of the experts who have a high importance to the organization. This field is very critical for the future success of organizations because it contains the **Knowledge Potential (KP)** of the organization and its knowledge workers. The term knowledge potential refers to the skills and experience each knowledge worker possesses based on the learning process to transform them into an excellent employee. The knowledge potential is about identifying, networking, and implementing the tacit knowledge of the experts quickly to achieve the company's strategic objectives. The knowledge potential of a knowledge worker covers customer capital, networking and communication skills, competitor information, content and culture knowledge, constant learning and training processes, information about knowledge management systems, information about the organizational knowledge structure, and the evaluation of the tacit knowledge of the experts. The quick implementing of a high quality solution, furthermore, influences the knowledge potential of an expert. The term *knowledge potential* expresses the knowledge a knowledge worker possesses in different categories (such as customer capital, networking and so on) and the quickness of applying these skills to guarantee the customer a high quality problem solution.

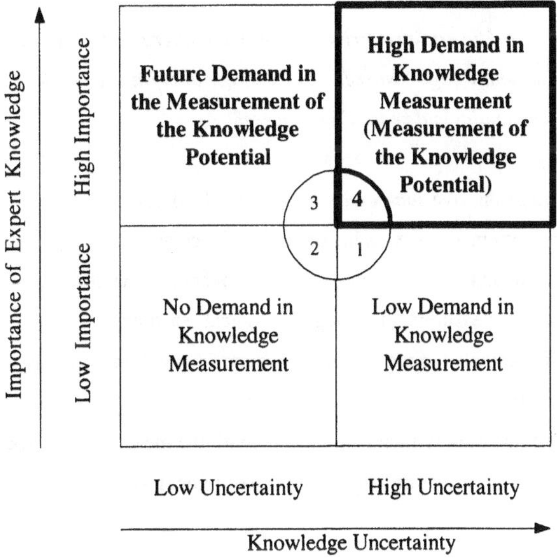

Figure 1: Research Area

It is the task of the management to motivate the experts to transfer and to share their tacit knowledge with other professionals. The management has to guide knowledge workers to make their knowledge potential transparent for the organization. Therefore, the *objective* of this book is to introduce a knowledge measurement system which enables each organization to make statements about the knowledge potential of each knowledge worker. Influenced by the circumstance that an uncertain character distinguishes the term knowledge, each organization has to find a measurement system to evaluate the knowledge potential of its highly important experts.

Derived from the matrix "Research Area", the forth area (4) covers the research area. Area three (3) represents the output of the knowledge measurement process because the knowledge potential of the professionals is measured already and a future action plan has to be implemented to motivate the experts to share their skills and experiences with other partners and to arrange learning and training programs to renew their existing knowledge. Based on the matrix, the **research question** can be formulated as follows:

Is it possible - based on the Uncertainty Principle of Heisenberg - to measure the knowledge potential of a knowledge worker by taking uncertainty factors into considerations by applying the analogical reasoning process?

Based on the key research question, five *sub-research fields* can be derived:

1. The exposition of measurement systems in cognitive science and in management;
2. The explanation of fundamental research areas in quantum mechanics, and its relevance for knowledge measurement through analogical reasoning;
3. The development of a knowledge measurement system for the knowledge potential of each knowledge worker;
4. The calculation of the uncertainty factors associated with the measurement process;
5. The reflection and evaluation of the knowledge measurement system through case studies.

In Chapter 1.3 the methodical framework and the expected results will be presented. Chapter 1.4 gives an overview of the content of each chapter.

1.3 Methodical Framework and Expected Results

From a methodical point of view, the state-of-the-art concerning the knowledge measurement research field is covered through a literature review. Knowledge management has many origins [Wiig00, pp. 5]. An understanding of the role and nature of knowledge once came from abstract philosophical thinking. According to Wiig, in the 20th Century perspectives broadened and efforts were made by theorists in psychology, cognitive science, artificial intelligence, social sciences, economics and business to analyze knowledge. There are two mainstream dimensions influencing the knowledge management and measurement field. The first one is the Cognitive Science approach [WiKe99], covering the philosophy, psychology, neurosciences, computational intelligence, linguistics and language, and finally culture, cognition and evolution. The second one is the management approach with its objective to measure the intellectual capital of a company [Broc96; Lev01; ReSc99]. The method of the literature review is valid for all five defined research fields. This means, the literature review method is not only applied to the knowledge measurement field, but it also is applied to quantum mechanic fundamentals, to the development of the knowledge potential measurement system, and to the derivation of the uncertainty factors. The *method of literature review* is a cross-section function to identify a gap in the current existing knowledge measurement systems. The gap covers the lack of a measurement system that enables a knowledge organization to make statements about the knowledge potential of individual knowledge workers. The knowledge potential is defined by nine knowledge variables that should allow a knowledge organization and its members to see which actions are necessary to receive an excellent knowledge potential value. Heinrich [Hein99, pp. 130] sees the gap analysis as part of the strategic information management. The purpose of the *gap analysis* is to identify the current system so precisely in order to initiate ideas to close the gap. The current state-of-the-art of knowledge measurement systems is introduced and discussed. The current system survey of the knowledge measurement approaches uncovers (see Chapter 2) the gap that inhibits the current measurement system from evaluating the individual knowledge potential of the knowledge workers. The current measurement system focus on metrics that can be divided into four categories: (1) monetary terms ($, €), (2) number (#), (3) percentage (%) or index, and (4) a combination of the three. However, the gap analyses show that the individual tacit knowledge of an expert is not measured (see Chapter 3).

The focus of the research is the development of a measurement system that reveals similarities to the quantum mechanical thinking. Concepts of the quantum mechanical view belong to physical/natural science. Since physical science concepts are applied to social and economic science phenomena, the *method of analogical reasoning* is a central deliberation. The research objects are measurable social and economic science phenomena measured with *statistical methods*. The knowledge measurement system will be empirically diagnosed and evaluated. Three methods are employed: *case studies, laboratory studies, and the theory of reflection.* Case studies [Gill00] are conducted at three companies in order to investigate how the knowledge measurement system is working in real-life situation. The case studies are reflected and evaluated according to the reflection theory of Schön [Schö82]. The knowledge measurement model also is evaluated in a laboratory study at the University of Innsbruck.

The method of analogical reasoning and the other named research methods effect the development of a measurement system under conditions of uncertainty factors. Sveiby describes the situation as follows [Svei97, p. 155]:

> *"Any measurement system is limited by Heisenberg's uncertainty principle ... If truth is in the eye of the beholder in the physical world, it is even more so in the world of business. There is no difference between financial measures and other measures. Both are uncertain; all depend on the observer."*

The topic of uncertainty is the guiding thought throughout the research of the knowledge measurement system. The uncertainty relationship has far-reaching implications to the value of the knowledge potential. The important point is that uncertainty does not represent any deficiency in the experiment used to measure knowledge potential. Through the analogical reasoning process, it is possible, in principle, to measure all nine dimensions of the knowledge potential. The method to gather data to measure the knowledge potential is through a *questionnaire* based on the literature review. The questionnaire is used to gather information from the knowledge workers about their behavior, their skills, and their attitudes towards knowledge management and towards learning processes. For Fife-Schaw

[Fife95, pp. 174], the questionnaire is one of the most common used research methods in social science.

The *expected results,* based on the applied research methods and the named research areas, is the development of a measurement system for the knowledge potential of the knowledge worker and the determination of the uncertainty factors for the knowledge potential of each knowledge-engineer. Courtney, Kirkland, Viguerie [CoKV99, pp. 1], in their article *Strategy under Uncertainty* discuss how managers choose strategies in an uncertain environment. The authors argue that uncertainty requires a new way of thinking and acting about a strategy. Companies acting in stable environments apply standard procedures to lay out a precise vision of future events which can be captured in discounted-cash-flows analyses. The situation will be completely different if the future is determined by uncertainty. The danger is that many executives think of uncertainty in a binary way [CoKV99, p, 3]. Thus, they see the world either as certain and therefore precise to predict or as uncertain and therefore not predictable. Courtney, Kirkland, Viguerie describe the situation as follows [CoKV99, p. 4]:

> *"Underestimating uncertainty can lead to strategies that neither defend against the threats not take advantage of the opportunities that higher levels of uncertainty may provide. ... assuming that the world is entirely unpredictable can lead managers to abandon the analytical rigor of their traditional planning processes altogether and base their strategic decisions primarily on gut instinct."*

The strategy of only setting actions is based on an instinct and misinformed belief, and it can lead to false future decisions. The described situation of choosing strategies based on uncertain information also applies to the knowledge measurement approach. Managers and executives have two alternate choices: either they do not measure the tacit knowledge residing in the heads of the knowledge worker and, therefore, make guesses about the value of the experts knowledge, or they take the challenge and measure the knowledge of the experts and develop a strategic plan to foster and renew the knowledge based on solid analysis. Knowledge is characterized by high uncertainty. Hence, executives cannot lay back and rely on speculations about the skills and experiences valuable for the organization to be competitive because the information about the knowledge potential has a significant impact on the future company strategy. The introduced knowledge measurement system in this book will allow executives and managers to predict the knowledge potential of each knowledge worker. Therefore, it will allow them to make reliable future decisions about how to deal with the uncertainty and in the development of a knowledge strategy. The uncertainty factors associated with the measurement process are taken into account, and the value of the knowledge potential is more precisely determined. This vital information and its analysis signals the managers and executives about possible future scenarios of how to renew the organizational knowledge. If managers and executives are able to identify and to analyze the knowledge potential and the level of uncertainty, they can formulate strategies and support their decision-making process to deal with the tacit knowledge of the experts in the future. The knowledge measurement model will give managers/executives an analytical framework:

- To utilize a current system survey for knowledge potential;
- To position experts in a knowledge classification schema, ranging from a poor knowledge worker to a standard knowledge worker, to an undefined knowledge worker, to a good knowledge worker, to an excellent knowledge worker. The clusters follow the skill acquisition schema from Dreyfus and Dreyfus [DrDr87];
- To take the uncertainty factor into consideration for the derivation of future strategies;
- To develop a portfolio of actions to improve, identify, network, and leverage the knowledge of the organization.

The level of uncertainty can be lowered through knowledge measurement. The measurement model that will be outlined in Chapter Five will guide managers/executives to judge the performance of employees, and it will assist them during the process for the implementation of a knowledge strategy.

1.4 Content Overview

This book is organized into seven chapters. In **Chapter One**, the research problem and the research question is discussed. The general framework of Chapter One follows the research guideline by Heinrich [http://www.winie.uni-linz.ac.at/, Date 2003-01-30] who divides the research process into three categories. Category one is called the definition of the research problem, and it has the objective of describing the research problem and the relevance of the research area. The second category is called the solution process, and it covers the systematic procedure to solve the research question. The third category is called expected results, and it gives the reader an expected solution. Chapter One introduces the general problem associated with knowledge management and measurement.

Chapter Two discusses the two mainstream research fields of measurement. The first one is the *cognitive science* approach with its six disciplines: philosophy, psychology, neurosciences, computational intelligence, linguistics and language, and finally culture, cognition and evolution. The second is the *management approach.* It begins with a brief review of the key management measurement systems, those by the authors Luthy [Luth98], Skyrme [Skyr98] and Sveiby [Svei97]. The presentation of the three measurement clusters leads to the differentiation of four sub-categories of knowledge measurement: Direct Intellectual Capital Methods (DIC), Market Capitalization Methods (MCM), Return on Assets Methods (ROA), and Scorecard Methods (SC). Each sub-category will be presented with its major measurement methods. Attention is mainly focused on how knowledge and/or intellectual capital is measured in an organizational context.

Chapter Three covers the detailed description of the knowledge potential view which is derived from the argumentation and criticism of the existing knowledge measurement systems discussed in Chapter Two. Chapter Three explains the basis for the measurement process in Chapter Five. The knowledge potential view is determined by nine key measurement variables: knowledge content, knowledge culture, knowledge networking, organizational knowledge and structure, knowledge worker skills, learning and training, customer knowledge, competitor benchmark, and Information and Communication Systems/Knowledge Management Systems.

The objective of **Chapter Four** is to give the reader basic background information about the quantum mechanical worldview. First, it will introduce the historical development of quantum mechanics with its major representatives such as Bohr, Einstein, Heisenberg, Planck, and Schrödinger. It will present major concepts such as the slit experiments, the wave-particle dualism or probability. The Copenhagener Interpretation is the standard explanation of the quantum world. It is the collection of quantum mechanical ideas: uncertainty, complementarity, probability, and the disturbance of the system being observed by the observer. The Uncertainty Principle of Heisenberg will be especially articulated because this principle is the basic theoretical framework for the measurement of the knowledge potential of an employee.

Chapter Five begins with the explanation of the analogical reasoning process. The Uncertainty Principle of Heisenberg functions as the framework for the measurement process of the knowledge potential of employees. As Kilmann [Kilm01, pp. 42] has pointed out in explaining the "Quantum-Relativistic View", there are similarities between nuclear particles and human beings because both objects have the freedom to go anywhere, a phenomenon generating uncertainty. However, it has to be noted that the measurement process concerning the knowledge worker is not a physical procedure. Rules applying to the quantum mechanical world will not apply to the knowledge measurement view. Chapter Five presents a measurement process for the knowledge potential of the knowledge workers. The objective is to measure knowledge potential based on the nine dimensions outlined in Chapter Three and to make forecasts to assign an employee to a knowledge classification. The questionnaire design covering the nine knowledge variables will be explained in Chapter Five. The development follows the knowledge architecture of Fink [Fink00a]. Furthermore, the uncertainty associated with the measurement process will be calculated in this chapter.

Chapter Six investigates the practical use of the measurement system through the application of case studies. The measurement process is reflected and evaluated at three American technology companies. In addition, the measurement model is evaluated in a laboratory study with students at the University of Innsbruck. The case studies investigate the research question formulated in Chapter 1.2.

The key research findings are summarized in **Chapter Seven** and information about future research work concludes this book.

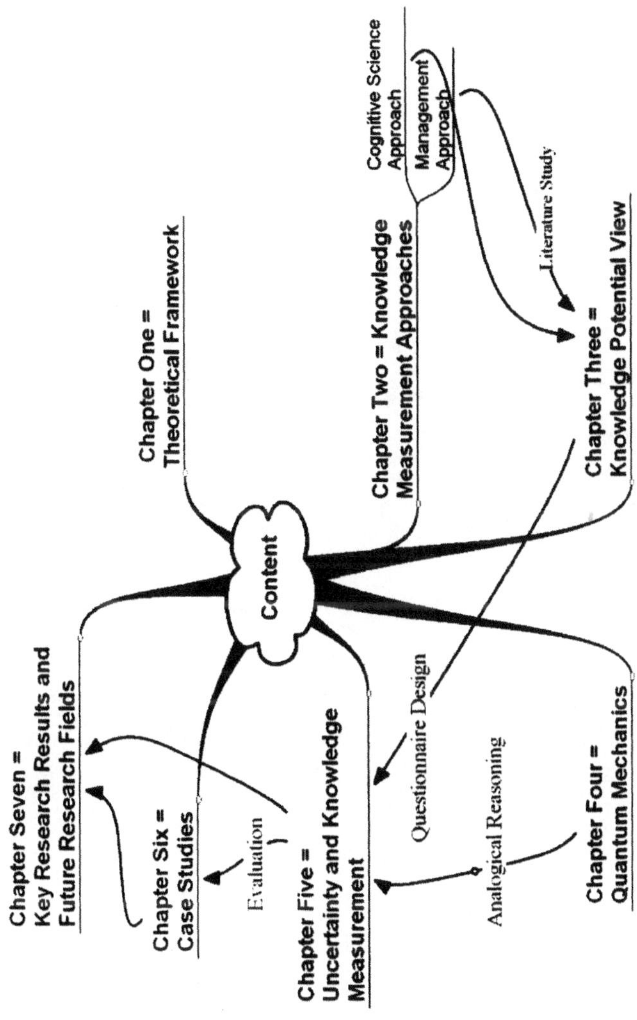

Figure 2: Mind Map of Content Overview

2 Knowledge Measurement Approaches

"Any investment in knowledge always gives the best return."
(Benjamin Franklin)

This chapter is organized in two main sub-chapters: Cognitive Science Approach and Management Measurement Approaches. Its objectives are to give the reader an overview of the different disciplines that constitute cognitive science and to discuss the state-of-the art of the current measurement approaches in the knowledge management literature. The study of cognitive science is interdisciplinary, and it covers the fields of philosophy, psychology, neurosciences, computational intelligence, linguistics and language, and finally culture, cognition and evolution, all of which will be discussed. For cognitive scientists the objects under study are behavior and cognition in humans, animals and machines. The examination of cognitive science can be seen as a basic explanation of how humans are perceiving, learning, thinking, speaking, and acting. Its main focus lies in the discussion of how individuals reason under conditions of uncertainty and how perceived information is processed in the brain to build knowledge. A detailed explanation of all views, concepts, methods and methodologies in cognitive science is beyond this research.

The second part of this chapter deals with the description of the current available measurement approaches in the field of knowledge management. The three major measurement models are from Luthy [Luth98], Sveiby [Svei02a], and Skyrme [Skyr98] and their importance will be examined. Furthermore, it will debate four measurement categories with their major measurement models that follow the measurement framework from Sveiby. The four categories are: Direct Intellectual Capital Methods (DIC), Market Capitalization Methods (MCM), Return on Assets Methods (ROA), and finally the Scorecard Methods (SC). In contemporary global environment, the measurement of knowledge is important for economics as well as for organizations. Traditional financial and accounting tools focus on the measurement of tangible assets, while the new approaches deal with the measurement of the intellectual capital of a company. The key issues are the quantification and measurement of the value of intellectual capital, especially measurement of the most valuable corporate asset - the knowledge and skills of the knowledge worker. There is a need for knowledge measurement in order to implement knowledge strategies successfully.

2.1 Cognitive Science Approach

"So far as the laws of mathematics refer
to reality they are not certain.
And so far as they are certain
they do not refer to reality."
(Albert Einstein)

2.1.1 Definition of Cognitive Science

In general, cognitive science deals with the nature of intelligence, and it rests on empirical studies that describe the performance of human subjects in cognitive tasks. These empirical studies involve verbal protocols, eye movement protocols, or memory performance. For Simon and Kaplan [SiKa89, p. 2] cognitive science

> *"is the study of intelligence and intelligent systems, with particular reference to intelligent behavior as computation. ... We say that people are behaving intelligently when they choose courses of action that are relevant to achieving their goals, when they reply coherently and appropriately to questions that are put to them, when they solve problems of lesser or greater difficulty, or when they create or design something useful or beautiful or novel."*

According to Eysenck, cognitive science grew out of three developments [Eyse90, pp. 66]:

1. The invention of computers and the attempts to design computer programs that could do human tasks;
2. The development of information-processing psychology with its goal to specify the internal processing involved in perception, language, memory, and thought;
3. The development of the theory of generative grammar and its related offshoots in linguistics.

Cognitive science can be approached in several ways. One way to define cognitive science is in terms of topic areas. Research is focused, according to Eysenck [Eyse90, pp. 67], on five major areas: knowledge representation, language, learning, thinking, and perception.

Another way to structure cognitive science is to understand that field more deeply and to know the disciplines that contributed to its foundation. Simon and Kaplan [SiKa89] identify six disciplines which determine the field: philosophy, psychology, neurosciences, artificial intelligence, language, and cognition. These six fields correspond to *The MIT Encyclopedia of the Cognitive Sciences* [WiKe99] that constitutes the foundation on the cognitive sciences. The Massachusetts Institute of Technology (MIT) clustering of the cognitive sciences into the fields of philosophy, psychology, neurosciences, computational intelligence, linguistics and language, and culture, cognition and evolution establish the basic framework for discussing the cognitive science approach because it is one of the most detailed approaches.

The cognitive science movement is far-reaching and diverse, containing within it several viewpoints. Since the primary focus of my research is the measurement procedure for knowledge in companies and the considerations of uncertainty factors, the cognitive science approach functions as the basic framework because it is the study of the acquisition and use of knowledge. Cognitive science is a synthesis of the six fields concerned with the kinds of knowledge that underlie human cognition, human cognitive processes, and computational modeling of the processes. It studies how the human mind works. Therefore, it is the initial process in building knowledge which can be measured by a company.

A discourse on the full range of all research areas in cognitive science is beyond the bounds of this book. In each chapter the major concepts, methods or methodologies will be presented, knowing that the field of cognitive science is so broad that only certain aspects can be discussed. For a more detailed discussion, see Wilson and Keil [WiKe99], Pinker [Pink97] or Pfeifer and Scheier [PfSc99] for more insight into the field of cognitive science.

2.1.2 Philosophy

2.1.2.1 Three Classic Philosophical Issues About the Mind

There are various areas of philosophy which contribute to the field of cognitive science, areas such as the philosophy of mind, formal and philosophical logic, and traditional metaphysics and epistemology. Wilson [Wils99a, pp. xv] denotes that the most direct connection between the philosophy of mind and cognitive science begins with the three

classic philosophical issues about the mind [Wils99a]. The relationship between mental and physical topics in classic philosophy of the mind is one of the deepest philosophical approaches, and it is still relevant today. The first one is the *mental-physical relation.* A topic of historical significance is the *mind-body problem* which is mostly associated with *René Descartes (1596-1650).* The mind-body problem [Faur00, pp. 473] is one of explaining how our mental states, events, and processes are related to the physical states, events, and processes in our body. Descartes [Wils99b, pp. 229] said that the mind is a nonbodily entity: a soul or a mental substance. This thesis is called "substance dualism" or "Cartesian dualism" because it argues that there are two kinds of substance in the world, mental and physical. If one believes in such dualism, it is based on the belief that the soul is immortal and that we have free will, phenomena which seem to require that the mind be a nonphysical thing because all physical things are subject to the laws of nature. To say it more commonly, people are of both a mind and a body. The question is how do they interact? However, the problem of causation between body and mind has been thought to pose a largely unanswered problem for Cartesian dualism. The materialists hold all that exists is material or physical in nature. Therefore, minds are somehow composed of other arrangements. So that even when the materialistic view is adopted, the physical mind has special properties like consciousness.

Throughout most of Descartes' writings, the demand for certainty was prominent. In his *Mediations*, he traces the path of the lonely meditator from doubt and disorientation to certain and reliable knowledge. Descartes offered in Latin a formal exposition of his central ideas in *Meditationes de Prima Philosophia* (Mediations on First Philosophy) in 1641. After an extended statement of the method of doubt, Descartes argued that most skepticism is overcome by the certainty of one's own existence as a thinking thing. From this beginning, he believed it possible to use our clear and distinct ideas to demonstrate the existence of God, to establish the reliability of our reason despite the possibility of error. On this ground, Descartes defended a strict dualism for which the mind and the body are wholly distinct even if they seem to interact. Descartes' aim is to reach certainty about the nature of life, and he starts by maintaining one should doubt everything at first. He doubted everything, and doubt was the only thing he was certain of. But one thing had to be true, and that was what he doubted. When he doubted, he had to be thinking, and, because he was thinking, he had to be certain he existed. Or, as he, himself, expressed it: *Cogito, ergo sum* which means, "I think, therefore I am". Descartes developed a "mechanist theory of nature, while also advocating a conception of the 'rational soul' as a distinct, immaterial entity, endowed by God with certain innate intellectual concepts" [Wils99b, p. 229]. The basic approach of Descartes is to understand the human (and animal) behavior by explaining the world by a mechanistic-materialistic view.

The second issue is the *structure of the mind and knowledge*. The dimension of the issue of the structure of the mind concerns the debate about rationalism versus empiricism, a debate for which there are different views of the nature of the human knowledge, the central concept in the Seventeenth and Eighteenth centuries. Some of the classical rationalists are René Descartes, Gottfried Leibnitz, and Baruch Spinoza. On the other side, classical empiricists are John Locke, George Berkeley, and David Hume; and in the Twentieth century, influential classical empiricists were Bernhard Russel and Hans Reichenbach. *Empiricism* [Alst98, pp. 298] is the view that all knowledge comes from experience. Knowledge of all matters of fact rests on inductively gained experience. Scientific knowledge is not based on *a priori* principles. Empiricism seemed attractive because it holds the promise for the rejection of irrationality, superstition, and obscurantism. On the other side, in *rationalism* [Mark98] experience is not the source of all knowledge. Some concepts are neither derived nor derivable from experience. In this view, reason has a higher calling. It furnishes *a priori* principles that are not only true, but also are necessary and recognizable. Rationalism is a theory which claims to be based on rational principles. In philosophy the word mainly is used to designate a certain kind of theory of knowledge springing from reasoning rather than experience. This means that representatives of empiricism argue human knowledge is derived from sensory, experimental, or empirical interaction with the world while representatives of rationalism disagree - knowledge does not derive from experience.

The third issue is the *first- and third-person perspectives*. This issue deals with the problem of the other mind, and, unlike the mind-body problem, it has disappeared from philosophical contributions to the cognitive sciences. Thus, "the problem of other minds is chiefly an *epistemological* problem, sometimes expressed as a form of skepticism about the justification that we have for attributing mental states to others" [Wils99a, p. xvii].

2.1.2.2 Logic and the Sciences of the Mind

A key issue in the discussion of the role of philosophy in the cognitive science approach is *logic* [Crai98]. The question is how people make logical decisions. The origin of dealing with logic and the object knowledge goes back as for as to the time of *Aristotle* (384-322 BC) [Dein00], who stated in his book *Metaphysics* that "all men by nature desire to know". Aristotle is the founder of the Ontology (the study of the nature of being), cosmology, and philosophical theology. The term comes from the metaphysical treatises of Aristotle, who presented a First Philosophy (as he called it) after physics, *meta-physic*. The logic of Aristotle has influenced the history of Western thought immensely, especially the theory of *syllogism* [Wils99a, p. xxxii]. Aristotle presented the logic of syllogism, an argument in which a conclusion follows from several premises. The definition by Aristotle implies that:

1. syllogisms are valid arguments;
2. syllogisms have two or more premises;
3. none of the premises is redundant.

Aristotle introduced the *categorical syllogism*. The following example demonstrates a syllogism (the letters A, B, and C are placeholders for terms) [Barn92]:

Every A is a B
Every B is a C
Every A is a C

The Aristotelian logic of demonstration revolves around a valid *deductive argument* (syllogism) which means that the premises are causally explanatory scientific principles for which the truth is known prior to the demonstration [http://ist-socrates.berkeley.com, Date 2003-02-18]. Aristotle defines the term deduction in his *Prior Analytics* I.2, 24b18-20 as: "A deduction is speech *(logos)* in which, certain things having been supposed, something different from those supposed results of necessity because of their being so" [Stanford Encyclopedia of Philosophy; http://plato.standford.edu/entries/aristotle-logic/, Date 2003-02-18].

For Aristotle, scientific knowledge follows a deduction. This means that all knowledge is demonstrative, and it must include the knowledge of causes and that things caused cannot be other than as it is. Demonstrations assume three types of knowledge: principles (definitions of the proper objects of the science in question), axioms (general principles of proof), and the existence of the proper objects of the science in question [http://ist-socrates.berkeley.edu/~fl3min4/25A/aristotlesepistemology.html, Date 2003-02-18].

The fundamental developments in logical theory perhaps have had the most widespread effect on the foundations of cognitive sciences [Wils99a, p. xxxiii]. They form the basis for much contemporary work across the cognitive science field: (1) in linguistic semantics, e.g., Modal Logic, Possible Worlds Semantics; (2) in metalogic, e.g., formal systems, Gödel's theorems; and (3) in artificial intelligence, e.g., logical reasoning systems, metareasoning, and temporal reasoning. However, even if the philosophical relevance of these developments in logical theory for thinking has had a great impact on the cognitive science field, the latest work in psychological research on human reasoning points to ways in which human reasoning is governed by structures very different from formal logic. Such new concepts (see Chapter 2.1.3) are judgement heuristics, causal reasoning, and mental models.

2.1.3 Psychology

2.1.3.1 The Place of Psychology within Cognitive Science

Psychology forms part of the core cognitive science field. According to the *Dictionary of Psychology*, cognitive psychology is defined as "the branch of psychology, concerned with all forms of cognition, including attention, perception, learning, memory, thinking, problem solving, decision making and language" [Colm01, pp. 143]. Cognitive psychology is highly related to information processing which focuses on cognitive functioning with the help of concepts borrowed from computer science. Holyoak defines psychology as "the science that investigates the representation and processing of information by complex organisms. … Humans are capable of the most complex and most domain-general forms of information processing of all species; for this reason, most of psychology aims directly or indirectly to understand the nature of human information processing and intelligence" [Holy99, p. xxxviiii]. Pfeifer and Scheier [PfSc99] state that the term intelligence is difficult to define because there is not much agreement. To have a better understanding of the term intelligence, Pfeifer and Scheier [PfSc99, pp. 7] introduce eight commonsense notions that specify certain capabilities typical of intelligent beings:

1. *Thinking and problem solving* is one essential characteristic of intelligence. The word thinking includes problem solving, logical reasoning, and less structured forms of mental activities (e.g., planning a weekend trip). Problem solving is the process of transforming a given situation into a desired situation or goal. The study of how humans solve problems belongs to cognitive psychology while computer-based problem solving belongs to the field of artificial intelligence [Simo99, p. 674].
2. *Learning and Memory*. The learning process itself does not make a human being intelligent; it provides the capability to learn. Closely associated with learning is memory as a capability to learn. Merely memorizing facts is not judged as an intelligent action, but its use for knowledge transference is referred to as an intelligent process. According to Reisberg [Reis99, p. 460], learning can "be understood as a change in an organism's capacities or behavior brought about by experience". Reisberg [Reis99, pp. 460] indicates that a diversity of learning forms exist, for example associative learning, acquisition of knowledge in cognitive maps, spatial learning, skill learning, inductive learning, learning through imagination, or deductive reasoning. Modern studies of memory distinguish between *implicit and explicit memory*. Traditionally, psychological studies have focused on conscious recollection or explicit memory for specific facts and episodes. However, in recent years the study of implicit memory - the interest in a nonconscious form of memory - has developed that does not require explicit recollection for specific episodes [GrMa93; Scha99, pp. 394]. Schachter [Scha99, pp. 395] states that the exploration of implicit memory has opened up new fields for the memory research and future empirical studies and theoretical analysis are needed for one to learn more about the implicit memory.
3. *Language*. A special human distinction is the capability to communicate with other people through language. For details see Chapter 2.1.6.
4. *Intuition and Creativity*. Many people, such as leaders or managers, act by intuition. The term intuition refers to coming to a conclusion without a train of logical thought that can be traced to its origins. Creativity also is a highly complex notion that depends not on the individual but also on society.
5. *Consciousness*. Like the commonsense notion of creativity and language, consciousness is a property of human beings. The term consciousness refers to

something that is difficult to describe and that is sometimes seen as mysterious and subjective.

6. *Emotions* are essential to human beings like consciousness. Coleman [Cole95, pp. 43] uses the term emotional intelligence to describe the skill about knowing one's emotions, managing the emotions, motivating oneself, recognizing emotions in others, and handling relationships.
7. *Surviving in a complex world* is seen as another commonsense notion of intelligence because humans and animals can survive in highly complex environments, and they have an astonishing behavior.
8. *Perceptual and Motor Abilities.* Perception is seen as one of the most important research fields in science. However, motor abilities, such as walking, are usually thought of as non-intelligent action.

Pfeifer and Scheier provide an overview of the variety of abilities and components involved with the term intelligence. To date, it seems that intelligence can be seen as a gradual rather than an absolute characteristic [PfSc99, p. 12].

Psychology has many major subdivisions [DoRT98; Holy99, p. xl] with different levels of connection to the cognitive sciences: *Cognitive psychology* deals with the representation and processing of information with emphasis on cognition in adult humans. *Developmental psychology* deals with the changes in cognitive, social, and emotional functioning. *Social psychology* investigates the cognitive and emotional factors involved in interactions between people. *Personality psychology* is involved with motivational and emotional aspects of human experience. *Clinical psychology* considers applied issues related to mental health. *Comparative psychology* deals with the commonalities and differences in cognition and behavior among different animal species. Finally, *behavioral neuroscience* provides the interface between research on molar cognition and behavior and their underlying neural substrate.

2.1.3.2 Probabilistic Reasoning under Conditions of Uncertainty

Holyoak [Holy99, pp. xl] points out that much of human inferences depend not on deduction, but on *inductive probabilistic reasoning under conditions of uncertainty.*

According to Henrion [Henr99, pp. 853], almost all information is subject to uncertainty. Uncertainty may arise from different sources like: (1) incomplete information; (2) linguistic impression; and (3) disagreement between information sources. Judgement and decision-making are pervasive and important intellectual activities. A successful expert should have the ability to make good and reliable judgements and to make wise and effective decisions. However, many decisions are based on beliefs concerning the likelihood of uncertain events, events such as the outcome of an election, the development of the stock market, or the judgement of the value of a knowledge worker, as will be shown later (Chapter 5). The key questions are how people assess the probability of an uncertain event or the value of an uncertain quantity. Tversky and Kahneman [TvKa86, pp. 38] introduce in their article "Judgement under Uncertainty: Heuristics and Biases" three heuristics used to make judgements under conditions of uncertainty. In general, people assess uncertain events by relying on heuristic principles which reduce complexity and probability assessments to simpler judgemental operations.

The first heuristics is **representativeness** [TvKa86, pp. 39], a phenomenon used when people are asked to judge the probability that object or event A belongs to class or process B. An example is explained in the following statement: Susan is a very open-minded person, likes to organize things, is very correct in her behavior and loves to talk to other people. She is very honest and is doing her work correctly, preparing important issues in advance. The question is how do people assess the probability that Susan is a secretary from a list of possible professions (i.e., physician, salesman, airline pilot, secretary)? In the representativeness heuristic, the probability that Susan is a secretary is derived from the situation, about how people think in stereotypes, and from the degree she is a representative of a certain profession. Tversky and Kahneman state that this kind of judgement of probability leads to serious errors because representativeness is not influenced by a number of factors that should affect judgements of probability [TvKa86, pp. 39]:

1. *Insensitivity to prior probability of outcomes*. They argue that prior probability, or the base-rate frequency, of outcomes should have a major impact on probability. However, prior probabilities are neglected in representativeness heuristics.
2. *Misconceptions of chance*. Tversky and Kahneman [TvKa86, p. 42] explain this effect as follows: "people expect that a sequence of events generated by a

random process will represent the essential characteristics of that process even when the sequence is short". A further consequence is the gambler effect. If a gambler observes a roulette wheel and a long black run, he will believe it is time for red to come. Chance is seen as a self-correcting process.

3. *Insensitivity to predictability.* If people make predictions solely on descriptions they favor most, their predictions will be insensitive to the reliability of the evidence and to the expected accuracy of the prediction.
4. *The illusion of validity.* Unwarranted confidence produced by a good fit between the predicted outcome and the input information is called the illusion of validity.
5. *Misconceptions of regression.* It is about the phenomenon known as regression towards the mean.

The second heuristic, **availability** [TvKa86, pp. 46] is often used when people are asked to assess the frequency of a class or the plausibility of a particular development. For example, one may evaluate the probability that a given business venture will fail by imaging various difficulties it could encounter. However, availability is affected by factors more than frequency and probability, and predictable biases must be taken into consideration: (1) biases due to the irretrievability of instances; (2) biases due to the effectiveness of a research set; (3) biases of imaginability; and (4) illusory correlations.

The third heuristic, **adjustment and anchoring** [TvKa86, pp. 49] means that people make estimates by starting from an initial value that is adjusted to yield the final answer. This means, different starting points, the initial value, yield different estimates which are biased toward the initial values. This phenomenon is called anchoring. Also, the third heuristic is determined by some biases: (1) insufficient adjustments; (2) biases in the evaluation of conjunctive and disjunctive events; and (3) anchoring in the assessments of subjective probability distributions. The three heuristics pointed out by Tversky and Kahneman focus on the difficult field of making decisions under uncertainty. However, a rational judge will make probability judgements compatible with personal knowledge by using his own heuristics with the biases, "the judgements must be compatible with the entire web of beliefs held by the individual" [TvKa86, p. 55]. An understanding of the three heuristics and their relating biases will improve judgements and decision in uncertain situations.

2.1.3.3 Mental Models

Another important research area in cognitive science and psychology is **mental model** [LuJa00] which try to examine the way people understand some human knowledge domain. Two research fields influence mental models: cognitive science and artificial intelligence. Gentner and Stevens [GeSt83] articulate three dimensions on which to characterize mental model research:

1. Nature of domains: it is necessary to center on the simplest possible domains to capture naturalistic human knowledge. To do so, domains should be chosen for which some normative knowledge exists that easily can be detailed and, therefore, made explicit. Mental model research focuses on simple physical systems or devices. Domains are simple physical or mathematical systems or artificial devices such as naive mechanics, or naive theories of heat.
2. Theoretical approach: these approaches focus in knowledge representation on computational semantics developed by artificial intelligence research. Data and processes are represented in formalism. Examples are constraint networks, production rules, and networks with attached procedures.
3. Methodology: the methodologies in this dimension are eclectic, and they include, for example, protocol analysis, traditional cognitive psychology experiments, developmental studies, expert-novice studies, or designed field observations for which an artificial domain is constructed with interesting relevance to the real domain.

For Norman [Norm83, pp. 7], mental models are naturally evolving models. In studying mental models, four issues have to be taken into consideration: the target system, the conceptual model of that target system, the user's mental model of the target system, and the scientist's conceptualization of that mental model. People form mental models of a system through interaction with the target system. A conceptual model is one invented to provide an appropriate representation of the target system. The person will modify the existing mental model through interaction influenced by a person's background, previous experiences, and the structure of the human information processing system. Norman further discusses how a particular mental model of a particular target system can be modelled. For doing so, Norman introduces a conceptual model of the system with the following variables:

t = Particular target system;

C(t) = Conceptual model of the system;

M(t) = User's mental model of the target system;

C(M(t)) = Our conceptualisation of a mental model.

Psychological experiments and observations are necessary to learn more about the mental model of the user. Furthermore, three functional properties have to be considered. The conceptual model of the mental model C(M(t)) should contain a model of the person's belief system. The belief system influences the mental model of a person. Its observability is the second property. In other words, in the conceptual model of the mental model, there should be a correspondence between the parameters and observable states of C(M(t)) and the observable aspects of t. Last, the model must have predictive power. The purpose of the mental model is its use to predict and to understand the physical system. Mental model research focuses on the relationship between the mental model M(t) and the conceptual model C(M(t)). One major purpose to mental model is to enable a person to predict the operation of a target system.

Rickheit and Sichelschmidt [RiSi99, pp. 16] discuss mental model research with the perspective of different views. Depending on the interpretation of the term mental model, different aspects are relevant. Rickheit and Sichelschmidt [RiSi99, pp. 17] make a distinction of four different approaches:

1. The first concept, *"cognitive maps"*, is a mental representation of spatial aspects of the environment, thus comprising the topology of an area. A cognitive map can be defined as a mental representation of a geographical surrounding. For Kitchin and Freundschuh [KiFr00, p. 1], cognitive mapping research "seeks to comprehend how we come to understand spatial relations gained through both primary experience and secondary media (e.g. maps)". Cognitive maps allow a person to navigate through familiar and unfamiliar areas by finding their path, landmarks, or other relevant districts. In the field of environmental cognition and urban planning, the concept of cognitive maps is used as a heuristic in studies of spatial orientation and the environmental behavior of persons. There are two entities represented in a cognitive map: (1) districts, which are sub-regions; and (2) landmarks defined as objects that serve as reference points in the localization of other landmarks. Kitchin and

Freundschuh differentiate the term cognitive mapping into three views: a descriptive term for the field of study that investigates how people learn, remember, and process spatial information about an environment; second, a title for how people think about spatial relations; and third, a descriptive phrase for a methodical approach to understand cognitive processes, the construction of cognitive maps.

2. The second concept discussed, *"naive physics"* is a mental model that represents natural or technical systems. The word naive is used because the commonsense idea about how nature works is incomplete or inconsistent, and it depends on metaphors and similarities. In physics, novices or even experts use simple models to explain highly complex physical systems. Such analogical comparisons are used to map the structure of complex systems. Naive physics mental models are used for two purposes: (1) to enable a person to decompose complex systems into smaller more units, each of which can be seen as a mental model of his own; (2) and to help people perform thought experiments.
3. The third view, *"reasoning by model"*, is a concept where a mental model is used for deductive reasoning. In contrast to the general belief that deductive reasoning is based on some logical structure, this view argues that reasoning is a semantic process based on the manipulation of mental models. People use their common knowledge as well as linguistic knowledge to construct their mental models and to draw a conclusion.
4. The last concept is called *"discourse model"*, *"situation model"*, or *"scenario"*. Mental models in this category are seen as mental representations of a verbal description of some real or virtual state of affairs. The mental model is closely related to knowledge perception and knowledge structures. Perception and knowledge are the principal sources for mental models. The perception of visual, auditive, tactile information is one side of the higher cognitive processes. Individual knowledge is on the other side.

Mental models are constructed in working memory, and they are the result of perception, comprehension of discourse, or imagination [John99, pp. 525]. If mental models are the end result of perception and comprehension they can underlie reasoning. Human beings use mental models to formulate conclusions and to test the strength of these conclusions by checking whether other mental models of the premises refuse them.

2.1.4 Neurosciences

The field of neurosciences covers a broad range of related disciplines with loosely defined boundaries. For Albright and Neville [AlNe99, pp. li], *cognitive neuroscience* investigates the fundamental question of knowledge and its representation by the brain. This means that cognitive neuroscience is a discipline of information processing. By using this definition, the field of cognitive neuroscience can be described with several research questions:

- Information acquisition (sensation);
- Interpretation to confer meaning (perception and recognition);
- Storage or modification (learning and memory);
- Use to ruminate (thinking and consciousness);
- Use to predict the future state of the environment and the consequences of action (decision making);
- Behavior guide (motor control); and
- Communication (language).

2.1.4.1 Neuron Development

One of the key research issues of neurosciences is **neuron development** [Chur86; Core01; Hofe81; Jose93; RaEs00]. To understand the mechanism of neurons helps to understand the learning process because learning is the process by which we acquire new knowledge. Figure "Principle Parts of a Neuron" illustrates the flow of information [Carl00, p. 419].

The nervous system is the center of consideration. Neurons communicate with each other and with other types of cells outside the nervous system. Carlson [Carl00, pp. 418] describes the nervous system as follows: some neurons serve as sensory receptors, detecting environmental stimuli and providing information required for perception. Other neurons have the task to monitor varies characteristics of the body, such as temperature or blood pressure. The main part of a neuron is called the *soma* which includes the nucleus that contains chromosomes. Attached to the soma of neurons are several treelike *dendrites* and a single axon which often branches extensively. Dendrites receive information from other neurons, and axons transmit the information to other neurons. The *axon* is a long hollow tube filled with a jellylike fluid. Most axons are insulated from other axons by the myelin sheath produced by glial cells. Each branch of the axon ends in a terminal button that forms part of a synapse.

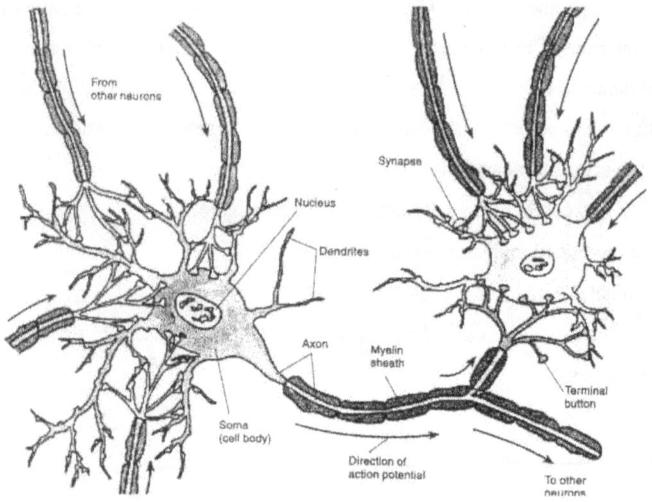

Figure 3: Principle Parts of a Neuron

The *synapse* is the junction through which information is passed from one neuron to another. The neuron that transmits information through a synapse is called the presynaptic neuron. The neuron that receives this information is called the postsynaptic neuron. The message carried by an axon is called an action potential. Although an action potential involves an electrical charge, it is a biological process rather than a simple transmission of electricity. An *action potential* consists of a brief impulse that travels at a speed up to 120m/sec. The membrane of an axon contains an electrical charge called the membrane potential. When at rest, the outside of the membrane is positively charged. When a neuron is stimulated, one or more action potentials are triggered in an axon. Each action potential consists of the entry of a small quantity of sodium ions which produce a brief reversal in the electrical charge. Action potentials begin at the junction of the axon with the soma and travel down each of the branches to their terminal buttons. Once an action potential is triggered in an axon of a given neuron, it is transmitted through all the branches to the terminal button. This observation is called the all-or-none law. When an action potential reaches a terminal button, it triggers the release of a small quantity of chemicals called *neurotransmitter* (a process called synapse). Different types of neurons release different types of neurotransmitters through their terminal button. The effect is divided into two categories: the excitatory effect which increases the rate at which action potentials occur in the axon of the postsynaptic neuron; and the inhibitory effect which decrease this rate.

Sensory neurons receive information from the environment and the gustatory neurons on the tongue and from olfactory neurons in the mucous membrane inside the nose that are sensitive to particular chemicals dissolved in salvia or contained in the air we breathe. Information received from all sensory neurons is transmitted to the central nervous system through a synaptic process with other neurons. Furthermore, neurons that are responsible for the control of muscle movements do so by means of synaptic connections with the cells of these organs.

2.1.4.2 The Brain

The *brain* contains several billion neurons which exchange information through synapses. The brain [OrCa91] and the spinal cord together form the central nervous system. The nerves connect the central nervous system with various sensory and motor structures throughout the body, and they make up the peripheral nervous system. The brain has three major divisions [Krec74, pp. 66]: the forebrain, the midbrain, and the hindbrain.

The ***forebrain*** includes the cerebrum, the thalamus and the hypothalamus. The *cerebrum* develops as an outgrowth near the front end of the forebrain, and there are two such enlargements referred to as cerebral hemispheres. On the exterior of each hemisphere is a layer of cortex. The cerebral cortex is essential to many complex functions. Within the hemispheres are several large nuclei, known as the basal ganglia, which are part of the neural system involved in the control of fine movement. The neurons whose cell bodies are concentrated in the cerebral cortex and the basal ganglia contribute many of their axons to the large mass of intermingled tracts that comprise much of the hemisphere interior. The tracts that run from one hemisphere to the other are known as commissures, and the most known one is the *corpus callosum*. *Thalamus and hypothalamus* are collective names for four groups of individual nuclei. The cells in the different thalamic nuclei send fibers to different areas of the cerebral cortex. Many of the thalamic nuclei receive fibers from sensory receptors enabling them to serve as way stations on pathways for incoming sensory information. For example, the lateral geniculate nucleus and the medial geniculate nucleus are thalamic nuclei involved in vision and audition.

The ***midbrain*** includes a large part of a structure called the reticular formation. The reticular formation initiates impulses that help to control the level of arousal and alertness of part of the central nervous system, particularly the cerebral cortex.

The cerebellum is part of the ***hindbrain***. It has a cortex much like the cerebrum, and it has many connections to the cerebral cortex, the basal ganglia, and the spinal cord. The cerebellum plays a role in regulating and coordinating motor activity. The *pons* is a prominent part of the hindbrain that serves as a way station for tracts running between the cerebrum and the cerebellum; it also includes nuclei that help control sleep and waking. The medulla is the most posterior part of the brain, and it resembles the spinal cord into which it blends in appearance and function. The spinal cord is the continuation of the central nervous system down one's back. It consists of cell bodies covered with fiber tracts to carry sensory and motor impulses between the rest of the body and the brain. The major structure of the brain is visualized in Figure "Brain Structure" [Krec74, p. 67]. All of the brain except the cerebral hemispheres and the cerebellum are referred to as the brain stem because it appears to form a stalk from which the cerebrum and cerebellum sprout.

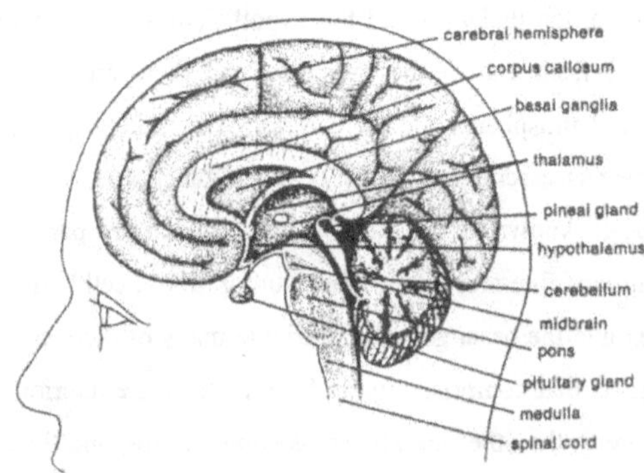

Figure 4: Brain Structure

In the early studies of cognitive neuroscience is the *localization of functions* [GeGa87; MoSe88; WhCi94, pp. 425]. The human brain has two anatomically and functionally different cerebral hemispheres, a property of the human brain is known as the cerebral asymmetry. The functional difference between the two hemispheres is that the left side is responsible for language functions and the right side is responsible for nonlanguage functions such as the control of spatial abilities. Furthermore, the left hemisphere is specialized in voice and music, and the production of certain types of complex movement such as writing. The right hemisphere focuses on complementary movements such as drawing, dressing, or constructing objects. Thus, the right hemisphere is superior to the left hemisphere for recognizing emotion and it plays an important role in the comprehension of humor.

2.1.4.3 Perception

The study of *perception* [Rock75] is one of the oldest enterprises in psychology. From the sounds and light waves and the pressure and chemicals that reach our body, the senses extract information about the world around us, enabling us to distinguish between different things, to note similarities, and to ignore irrelevancies. Norman and Rumelhart describe the general system for perception and memory illustrated in Figure "General Perception System" [NoRu70, p. 21].

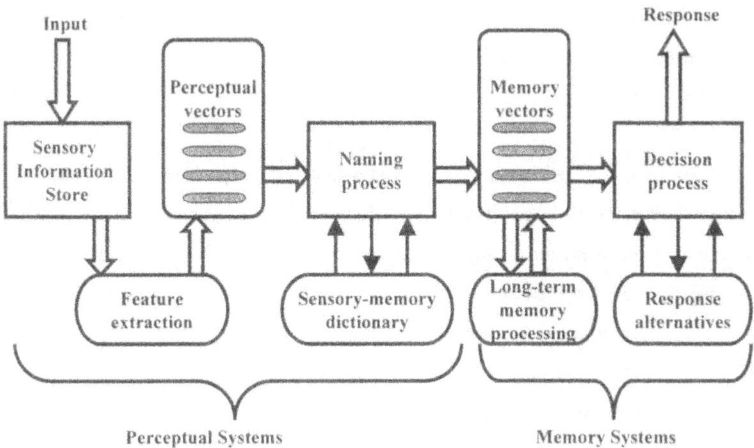

Figure 5: General Perception System

Norman and Rumelhart [NoRu70, pp. 21] define the terms perception and memory. Perception includes "those processes involved in the initial transduction of the physical signal into some sensory image, the extraction of relevant features from the sensory image, and the identification of that list of features with a previously learned structure. By memory, we mean the processes that act to retain the material that was sent to it from the perceptual system".

Figure "General Perception System" describes the *perceptual and memory system*. Physical *inputs* are transformed by the sensory system into a sensory image temporarily stored in the *sensory information system*. Information can be represented by means of a list of its features or attributes. For example, spoken words might be represented by a list of its phonemes or distinctive features. These lists are represented as *vectors* in the model. Critical features are extracted from each item and placed in the appropriate perceptual vector. The *naming* system transforms the vectors of perceptual features into vectors of memory attributes. The use of a dictionary helps one match physical features with psychological features. The naming process usually takes place in a rush with the perception of the physical system being incomplete and noisy, one where several things are competing for attention. The output of the naming dictionary is an ordered list of attributes formed into a *memory vector* that contains the name of the stimulus item. The type of *response* depends on three influences: (1) questions asked of the *decision process*; (2) the set of possible response *alternatives*; and (3) the attributes that remain in each memory vector, either temporarily (as *short term memory* attributes) or more permanently (as *long term memory* attributes).

Direct perception is the basis of knowledge and a source for information. If human beings do not trust their perception they will not be able to come to a conclusion about the world, and they will achieve no reasoning or interference [Arno84, pp. 3]. Sekuler and Blake [SeBl85, pp. 423] discuss the relationship between *uncertainty and perception*. One way to discover the importance of knowledge to perception is to examine perception under conditions of uncertainty. One example to illustrate this situation is the study of hearing. If a listener does not know what frequency to expect, then he finds it harder to hear a faint tone. Giving the listener cues will make it easier to overcome the lack of knowledge about the frequency and to hear the tone. To eliminate uncertainty is by giving cues to the person.

The perceiver's knowledge of the world has an important impact on perception such as knowledge of memories from lifetime experience or from cues immediately preceding some event.

2.1.5 Computational Intelligence

2.1.5.1 History of Artificial Intelligence

In the *MIT Encyclopedia of Cognitive Sciences*, Jordon and Russel [JoRu99, pp. lxxiii] use the term computational intelligence to express both existing views of artificial intelligence (AI): an engineering discipline concerned with the creation of intelligent machines and an empirical science involved in the computational modelling of human intelligence. The term computational intelligence is a neutral one for both AI views, a common understanding of intelligence in computational terms. Artificial Intelligence is a new generation of computing technology and capability that seeks to achieve intelligence through computation. Any computation requires a representation of some entity and a procedure to manipulate it. Applied AI is the engineering counterpart to some parts of cognitive science. While philosophy, psychology, neurosciences, and linguistics focus on detailed explanations for individual human intelligence and on descriptions of the human brain, AI is an approach that requires the development of programs, databases, and algorithms to exhibit human behavior. For Nilsson [Nils98, p. 1], AI "is concerned with intelligent behavior in artefacts. Intelligent behavior, in turn, involves perception, reasoning, learning, communicating, and acting in complex situations. AI has one of its long-term goals the development of machines that can do these things as well as humans can, or possible even better. Another goal of AI is to understand this kind of behavior whether it occurs in machines or in humans or other animals".

Russel and Norvig [RuNo95, pp. 16] see the 1952 to 1969 period as the early years of AI, years full of enthusiasm and successes. The dream of creating intelligent artefacts has existed for many centuries. The birth of AI is considered at the Dartmouth College conference in summer of 1956. Minsky and McCarthy organized the conference, and McCarthy coined the name "artificial intelligence". Among the conference members were Simon and Newell, who had already implemented the Logic Theorist Program at the Rand Corporation. Minsky and McCarthy went on to found the AI laboratory at the

Massachusetts Institute of Technology and Simon and Newell founded the AI laboratory at Carnegie Mellon University. Later McCarthy moved to Stanford, and he founded the AI laboratory there. In 1963 the first AI text was *Computers and Thought* edited by Feigenbaum and Feldman, a collection of 21 papers by the early AI researchers. In the mid to late 1960s, regular AI conferences began to be held. In recent years, the *Probabilistic Reasoning in Intelligent System* by Judea Pearl influences a new acceptance of probability and decision making theory in AI. Furthermore, the belief network formalism was invented to facilitate reasoning about uncertain evidence. This approach has come to dominate AI research on uncertain reasoning and expert systems. Since the main focus of this book is uncertainty and knowledge measurement, its primary exposition is the process of reasoning and decision making with uncertain information.

2.1.5.2 Representation and Reasoning under Uncertainty

Probability theory [JoRu99, pp. lxxiii] is the tool to handle uncertain information. It is a tool for dealing with degrees of belief; i.e., a sentence is assigned a numerical degree of belief between 0 and 1 [RuNo95, pp. 415]. For example, if a patient has a toothache, we believe that there is an 80% (probability of 0.8) chance that the patient has a cavity. This probability could be derived from statistical data that 80% of the toothache patients have cavities, or it can be derived from general medical information or a combination of both. Standard probability theory distinguishes between two kinds of knowledge: prior knowledge and posterior knowledge, the latter defined by Jordan and Russell [JoRu99, p. lxxxii] as knowledge that "comes in form of *prior* probability distributions over the possible assignments of values to sub-sets of the random variables. Then, when evidence is obtained about the values of some of the variables, inference algorithms can infer *posterior* probabilities for the remaining unknown variables".

The prior probability is also called *unconditional probability* and the notation P(A) (proposition A is true) is used. P(A) only can be used when no other information is available. The moment new information B is known, the reasoning process must use the conditional probability. Posterior probability is referred to as *conditional probability* with the notation that P(A|B) can be interpreted as probability of A given that all we know is B.

The *Bayesian approach to uncertainty* [FrSm97; Lee97; LuSt89; Vier87] is based on formal probability theory, and it shows up in several areas of AI research, research areas such as pattern recognition and classification problems. Assuming the random distribution of events, probability theory allows the calculation of more complex probabilities from previously known results. Probability theory provides a mechanism for drawing plausible conclusions from uncertain premises. In mathematical probability theory, individual probability instances are worked out by sampling and by combinations of probabilities, using the formula below [LuSt89, p. 310]:

Probability (A and B) = probability (A) * probability (B)

where A and B are independent events.

The contribution of Bayes' research consists of a unique method for calculating conditional probabilities. The *Bayes' Theorem* is one of the most important results of probability. Bayes' results provide a way of computing the probability for a hypothesis following from a particular piece of evidence given only the probability with which the evidence follows from actual causes (hypotheses). The Bayes' equation underlies all modern AI systems for probabilistic inference [RuNo95, p. 426]. The Bayes' Theorem, also referred to as Bayes' rule or Bayes' rule, is formulated as follows [LuSt89, p. 310]:

$$P(H_i / E) = \frac{P(E / H_i) * P(H_i)}{\sum_{k=1}^{n} (P(E / H_k) * P(H_k))}$$

where

$P(H_i / E)$ = Probability that H_i is true given evidence of E;

$P(H_i)$ = Probability that H_i is true overall;

$P(E / H_i)$ = Probability of observing evidence E when H_i is true;

n = Number of possible hypotheses.

The representation of uncertainty about parameters or hypotheses as probabilities is central to Bayesian interference [Cong97]. In other words, under his framework, it is possible to calculate the probability that a parameter lies in a given interval or the probability of a hypothesis about a parameter or a set of parameters. Congdon [Cong97, p. 3] states, "the learning process involved in Bayesian inference is one of modifying one's initial probability statements about the parameters prior to observing the data to updated or posterior knowledge incorporating both prior knowledge and the data at hand. Thus prior subject matter knowledge about a parameter ... are an important aspect of the inference process". This means [Cong97, p. 3]:

$$posterior\ distribution = \frac{likelihood * prior\ distribution}{\sum(likelihood * prior)}$$

where the dominator (the likelihood accumulated over all possible prior values) is a fixed normalizing factor which ensures that the posterior probabilities sum to 1.

The Bayesian approach encodes all uncertainty about model parameters and structure as possibilities. The *probability network*, often called Bayes network or *belief network*, was conceptualized in the late 1970s, and Bayesian networks have emerged as a general representation schema for uncertain knowledge. For Pearl [Pear99, pp. 72], Bayesian networks can be described as a directed, acyclic graphs (DAGs) whose nodes represent variables of interest (e.g., the temperature of a device) and the links represent informational or causal dependencies among the variables. The strength of a dependency is represented by conditional probabilities attached to each cluster of parent-child nodes in the network. Figure "Bayesian Network" below illustrates a Bayesian network with six variables [Pear90, p. 350].

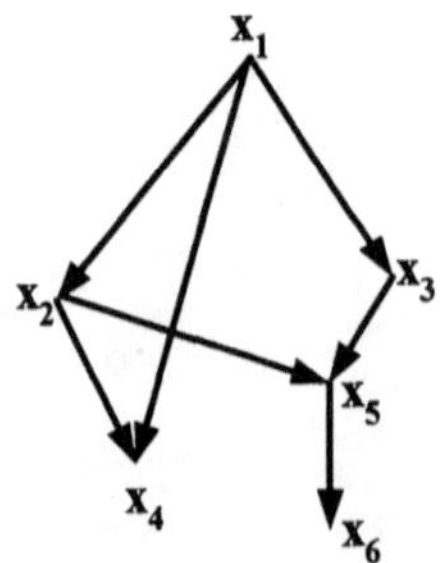

Figure 6: Bayesian Network

Pearl [Pear90, pp. 350] explains the "Bayesian Network" figure as follows: if the graph contains the variables x_1, ... x_n and S_i is the set of parameters of parents for variable x_i, a complete and consistent quantification can be attained by specifying for each node $x_{i,}$ a subjective assessment P (x_i | S_i) of the likelihood that x_i will attain a specific value given the possible states of S_i. The product of all these assessments,

$$P(x_i,....x_n) = \prod_i P(x_i \mid S_i)$$

constitutes a joint-probability[4] model that supports the assessed quantities. That means, if the conditional probabilities P (x_i | S_i) dictated by P(x_1, ... x_n) are computed, it recovers the original assessments. The advantage of the Bayesian network is that it can be seen as a clear graphical representation of many independent relationships embedded in the underlying probabilistic model. In the book *Readings in Uncertain Reasoning* [Pear90, p. 351] Pearl notes that Bayesian methods "provide coherent prescriptions for choosing actions and meaningful guarantees of the quality of these choices. The prescription is based on the realization that normative knowledge – that is, judgements about values, preferences, and desirability – represents a valuable abstraction of actual human experience and that, like its factual knowledge counterpart, it can be encoded and manipulated to produce recommendations". The occurrence of events is quantified by probabilities, and, alternatively, the desirability of action-consequences is quantified by utilities.

For Morris et al. [MoCN97], Figure "Bayesian Network Example" [MoCN97, p. 385; Pear99, p. 73] represents a network in which the variables have to do with the causal mechanisms underlying how the pavement could get wet. This means, for example, the pavement will not get wet even when the sprinkler is on if the pavement is covered with a blanket. There is no arrow from K to L because the sprinkler does not directly cause a slippery pavement. However, if we learned the sprinkler was on, then the probability will increase that the pavement would be slippery because it would be more probable that the pavement is wet. There are only arrows from direct causes to effects. According to Pearl

[4] A joint probability distribution specifies an agent's probability assignments to all propositions in the domain [JoNo95, p. 425].

[Pear99, p. 73], a belief network is a model of the environment rather than a model for the reasoning processes.

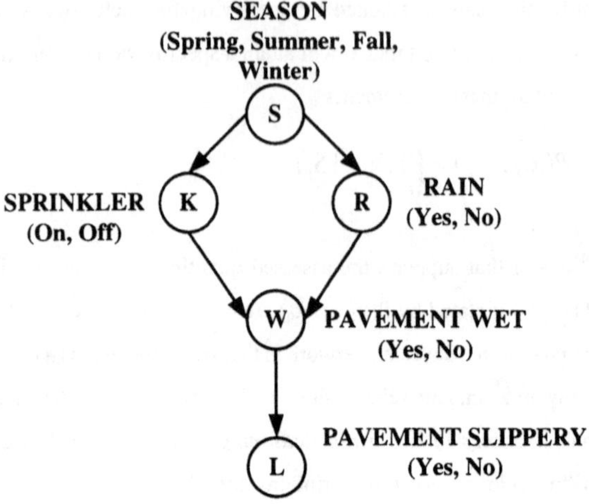

Figure 7: Bayesian Network Example

An alternative approach to Bayesian reasoning is the *certainty factor theory* [Negn02, pp. 74; Pars01, pp. 66]. The general principles of this theory were first introduced in MYCIN which is an expert system designed for the diagnosis of and therapy for blood infections and meningitis. The developers of MYCIN could not use the classical probability approach because medical experts expressed their beliefs in terms that were neither logical nor consistent. Therefore, they introduced a certainty factor (cf) which is a number to measure the belief of an expert. The maximum value of the certainty factor is +1 (definitely true) and the minimum value is –1 (definitely false). Thus, a positive value is a degree of belief and a negative value is a degree of disbelief. The certainty factor theory has the following syntax [Negn02, p. 74]:

IF < evidence E >
THEN < hypothesis H > {cf}

The certainty factor represents the belief in hypothesis H given the occurrence of evidence E. Furthermore, the certainty factor theory is based on two functions: the first function measuring belief MB(H,E) and the second function measuring the disbelief MD(H,E). The values for MB(H,E) and MD(H,E) range between 0 and 1. Negnevitsky [Negn02, p. 75] states that these two functions are indicators of the degree to which the belief in hypothesis H would be increased if evidence E were observed and the degree to which the disbelief in hypothesis H would be increased by observing the same evidence E.

Another important model is the *theory of fuzzy logic and fuzzy sets* [KaTe01] which was introduced in 1965 by Zadeh [RuBP98; SaSZ97; Zade99, pp. 335]. Fuzzy sets can be defined as sets with boundaries that are not required to be precise. Each fuzzy set can be characterized by a function that assigns a degree of membership in the fuzzy set to each element of a set. Fuzzy sets use the continuum of values between 0 and 1. This function is called a membership function. For Zadeh, fuzzy logic "is a body of concepts, constructs, and techniques that relate to modes of reasoning that are approximate rather than exact. Much of – perhaps most – human reasoning is approximate in nature. In this perspective, the role model for fuzzy logic is the human mind" [Zade99, p. 335]. Fuzzy logic reflects the pervasive imprecision of human reasoning, therefore it is much better suited to serve as logic of human cognition. Parson makes the point that fuzzy sets are used to model vague information rather than uncertain information. Fuzzy logic has been very successful in control systems for products [NoRu95, p. 463] such as automatic transmissions, trains, video cameras, and electric shavers.

2.1.6 Linguistics and Language

Language plays a key role in understanding cognitive phenomena [Chie99, pp. xci; Chom98]. Language has a dynamic character because it changes across time and space, it varies along social and gender dimensions, and it differs sometimes in idiosyncratic ways from speakers to speaker. For Chomsky [Chom75, p. 4] "language is a mirror of mind in a deep and significant sense. It is a product of human intelligence, created anew in each individual by operations that lie for beyond the reach of will or consciousness". Every human being uses language which is a complex symbolic system of communication. The language user can express the full range of their experience by joining words into clauses, sentences, and connected discourse. Human language developed because the human brain has unique characteristics that make symbolic thought and grammatical structure possible. Human language can be structured into a number of subsystems [FrRo83]:

1. *Phonology* is a research area which includes all the significant sounds used in a language and the rules for combining them. The study of speech sounds (phones) is called *phonetics*. Phonemes are defined as the sounds that the speakers of a language regard as different from one another. To describe speech sounds, a person has to decide what an individual sound is and how it differs from another. In order to understand the nature of a language, one has to understand the nature of these sounds and their pronunciation. Articulatory phonetics is a framework for this problem. The production of any speech sound involves the movement of an airstream. Most speech sounds are produced by pushing lung air out of the body through the mouth and sometimes through the nose (voiced vs. voiceless sounds, nasal vs. oral sound). So, phonology is the study of sound patterns found in human language and the knowledge a speaker has about the sound patterns of their particular language.
2. *Morphology* of a language includes rules for word formation and variation. Morphemes are the smallest units in a language, and they carry a definable meaning or grammatical function. In each language rules exist related to the formation of words, the so called morphological rules which determine how morphemes combine to form new words. There are derivational morphemes because a new word is derived when morphemes are conjoined to others. For example, when a verb is conjoined with the suffix –able, the result in an adjective, as in desire+able, or health+ful. Furthermore, one morpheme may have different pronunciations that are different phonetic forms in different contexts.
3. *Lexicon and Semantics.* The lexicon and semantics of language are its individual words (lexicon) and the meanings attached to them (semantics). Semantics concerns the study of word and morpheme meanings as well as the study of the rules for combining meanings. The meanings of morphemes and words are defined by their semantic properties. When two words have the same sound but differ semantically, they are homonyms or homophones. The use of homophones in a sentence may lead to ambiguity which occurs when a single utterance has more than one meaning or because of the structure of the sentence. The study of how context influences the way we interpret sentences in called pragmatics.

4. *Syntax.* The part of our linguistic knowledge that concerns the structure of sentences is called syntax. Syntax includes the rules for combining or rearranging words to produce different kinds of utterances: declarative sentence, imperatives, questions, or negative statements. By knowing a language, one knows which combinations or strings of morphemes are permitted by the syntactic rules and which are not. Those that conform to the syntactic rules are called sentences of the language.

Figure "Language Structure" [Chie99, p. xciv] shows a road map of the major modules that deal with language.

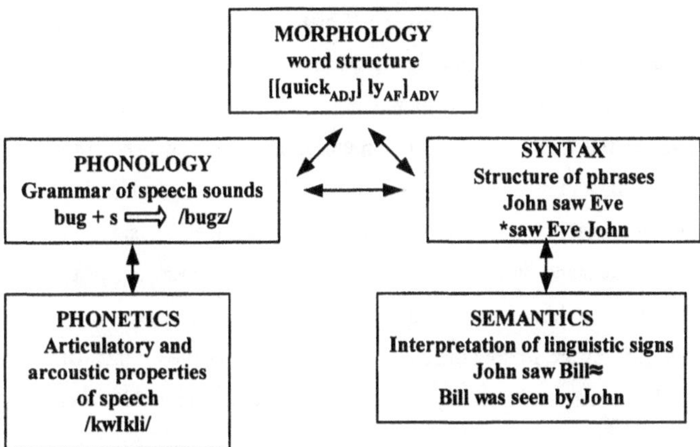

Figure 8: Language Structure

Language and culture [Levi99, pp. 441] have a high impact on each other. There are about 7000 or more distinct languages in the world and at least 20 language families. Each language is adapted to a cultural and social environment. Through language, human beings can participate on special cultural ideas, practices, and technological innovations. Also, Kess [Kess92, pp. 105] notes that language and society are interrelated and society, as we know it today, would not exist without language. To learn a language is not just the process of knowing semantic and grammatical references it is also a way individuals are helped to manage social interaction between those who speak. Through the choice of specific items from the linguistic *repertoire*, the attitudes, beliefs and thoughts of a speaker are expressed, and they may lay open the entire social and cultural context. For Kess [Kess92, p. 106], interaction by speech is a far more ritualistic activity than we may imagine. Each individual has the desire to interact with other members of the society and speech is a medium to communicate one's thoughts and feelings. However, interaction by speech can lead to misunderstanding, hostility, or even rejection if the norms of sociolinguistic interaction are not known. This process can go so far that people may cultivate certain styles of speech in order to belong to a certain group in society and to be recognized as a member of this group.

Language is the main human tool through which each individual can express their thoughts, and the modes of reasoning become manifest. For Chierchia [Chie99, p. cviii], language pathologies reveal aspects of the functioning of the brain on one hand and the use of language in human-computer interaction on the other, especially the research field of *speech recognition*. At the human-machine communication level, the need for a voice interface between humans and machines was evident, and it has been provided by speech-processing systems that enable a machine to speak (speech synthesis systems) and that enable a machine to understand human speech (speech-recognition systems) [Rabi99, pp. 790]. Linguistics is still searching for and collecting facts about the language of the world, but it experienced a shift toward finding mental mechanisms responsible for linguistic facts. Language research has a cross-disciplinary interaction with the other fields of cognitive science.

2.1.7 Culture, Cognition, and Evolution

The sixth discipline in cognitive science deals with culture, cognition, and evolution [SpHi99, pp. cxi]. Sperber and Hirschfeld [SpHi99] divide this research field into three categories: (1) cognition in a comparative and evolutionary perspective; (2) culture in an evolutionary and cognitive perspective; and (3) cognition in an ecological, social and cultural perspective. The third view will be the primary focus of in this sub-chapter because it relates most to the knowledge research. Cognitive activity takes place in a complex, information-rich, and ever-changing environment. Tomasello [Toma99] notes that all human beings share their cognitive skills and knowledge with other individuals; meaning that "all primate species use their skills and knowledge to formulate creative and insightful strategies when problems arise in either the physical or the social domain. … In the current hypothesis human beings do indeed possess a species-unique cognitive adaptation, and it is in many ways an especially powerful cognitive adaptation because it changes in fundamental ways the *process* of cognitive evolution." [Toma99, p. 201]. The try to understand other persons, changes the way of interaction and social learning.

Cultures are not static; they change over time when one culture comes into contact with another culture. Berry uses the term acculturation [Berr00, p. 395] to express the process of change that involves either group or collective phenomena or individual or psychological phenomena. Examples for the first change process are language, politics, religion, work, school, or social relationships, and examples for the second encompass phenomena such as identifies, beliefs, values, attitudes, and abilities. Intercultural contacts influence the way individuals behave and act.

Social cognition is the sub-field of social psychology that studies mental representations and processes that underlie social perception, social judgment, and social influence. Culture is the prime determinant of individual learning processes. Learning is affected by the culture, including, for example, the culture of a family environment. *Vygotsky* (1896-1934) was concerned with the issue of how human mental functioning is shaped by its historical, cultural, and institutional context. The framework Vygotsky developed can be summarized in a few issues [Wert99, pp. 878]:

- He used a genetic, or developmental, method, meaning that mental functioning can only be understood by examining its origins and the transformations it undergoes in development.
- Vygotsky claimed that higher, uniquely human mental functioning in an individual has its origins in social processes, and it retains a "quasi-social" nature.
- Higher mental processes are mediated by social-culturally evolved tools and signs.

Central to social psychology is rationality and the study of reasoning in general. One area tries to model the actual behavior of economic agents. Assumptions about individual behavior play a key role in economic theorizing. The second area is determined by Kahneman and Tversky who introduced three judgment heuristics and their associated biases on how individuals reason under conditions of uncertainty.

2.2 Management Measurement Approach

"Measure for Learning not for Control!
In this way we will never destroy the
Wellspring of Knowledge – only help
each other to protect it and to utilise it better."

(Karl-Erik Sveiby)

2.2.1 Categorization Clusters for Knowledge Measurement Methods/Models

Over the years, research into measuring the value of company intangible assets or intellectual capital (IC) has produced many methods and theories. Knowledge measuring solutions can accelerate decision making processes, help enhance the speed of the business process, and deliver a decisive competitive advantage. If organizations want to be more successful today, they need have effective knowledge measuring systems. The success of professional knowledge organizations depends on how efficiently they can identify their knowledge potential, their knowledge workers, their critical knowledge, and their missing knowledge to locate the expertise and experience within the organization. However, measurement the effectiveness of knowledge management is not a simple task. As knowledge measuring becomes more structured and widespread, the need to establish different models and methods becomes more important. Skyrme [Skyr98, p. 1] identifies four factors that lead to pressure to measure:

- The growing irrelevance of existing measures. Organizations have recognized that intellectual assets, rather than physical assets, are the future. Traditional economic measures, such as conventional balance sheets, are not enough to establish the value of the organization.
- Growing recognition that intangible assets are more important to gain competitive advantages. The intangible assets range from brand names to the expertise of a knowledge worker.
- The focus on long-term shareholder value as a corporate goal. The shareholders want to get a better understanding of the company.
- Concerns about corporate governance. As seen in recent years, many successful companies failed due to their weakness in understanding the value of their knowledge and because they ignored the potential of intangible assets.

Based on these factors, new types of measurement systems are needed to help investors, managers, and policy-makers make decisions about the value of organization's knowledge. Also Housel and Bell [HoBe01] argue new metrics for knowledge assets must be developed in addition to traditional accounting and financial data. There are different groups, such as investors, management, and customers that need metrics for the knowledge potential of a company. Without the development of knowledge metrics, this valuable resource will result in some unused assets. Housel and Bell state, "knowledge metrics must be based on quantifiable, real-world-based raw data that can be rigorously and adequately captured in a common unit of measurement. In this way, they may be used to track and manage the direct impact of knowledge assets on value production" [HoBe01, p. 80]. Companies should shift to a knowledge-value-added methodology [HoBe01, pp. 91] that should help managers and executives to leverage and measure the knowledge that resides in the employees, information technology, and core processes. Contractor [Cont01] identifies six principal business circumstances in which intangible assets needs to be measured:

1. *Company sales, mergers and acquisitions.* In a merger and acquisition deal, the acquiring company wants not only have information about physical assets but also about the knowledge. It also could be of much interest if there are incompatibilities such as knowledge transfer cost or cultural compatibility problems between the merging companies.
2. *Sale, purchase, or licensing of separable assets.* Separable assets are, for example, brands, patents, copyrights, databases, or technologies that can be detached from the company that possesses them and transferred to another company. In this case, only a part of the company is spun off to another company. The question is, how much should the company pay for licensing or acquiring these assets.
3. *Lawsuits involving intellectual property infringement.* The court has to determine infringement costs and penalties.
4. *Tax liability.* The calculation of the tax liability in the context of the transfer of intangible assets plays a significant role.
5. *Corporate Alliances.* The valuations of the knowledge during a joint venture negotiation, or during other strategic alliances, plays a key role. The result decides the equity share and other fees of joint venture partners.
6. *R&D management.* The valuation of future knowledge generated by R&D investments is a key issue for the selection of competing of R&D projects. Another

issue concerns the valuation of R&D projects in the case of a joint R&D strategy between partners.

In the global economy, the measurement problem has become a key aspect because intangible assets are shared across borders between partners and among strategic alliances [Cont01, pp. 21]. Such knowledge transfer activities require a monetary value for the knowledge package, and the establishment of its value must be a management function. The landscape for clustering the different measurement methods and models for intangible assets is primarily influenced by three authors: Luthy [Luth98], Skyrme [Skyr98] and Sveiby [Svei02a]. Depending on the research approach of each of the three authors, the proposed methods and models for measuring intangible assets can be assigned to different classification schemes. Figure "Comparison of the Measurement Classification Schemas" was constructed by the author to differentiate the views.

<table>
<tr><th>SVEIBY (2002)</th><th>SKYRME (1998)</th><th>LUTHY (1998)</th></tr>
<tr><td>Organization Level + $-Valuation:
- MCM
- ROA</td><td rowspan="2">Asset Focus:
- Value-based Models</td><td rowspan="3">Financial Valuation and Organization Level</td></tr>
<tr><td rowspan="4">Component Level and $-Valuation:
- DIC</td></tr>
<tr><td rowspan="2">Benefit Focus</td></tr>
<tr><td rowspan="4">Component-by-component Evaluation</td></tr>
<tr><td rowspan="2">IC Measurement Focus</td></tr>
<tr><td rowspan="2">Component Level and No $-Evlauation:
- SC Methods</td></tr>
<tr><td>Action Focus:
- Performance Measurement</td></tr>
<tr><td>Organization Level + No $ Valuation</td><td>-</td><td>-</td></tr>
</table>

Figure 9: Comparison of the Measurement Classification Schemas

The delimitation of one classification to another is not definite as seen in the following discussion of the basic concepts of each author. ***Skyrme*** [Skyr98; Skyr00] uses three major motivation strategies for measuring intellectual assets as a classification schema: asset focus, action focus, and benefit focus. In addition to these three foci, a new generation of measurement methods is distinguished focuses on intellectual capital measurement models. In his report about measuring the value of knowledge, Skyrme [Skyr98, p. 14] clusters the different types of measurement systems into four motivation forms of measuring intellectual capital:

1. The *asset focus* provides a basis for a company valuation. It is used for trading assets or for analysts to value the company properly in the marketplace in order to earn a proper return for shareholders.
2. The *action focus* comprises performance measurement methods which use nonfinancial measures alongside financial measures, such methods as the Balanced Scorecard.
3. The *benefit focus* measures the outcomes of management actions and of investments (e.g., in a knowledge management program). These systems, having several characteristics in common, distinguish among different types of intellectual capital: such as human capital, structural capital, and customer capital.
4. A *new measurement focus* measures the intellectual capital of a company.

The measurement cluster from Sveiby is an extension of the suggested cluster from Luthy. ***Luthy*** [Luth98] distinguishes two general methods for measuring intellectual capital. The first, a *component-by-component* evaluation, includes measures appropriate for each component. Examples are market share or the value of patents. Different measures have a different relevance and usefulness at different levels in an organization. The second measurement method measures the value of intellectual assets in financial terms at the *organization level* without reference to the individual components of intellectual capital (e.g., shareholder value).

Sveiby [Svei02a, http://www.sveiby.com/Articles/IntangibleMethods.htm, Date 2003-02-16] uses the classification schema from Luthy as his basic framework, and he extends it to the existing model by dividing the measurement models into four clusters: (1) organization level and No $-Evaluation; (2) organizational level and $-Evaluation; (3) component level and No $-Evaluation; and (4) component level and $-Evaluation. Sveiby assigns the different knowledge approaches to four measurement categories:

1. *Direct Intellectual Capital Methods (DIC).* The DIC methods estimate the \$-value of intangible assets by identifying various components. Once the components are identified, they can be evaluated directly either individually or as an aggregated coefficient.
2. *Market Capitalization Methods (MCM).* The MCM calculate the difference between a company's market capitalization and its stockholders equity as the value of its intellectual capital or intangible assets.
3. *Return on Assets Methods (ROA).* The ROA methods divide the average pre-tax earnings of an organization for a period of time by the average tangible assets of the company. The result is the ROA of a company, and it is compared with the industry average. The difference is multiplied by the organization's average tangible assets to compute the average annual earnings from the organization's intellectual capital. Dividing the intellectual capital earnings by the company's average cost of capital or by a reference interest rate results in an estimate of the value of an organization's intellectual capital.
4. *Scorecard Methods (SC).* SC methods identify different components of intellectual capital and corresponding indicators which are generated in scorecards or graphs. According to Sveiby, the SC methods are similar to the DIC methods but without making a \$-value of the intangible assets.

The transition from one measurement cluster to the other is fluid and it cannot be very sharp. If one compares the clustering approach from Sveiby with that of Skyrme, they are similar in the sense that they make a distinction in models which focus on the measurement of the \$-value and on the measurement of some components within the company. Sveiby gives the most detailed state-of-the art of knowledge measurement methods. Therefore, the following sub-chapters are oriented to his clustering model. Methods concerning the \$-valuations clusters, which are DIC, MCM and ROA, will be explained and discussed because they focus on monetary valuation. The scorecard methods measure on the basis of non-\$-valuation, and they are explained in more detail because of this reason and because they are the basic framework for the derivation of the knowledge potential view (see Chapter 3).

2.2.2 Direct Intellectual Capital Methods (DIC)

2.2.2.1 Technology Factor and Citation Weighed Patents

Citation Weighed Patents is discussed by Bontis [Bont96; Bont00], who introduces the situation of Dow Chemical which was one of the first companies to use patents as a proxy for intellectual capital measurement. Central is the determination of the Technology Factor. This methodology, first developed by Arthur D. Little, was adjusted by Khoury [Khou02] during his stay at Dow Chemical. The Technology Factor (TF) measures the extent to which cash flow is derived from the technology itself.

In the case of Dow Chemical [Bont00, p. 30], the TF is estimated to identify the impact of R&D efforts that lead to the creation of intellectual property. The indicators used are, for example, R&D expense per sale dollar, number of patents, income per R&D expense, and project life-cycle cost per sales dollar. According to Khoury [Khou02], the TF is a hybrid of the market and income methods, and it minimizes their weaknesses by drawing on both market data and income data. The TF approach seeks the most specific market and income information available, and it places this information in a reasoned context. For Dow Chemical competitive advantages are gained through key value drivers. Examples of Dow Chemical intellectual properties are: patents, trademarks, trade secrets, know-how, engineering drawings, and computer software. These intellectual properties have a value which can be calculated based on the economic impact of the technology on the business enterprise. Calculation of the valuation of the Technology Factor method can be done with the following formula [Khou02, p. 339]:

$$\text{Value of the Intangibles} = \text{Technology Factor (TF)} * \text{Incremental Business NPV}$$

$$0\,\% \leq \text{TF} \leq 100\%$$

where

NPV = Net present value of the income from products or processes that are directly tied to the technology being evaluated. This NPV is a preliminary figure, a cash flow that only has been discounted based on an expected rate of return, such as 12 percent. It has not yet been discounted by the TF to reflect a specific business situation and competitive environment;

and

TF = 0%-30% = Low Value;

TF = 30%-50% = Medium Value;

TF = 50%-70% = High Value.

Considering all existing attributes of technology develops the Technology Factor. These attributes fall into two categories. The first is *utility issues* which include attributes such as the usefulness of the technology to the company, the usefulness of the technology to others, the time required for implementation, and the expected useful life of the technology. The second category concerns *competitive advantage issues* such as the differentiation of technology, possible alternative technologies, legal strength, competitors' technology, the teaching value of the patent, and the owner's right to use the technology. The next step calculation of the technology factor involves, different internal persons of a company and external members, even representatives from a company which want to purchase the technology and they form a valuation task force. Each member of the task force then will be asked to evaluate the utility and competitive advantage issues. The following scores are possible: (+) add value; (-) destroy value; and (0) no impact. Finally, through task force group consensus, one single technology factor percentage is derived by taking the positive and negative judgments into consideration. Putting these TF characteristics together, the valuation procedure can be described as follows [http://www.inavisis.com/techfactor.html, Date 2002-07-23]:

1. Calculate the present value (PV) of the business cash flow;
2. Calculate the technology factor by using utility issues and competitive issues;
3. Value of a Technology = PV * TF.

The TF quality depends greatly on the quality of the assumptions and inputs. In addition, the composition of the task force and the special expertise of the task force members for the valuating technology are critical success factors. Khoury suggests that at least one other methodology that fits the specific objectives of the valuation should be applied in addition to the calculation of the technology factor.

Furthermore, Hall, Jaffe, and Trajtenberg [HaJT01] make a distinction between patents and their citations. The authors note that "the idea of using subsequent citations to a patent as a measure of the patent's value rests on the argument that valuable technological knowledge within the firm tends to generate patents that future researchers build on (and therefore cite) when doing their own innovation. ... We find that augmenting firms' patent counts with citation intensity information produces a proxy for the firms' knowledge stocks that is considerably more value-relevant than the simple patent count itself. It remains true that, for most of the time period, patent-related measures cannot win a 'horserace' with R&D as an explanator of market value" [HaJT01, p. 13 and p. 22]. Hall et al. argue that the citation of patents gives an idea about its technological impact. Patents are seen as a proxy for inventive output, and patent citations are a proxy for knowledge flows or knowledge impacts. If there is evidence that patent-related measures are correlated with market values, it is evidence they are proxies for the private economic value of the firm's knowledge stock. If persons other than the citing inventor identify a patent, it is an indication of the patent's importance, impact or even economic value. Hall et al. suggest that the citation-weighed patents are a better measure of innovative output than pure patent counts.

2.2.2.2 Inclusive Valuation Methodology

McPherson introduced the Inclusive Valuation Methodology [cited in Skyr98, pp. 70]. He argues that traditional accounting methods use additive as opposed to combinatorial measures. In his methodology, McPherson combines information and monetary value by taking aspects of measurement theory and combinatorial mathematics into account. McPherson describes the focus of his research as the use and value of information [cited in Skyr98, p. 70]:

> *"If we are to stalk the value of information to a business, a useful start can be made by viewing the business as a knowledge machine that converts information into useful or enjoyable products that are potentially valuable."*

In general, McPherson sees cash flow as the ultimate measure for tangible assets. In a second step, intangible assets can be taken into account. This methodology uses combined hierarchies of weighted indicators, and it focuses on relative rather than absolute values. Figure "McPherson's Inclusive Valuation Methodology" [Skyr98, p. 72] visualizes the process of measurement of tangible and intangible assets.

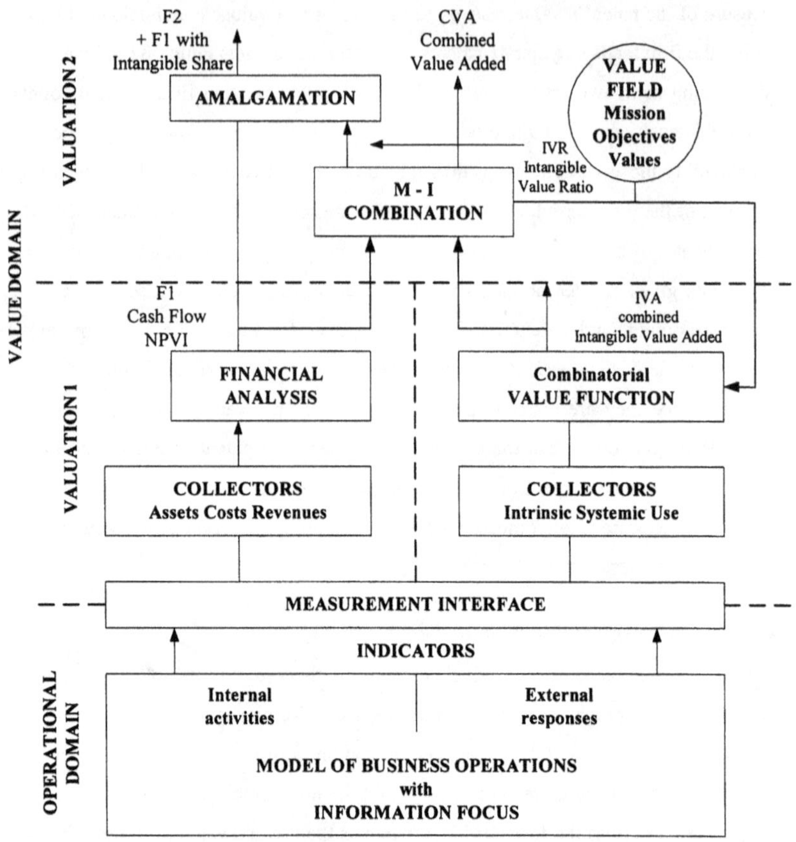

Figure 10: McPherson's Inclusive Valuation Methodology

McPherson combines two levels of valuation: the financial side (left side of Figure "McPherson's Inclusive Valuation Methodology") and the intangible measurement side (right side of Figure "McPherson's Inclusive Valuation Methodology"). For McPherson the measurement value for tangible assets is the cash flow. Therefore, the first level of valuation for the financial side is the calculation of the discounted net present value of cash flow. On the intangible side, the value is estimated by a number of attributes. These intangible attributes include: (1) input measures such as the availability of information and the efficiency of information gathering; (2) business output measures such as the contribution of individuals′ cognitive effectiveness; and (3) value in use such as contribution to the achievement of the business strategy. The second level of the McPherson Inclusive Valuation Methodology is the combination of monetary and intangible values into a coherent framework. The key formula of McPherson is [Skyr98, p. 73]:

$$CVA = MVA \circ IVA$$

where

CVA = Combined Value Added;

MVA = Monetary Value Added;

IVA = Intangible Value Added;

$\circ$ denotes a combinatorial operation.

The components of the formula are placed into three-dimensional value-space diagrams and binary combination planes. Furthermore, the methodology is implemented by means of a computer program which allows the manipulation of weights and hierarchies in real time. This means, McPherson functions as a mediator between the managers and his methodology, and he can change the weights and hierarchies during the managers' discussion. However, McPherson admits that his methodology is characterized by a high level of complexity and that managers are overwhelmed at first by the measurement procedure. The Inclusive Valuation Methodology has the objective of bringing managers and senior executives to think about the impact of information, knowledge, and bottom-line performance.

2.2.2.3 Value Explorer

The Value Explorer is advocated by Tiessen and Andriessen [TiAD00]. This approach is an accounting methodology proposed by KMPG Netherlands, and it focuses on a company's economic value or monetary value assigned to its intellectual capital. The Value Explorer uses a three step-measuring model [TiAD00, pp. 54]:

1. The Value Explorer measures a company's intrinsic strengths by analyzing the intangible assets hidden in a company's *core competencies*. The measurement of these strengths enables the rating of the intangible assets that make up the company's intellectual capital.

2. The Value Explorer identifies *strengths and weaknesses* for each of these competencies[5] using five different tests:
   a. the first test focuses on the value the competence adds for a customer (added-value test);
   b. the second test determines its competitiveness (competitiveness test);
   c. the third test evaluates the future potential (potentiality test);
   d. the forth test looks at the sustainability (sustainability test); and
   e. the last test assesses robustness (robustness test).
3. Finally, it rates and assigns a *monetary value* based on their economic potential to the core competencies of the company.

KPMG is distinguishing and allocating value to five types of intangibles [TiAD00, p. 55]:

1. *Assets and endowments*: The focus lies on the image, networking ability, and client relationship of a company.
2. *Competencies and implicit knowledge* should be built in order to gain new knowledge professionals. A mixture of competencies such as social (networking, team work, dialog), cognitive (reflection, creation, analysis) and information (questioning, sourcing, sensing) are necessary for professionals.
3. *Culture and values* deal with the reliability, quality, and client focused values.
4. *Technology and explicit knowledge* resides in patents, manuals and procedures.
5. *Management processes* focuses on management information and communication processes as well as on leadership questions.

Andriessen and Tiessen [TiAD00, p. 56] point out that the Value Explorer has three major benefits: (1) *The Value Explorer establishes a strategic management agenda.* It gives the Board of Directors and the CEO the ability to evaluate the reports on intangible assets; (2) *Direct Investments.* The Value Explorer calculates the value of the core competencies of a company in dollar terms, giving managers a decision platform to decide which intangible assets should be strengthened and which ones are not for further investment; and (3) *leads mergers and acquisitions.* Since the Value Explorer is determining the strengths and

[5] Competencies is the term used in much of the available literature. However, alternative words are abilities or skills. Because of the widespread use of competencies that word will be used throughout this book.

weaknesses of a company by quantifying core competencies in dollar values, it gives bankers and companies an in-depth insight for making buy and sell decisions. Knowledge of the strength and weaknesses of a company's intangible assets is a good basis for mergers and acquisitions.

The success of a knowledge company in the knowledge-driven society greatly depends on four guiding principles. First, the overall intangible *market value* of the company must be enhanced. Even if the management is aware of the importance of the knowledge resource, it has to find new ways of measuring and monitoring the knowledge. The fact is that every company has its in-house knowledge, and managers must find ways to calculate the value of that knowledge and to develop strategies to protect this valuable knowledge so it does not leave the company. The Value Explorer is one method of measuring the economic potential of a company. To accomplish the first principle, the identified knowledge of the company should add to the creation of *value for the customers*. The competitive advantage of the company depends on the knowledge of what the customer will want in five to ten years according to the French scientist and consultant Claude Fussler [TiAD00, p. 59]. The third principle focuses on the fact that a company also should add *value to society* and not only concentrate on increasing shareholder value. Tissen, Andriessen et al. [TiAD00] point out that there has to be a shift in thinking about doing business, a shift from the principle of being "built-to-compete" to the principle "built-to-last". The last principle is increasing the *value to people*. In recent years companies have recognized that their value rests on the experience and knowledge of their professionals who act and think independently. The work environment has changed dramatically from being repetitive, little judgement, task oriented, and the use of existing frameworks to a new work environment which is non-repetitive, encourages independent judgement, team oriented, and networked.

2.2.2.4 Intellectual Asset Valuation

Sullivan [Sull00] investigates a value-driven approach to intellectual capital. Value measurements are a basis for decision making especially in a business context. In an intellectual capital based view, managers know the value of an intangible asset or a piece of an intangible asset, this is the foundation of further decisions such as making more investments. Highly related to value measurement is the vision of a firm. If a firm knows its vision, then it has the ability to determine what part of its intellectual capital will help the company towards the vision. Since vision is a long-term issue, it can help the company to establish the present value of an intangible asset. Sullivan [Sull00, p. 93] distinguishes between two separate ways for thinking about intellectual capital. One is called the knowledge and brainpower path, and it focuses on creating and expanding the firm's knowledge. Major representatives of the view are Sveiby, Edvinsson, and Stewart. The second is the resource-based perspective which is concerned with the creation of profit from a firm's unique combination of intellectual capital and tangible resources. Representatives of this view are Sullivan, Teece, and Itami. At the 1995 ICM Gathering, intellectual capital was defined as "knowledge that can be converted into profit". The objective of the ICM Gathering was to get representatives of different views together to talk about methods for extracting value from intangible assets. There are two major elements of intellectual capital:

1. The first, humans and their embedded tacit knowledge, is called the Value Creation Component.
2. The second, named Value Extraction, focuses on intellectual assets which is a firm's codified knowledge. Some of these codified assets are legally protected, and they are referred to by the legal term "intellectual property". Examples of intellectual properties are patents, copyrights, trademarks, trade secrets, and semiconductor masks.

In the context of intellectual capital two kinds [Sull00, pp. 92] of values have to be distinguished: (1) *strategic position* which is similar for Sullivan with qualitative measures such as the image and competitive posture; and (2) *financial and economic value* which is easy to quantify in terms of price, share, or cash flow. At a more recent ICM meeting, they gave a list of different kinds of company values derived from their intellectual capital: (1) profit generation from income from products and services through sales, licensing royalties, and strategic alliance income; (2) profit generation from the intellectual property itself through sale, and price premiums; (3) strategic positioning through market share, leadership, and name recognition (e.g., branding, trademarking, reputation); (4) acquisition of the innovations of others; (5) customer loyalty; (6) cost reductions; and (7) improved productivity.

Concerning measurement, they are either qualitative or quantitative. Qualitative measures are judgement-based, and they are often used when it is not possible to assign a precise measurement. If it is difficult to measure the impact of intellectual capital directly, companies use indicators. Another way is to use vectors because they provide information on the direction as well as on the amount. To determine the quantitative value of a company, different management views, such as accounting, economics, intellectual capital, and shareholder value approaches, have to be taken into account. Table "Measurement Examples according to Sullivan" [HaSu00, p. 44] gives examples of measures for intellectual capital.

Qualitative Measures		**Quantitative Measures**	
Value Based	*Vector Based*	*Non-Dollar $*	*Dollar $*
• Value Category • Alignment with Vision & Strategy • Satisfaction • Quality	• Rate of Addition • Rate of Deletion • Backlog • Market Share Forecast • Coverage • Comprehensiveness • Stock Price	• Techniques Available • # of staff • Age • Remaining Life	• $ Invested • $ Received • Forecast Income • Costs to date • Forecast Cost

Table 1: Measurement Examples according to Sullivan

For a variety of people, like the CEO or financial analyst, it is of interest to determine the value of a knowledge company [Sull00, pp. 115]. According to Sullivan, a knowledge company has two fundamental sources of value: its innovations and its complementary business assets that are applied to their commercialization. There are six ways to convert these sources of value into profit: sale, out-licensing, joint venture to obtain and use needed complementary business assets, strategic alliance to obtain and exploit markets, integration, and donation. These six are understood by Sullivan as an all-inclusive package. The equation for the market value of a going concern can be written down as follows [Sull00, p. 120]:

$$V_m = VTA + DCF$$

where

V_m = Stock market value;

VTA = Values of the firm's tangible assets;

DCF = Discounted Cash Flow.

The equation means that the value of a company can be calculated as the sum of the value of its tangible assets and the net present value of its future cash flows. In terms of intellectual capital, the equation is modified in the following way:

$$V_m = V_{SC} + vdcf_{ic}$$

where

V_m = Stock market value;

sc = Structural capital;

dcf_{ic} = Discounted cash flows arising from the innovations of the company's IC.

This means, that the value of a knowledge company is the sum of the value of its tangible assets and the discounted value of the cash flow generated largely by the firm's intellectual capital. So intellectual capital is the creator of cash flow.

Furthermore, Sullivan introduced a formula to forecast the earnings of a firm. In this special case, three issues must be included in the calculation: (1) the earnings streams associated with the income generated by a company's intellectual capital; (2) a term to account for the earnings generated by the firm's complementary business assets; and (3) a term to account for any earnings associated with the firm's generic structural capital. These considerations lead to the following equation for total earnings [Sull00, p. 122]:

$$\begin{aligned} V_m = V_{TA} &+ \text{NPV of earnings from the firm's intellectual capital} \\ &+ \text{NPV of earnings from the firm's complementary business assets} \\ &+ \text{NPV of earnings from the firm's generic structural capital} \end{aligned}$$

where

V_{TA} = Value of the firm's tangible assets;

NPV = Net Present Value.

In general, the ability of a firm to leverage ideas into cash flow changes from one company to the next. If a company believes its intellectual capital is a source of the cash flow, then the above formulas help it forecast the income streams and earnings, expected to result from the resources: intellectual capital, complementary business assets, and generic structural capital. Sullivan goes one step further, and he discusses a method for valuing companies for mergers and acquisition [Sull00, pp. 103]. In a mergers and acquisition deal, company A absorbs the intellectual capital of company B which, when matched with company A's complementary business assets, produces a high return. This means that the new formula looks like the following equation, when company A is acquiring company B:

$$\text{Tangible assets of the new organization} = TA_A + TA_B$$

This equation expresses the situation that the value of the new organization is the sum of the tangible assets of company A and company B and their discounted cash flows, and it is derived from the following four combinations:

1. The Intellectual Capital (IC) of Company A and the complementary business assets of company A;
2. The IC of Company A and the complementary business assets of company B;
3. The IC of Company B and the complementary business assets of company A;
4. The IC of Company B and the complementary business assets of company B.

The new formula can be written as follows [Sull00, p. 104]:

$$V(\text{new organization}) = [VTA_A + VTA_B] + [f(V(IC)_A, CBA_A) + f(V(IC)_A, CBA_B) + f(V(IC)_B + CBA_A) + f(V(IC)_B + CBA_B)]$$

If one looks a little closer at the four combinations, not all combinations are relevant for the merger and acquisition deal. The first combination need not be calculated since it is already known; the second combination is of no interest since company A is not acquiring company B for its complementary business. The fourth combination also is probably not of much interest because company A purchased company B to match up the intellectual capital of company B with company A's complementary business assets. So, the only relevant combination is the third one because the intellectual capital of company B is of interest for company A. Therefore, the equation above can be modified as follows [Sull00, p. 105]:

$$V(\text{new organization}) = [VTA_A + VTA_B] + [f(V(IC)_A, CBA_A) + f(V(IC)_B\,, CBA_A)]$$

The equation can be interpreted as follows: the value of the new organization resulting from the merger and acquisition deal is the sum of the tangible assets of company A and company B and the sum of the value of the combination of the intellectual capital of company B and the complementary business assets of company A. In the above equation all values are known except for the value of the intellectual capital of company B and the complementary business assets of company A. The purchase price requires the calculation of the intellectual capital of the acquired company for the acquiring company.

2.2.3 Market Capitalization Methods (MCM)

Stewart [Stew97] also sees an emerging necessity to measure the acquisition and the use of knowledge assets. Even if it were not easy to mingle measures of intellectual capital with financial data, it would be a mistake not to try to measure it. He states "undoubtedly measuring knowledge assets must be imprecise, but there is a lot of informed guesswork in 'hard' numbers, too" [Stew97, p. 223]. Stewart advocates three measures for the overall value of intangible assets at the organizational level [Stew97, pp. 224]: the market-to-book ratio, Tobin's Q, and Calculated Intangible Assets (which is assigned from Sveiby to the ROA-Methods).

2.2.3.1 Market-To-Book Ratio

The general idea of the market-to-book ratio [Stew97, pp. 224] is the calculation of the difference between the company's stock market value and the company's book value. This means, the difference between book value shown on the company's balance sheet and its market value gives an approximate measure of its intellectual capital. The market-to-book ratio assumes that the worth of a company is calculated by its market value which is defined as the price per share times the total number of shares outstanding. Stewart indicates that everything left in the market value after accounting for the fixed assets must be an intangible asset. The advantage of this market-to-book ratio is that it is quick to calculate and easy to measure. Alternatively, there are several problems related to this ratio. First, stock prices are affected by many economic factors, and the stock market is volatile. For example, if the Federal Reserve Board raises the interest rate and the value of a company's stock drops 10 percent, does this imply that the value of the intellectual also dropped? Second, often the book value and the market value are understated. Therefore, it would be better to look at the ratio between the two rather than the raw numbers. As a consequence, the reliability and usefulness of the measurement can be improved because the value of the company can be compared, for example, within an industry. And finally Stewart emphasizes, that it is difficult for managers and investors to make reliable statements about the company's knowledge assets by relying on the market-to-book ratio. What does this information mean for the real company's knowledge value?

2.2.3.2 Tobin's Q

Tobin's Q [Tobi71; Tobi75] is advocated by Stewart [Stew97, pp. 225] and by Bontis [Bont00]. This ratio is named after the Economics Nobel Laureate James Tobin of Yale University. According to the Forbes Financial Glossary [http://www.forbes.com, Date 2003-02-24] the Q-Ratio is defined as the follows:

$$\text{Q-Ratio} = \frac{\text{Market value of a firms assets}}{\text{Replacement Value of the firms assets}}$$

where

Market Value = The value investors believe a firm is worth calculated by multiplying the number of shares outstanding by the current market price of a firm's shares;

Replacement Value = Current cost of replacing the firm's assets.

Tobin hypothesized that the combined market value of all the companies on the stock market should be equal to their replacement costs. In other words, the ratio of all the combined stock market valuations to the combined replacement costs should be around one. This means, if the Q-Ratio is greater than one and greater than the competitor's Q-Ratio then the company's intangible assets are high because it has the ability to produce higher profits than other similar companies. Changes in Q provide a proxy for measuring effective performance but not a firm's intellectual capital. In general, Tobin's Q was not developed to measure intangible assets. However, according to Stewart [Stew97, p. 226], it is a good measure because it says something about diminishing returns, and, therefore it says something about the value of the company's assets, e.g., people, systems, or customers. If Q is very high, then a firm is getting extraordinary return on that class of asset. Compared to the market-to-book ratio, the Tobin Q-Ratio neutralizes different depreciation policies by taking the book value of a company, adding back accumulated depreciations, and making appropriate adjustments for price changes in different classes of assets from the time of purchase.

2.2.4 Return on Assets Methods (ROA)

2.2.4.1 Calculated Intangible Value (CIV)

Sveiby assigns the Calculated Intangible Value discussed by Stewart [Stew97, pp. 226], to the ROA-Method. This approach calculates the excess return on hard assets, and it then uses this figure as a basis for determining the proportion of return attributable to intangible assets. Seven steps are necessary to establish the Calculated Intangible Value (CIV) [Stew97, pp. 227]:

1. Calculate average pre-tax earnings for the past three years;
2. Go to the balance sheet and get the average year-end tangible assets for three years;
3. Divide earnings by assets to get the return on assets;
4. For the same three years, find the industry's average ROA;
5. Calculate the "excess return". Multiply the industry-average ROA by the company's average tangible assets and than subtract that from the pre-tax earnings in step one;
6. Calculate the three-year-average income tax rate, and multiply this by the excess return. Subtract the result from the excess return to get an after-tax number. The result is the premium attributable to intangible assets;
7. Calculate the net present value of the premium by dividing the premium by an appropriate percentage, such as the company's cost of capital.

Stewart uses the calculation of the CIV for Merck & Co. [Stew97, pp. 227] as an example:

1. Average pre-tax earnings for three years is for Merck: $3.694 billion;
2. Average year-end tangible assets for three years is for Merck: $ 12.953 billion;

3. Division of earning by assets: 29%;
4. Industry's average ROA: 10%;
5. Calculation of the excess return:
   (\$12.953 * 10%) – (\$3.684) = \$2.39 billion;
6. Average income rate for Merck is 31%, so the after-tax number is \$ 1.65 billion;
7. Appropriate percentage for Merck is 15%, and its CIV = \$11 billion.

The CIV has the advantage that it permits a company-to-company comparison because it uses audited financial data. Furthermore, it can function as a benchmark measure, and the CIV is an indicator whether the value of a firm is fading or whether it has a value that is not reflected in the financial balance sheet. Stewart finds the CIV a good measure for intangible assets because a company with few tangible assets can take this indicator to the bank along with their financial statements to show its true value.

2.2.4.2 Economic Value Added (EVA)

EVA is the Economic Value Added [StSR01]. In 1989 EVA was launched by Stern Stewart & Co. In general, EVA is not new; it refers to what economists have long called economic profit. However, a method to measure the EVA was lacking. Since 1989, many companies such as Coca-Cola, Siemens, Monsato, JCPenney and U.S. Postal Service have implemented the EVA method. If the EVA is implemented correctly, it attracts managers as well as shareholders, ending the long conflict of interest between these two parties. EVA is a mover for shareholder value, and it is linked to another measure, also introduced by Stern Stewart, the Market Value Added (MVA) method. MVA is defined as the difference between the market value of a company and the sums invested in it over the years. From an accounting perspective, EVA is defined as net operating profit after tax (NOPAT) less a capital charge that reflects a firm's cost of capital. It can be defined in more general terms mathematically [Gran97, pp. 2]:

$$EVA = NOPAT - \$Cost\ of\ Capital$$

The firm's dollar cost of capital is calculated by multiplying its percentage cost of capital times its capital investment according to:

$$\$\ Cost\ of\ capital = [\%\ Cost\ of\ Capital/100] * Investment$$

The percentage cost of capital is obtained by the following formula:

% Cost of Capital = [Dept Weight * % After-Tax Debt Cost + Equity Weight * % Cost of Equity]

Since EVA and MVA are related, MVA is the present value of the firm's expected future EVA. In more formal terms, the linkage between MVA and EVA can be written as follows:

MVA = Firm Value – Total Capital

This means in more detail:

MVA = [Dept + Equity Value] – Total Capital

This results in the formula:

MVA = Present Value of Expected Future EVA

Stern et al. [StSR01, p. 19] give a simple example for calculating the EVA. They assume that the company's capital is $5000 and its cost is 12%, the capital charge therefore is $600. If the NOPAT is assumed with a value of $1000, then the $600 charge is deducted, and the result is the EVA of $400. The authors state that the major advantage of the EVA is its adaptability because the measurement system can be taken for different purposes, e.g., measuring the whole company, a factory, a division, or a store. EVA is a measurement tool that is good information for investors, and it is a basis for an incentive compensation system for managers. However, there also are several factors which can lead to failure [StSR01, pp. 159] of the EVA method. The first issue causing a failure is a missing commitment from the CEO: the success of EVA depends to a high degree on the CEO, who has to stand behind the concept and who also should be the chair of the steering committee. The role in this committee, composed of members from the financial department, the chief operation officer (COO), and other key executive members, is a coordination function, resolving conflicts and enforcing the timetable for action. A second possible EVA failure is when the executives are overpaid for a poor performance. Under EVA, they would earn less. A third issue is the expectation that a person on an EVA incentive program is to deliver an excellent performance. Due to the circumstance that the person might not have the required skills, then the goals are too high for him, and they might end in frustration. The last failure concerns the corporate culture. The measuring method has to be negotiated and clearly understood by the employees. EVA had many difficulties being accepted in European countries because companies were not focused on increasing shareholder value by employing capital efficiently [StSR01, pp. 164]. Their objective was more on producing excellent products and increasing the company's market share.

2.2.4.3 Value Added Intellectual Coefficient

The Value Added Intellectual Capital Coefficient (VAIC™) is a trademark of Pulic and the International Management Center at the University of Graz (Austria). According to Pulic [Puli97], VAIC™ measures the performance of physical and of intellectual capital. The VAIC™ is a methodology that not only can be applied to a company but also to a national economy. The author points out the importance of this concept is that it considers all the employees of a company as contributors to corporate success. Since the physical capital of a company is expressed in monetary terms, the intellectual capital of a company also should be expressed in monetary terms. This means, for Pulic, that the labor expenses are an indicator of intellectual capital, meaning "that labour expenses do not express the value of intellectual capital, ... [they are] only a compensation to the employees for their effort to make business possible" [Puli97]. Physical and intellectual capital are the basis for calculating the VAIC™. The measurement process consists of five steps [Puli00]:

1. *Creation of Value Added (VA).* Is a company able to create Value Added?

$$VA = OUT - IN$$

where

VA = Value Added expresses the newly created wealth for a specified period;

OUT = Output, represents the overall income from all the products and services sold on the market;

IN = Inputs which include all the expenses except labor expenses.

2. *Calculation of the Efficiency of the Value Added.*

$$VACA = \frac{VA}{CE}$$

where

VACA =Value Added Capital Coefficient; it is an indicator for the Value Added created by one unit of capital employed;

CE = Capital Employed.

Value Added is a combination of physical and intellectual capital. For a company it is only important that a value added is created regardless of the number of employees. What matters for a company is the amount of funds used whether it is 10 or 100 million. The VACA is an indicator of how much value added is created by one unit of physical capital.

3. *Calculation of the Efficiency of the Intellectual Capital.*

   The third step is the calculation of the intellectual capital and of its two components, human and structural capital. Pulic defends the thesis that human capital can be expressed by expenditures for the employees. The VAIC^{TM} coefficient is based on the balance sheet of a company, and, therefore, Pulic considers the payroll cost as expenses for human capital. The new relationship focuses on value added and employed human capital:

$$VAHU = \frac{VA}{HC}$$

   where

   VAHU =Value Added Human Capital Coefficient;

   HC = Human Capital;

   VA = Value Added.

   The VAHU is a coefficient that shows how much value added was created by 1$ spent on the employees. The relationship between VA and HC is an indicator of the ability of human capital to create value in a company.

4. *Successfulness of Structural Capital for Value Creation.*

   The forth step focuses on the question how structural capital (SC) fits into the value creation. Structural capital is defined as intellectual capital minus human capital. HC and SC are reverse proportional related, meaning the less HC related to the value creation process, the more SC contributes to it. Pulic then formulates the relationship STVA which indicates the share of intellectual capital in the creation of value added:

$$STVA = \frac{SC}{VA}$$

where

STVA = Coefficient to measure the share of Structural Capital to Value Added;

SC = Structural Capital;

VA = Value Added.

Pulic points out that the indicator is very objective because the collected data is from the balance sheet. The STVA should enable management to calculate the efficiency of capital employed and intellectual capital.

5. *Calculation of the VAIC™*

$$VAIC^{TM} = \frac{VA}{IC}$$

where

VAIC™ =Value Added Intellectual Coefficient;

IC = Intellectual Capital;

VA = Value Added.

The VAIC™ is an indicator for how successful intellectual capital is for the creation of value added, and it evaluates the performance of all employees of a company. In other words, the VAIC™ is a coefficient to measure the value creation efficiency of tangible and intangible assets within a company.

Pulic conducted some empirical studies for Austrian Banks [Puli97]. Table "VAIC™ Schoeller Bank and Steiermärkische Hypo" shows the value of the VAIC™ coefficient.

Bank	*CE*	*IC*	*VA*	*VACA*	*VAIC™*
Schoeller Bank	1.246	349	476	0.38	1.365
Steiermärkerische Hypo	1.258	246	476	0.38	1.946

Table 2: VAIC™ Schoeller Bank and Steiermärkische Hypo

From Table "VAIC™ Schoeller Bank and Steiermärkische Hypo" both banks have the same amount of capital employed and value added. If a shareholder takes only these two indicators for an evaluation of the banks, both banks appear equally successful. However, the VAIC™ coefficient distinguishes the banks because the Steiermärkische Hypo employed only 70% of intellectual capital in comparison to Schoeller Bank.

Bornemann [Born98] applied the VAIC™ method to benchmark companies in one branch of different national economy. He used the VAIC™ coefficient for the multinational group Karstadt to learn how segments of one group perform. Bornemann gave special attention to Neckermann Versand, a company that does business in the mail order sector. From an organizational point of view, Neckermann Versand is part of the German Karstadt company which is part of Karstadt Group. Bornemann applied the VAIC™ method to subsidiary levels in both Germany and Austria. Neckermann Austria is the headquarter for Eastern European countries, and it is in charge of the development of the mail order sector in these new markets. Table "VAIC™ Karstadt Group"[6] contains the key research results from Bornemann [Born98] for the years 1995 and 1996.

Company / *Year*	*Karstadt Group*	*Karstadt AG*	*Neckermann Versand AG*	*Neckermann Austria AG*
1995	0.75	0.8	0.8	-0.2
1996	0.9	0.9	1.1	0.1

Table 3: VAIC™ Karstadt Group

The explanation for the negative results for Neckermann Austria in 1995 is related to the 1994 loss when Neckermann Austria bought Kastner & Öhler, and it invested in restructuring and building a new infrastructure (the 1997 forecast for the year was the return into black figures).

[6] In the original paper, Bornemann used a three-dimensional diagram to illustrate the VAIC™.

2.2.5 Scorecard Methods (SC)

2.2.5.1 SKANDIA Navigator

Skandia Navigator [EdMa97] has its origin in a Swedish company. Knowledge navigation originates in Skandia's Assurance & Financial Services business unit (AFS). AFS is responsible for the global savings and life insurance segments. In 1980, the company's then-CEO, Bjorn Wolrath, and Jan Carendi, recognized that a knowledge intensive service competitive strength was decreasingly built on traditional accounting assets such as buildings, equipment, or inventories. Rather, it was built on new intangible factors like individual talent, synergistic market relationships, and the ability to manage the flow of competence. In the words of Wolrath [EdMa97, p. 17]:

> *"Measurement of intellectual capital and a balanced reporting represent an important milestone in the shift from the Industrial Era into the Knowledge Economy ... This broadened, balanced type of accounting and reporting results in a more systematic description of the company's ability and potential to transform intellectual capital into financial capital."*

In September 1991, Skandia created the very first intellectual capital function, and it appointed Leif Edvinsson as its director. His task was to capture and cultivate the hidden value in Skandia by developing new measurement tools and to visualize its intellectual capital as a complement of the balance sheet. In 1995 Skandia first described the Skandia Navigator [EdMa97] which incorporates measures of intellectual capital in a supplement to its Annual Report entitled "Visualizing Intellectual Capital in Skandia". The key idea for the IC model was that the true value of a company's performance lies in the company having a clear business vision and a resulting strategy. The strategy is the starting point for the determination of success factors. A company must develop an understanding of its hidden values, values which can only flourish when the culture of the company supports an atmosphere of innovation and creativity and when the company leadership recognizes changes and tries to build partnerships with suppliers, customers, and manufactures. Therefore, the definition of hidden value for Skandia is its intellectual capital which summarizes the knowledge, applied experience, organizational technology, customer relationships and professional skills [EdMa97, p. 44]. The recognition of hidden value is a major challenge for companies because these intangible assets can be converted into financial returns. Skandia recognized several nonfinancial components that create value and that are responsible for the gap between book value and market value. Skandia clustered its market value into the following structure [EdMa97, p. 52]:

Market Value = Financial Capital + Intellectual Capital

Intellectual Capital = Human Capital + Structural Capital

Structural Capital = Customer Capital + Organizational Capital

Organizational Capital = Innovation Capital + Process Capital

Analysis of the value of intellectual capital offers the ability to make those factors responsible for the company's success transparent. Skandia identified five success factors which help to add value to the company:

1. Financial Focus;
2. Customer Focus;
3. Process Focus;
4. Renewal & Development Focus; and
5. Human Focus.

Each focus on its own does not add value to the company; only the combination of all five components brings competitive advantages to the company. To illustrate this, Skandia developed the Skandia Navigator which is a system for making detailed statements about the success of the company. Skandia used the metaphor of a house to illustrate the linkages between the five foci. The detailed structure of its Navigator is visualized in Figure "Skandia Navigator" [EdMa97, p. 68]. The roof of the intellectual capital house is the financial focus containing the traditional balance sheet; the walls are the customer and process focus; the basement is the company future, encompassing the renewal and development focus and, finally, the human focus is the center of the house touching the other four foci, and it consists of the experience, knowledge, and competence of the employees.

Skandia assigns measurement indicators to each of the five foci. Four different types of *indices* can be identified:

1. *Cumulative indices*: this group belongs to the direct measures of finance-related business activities, and it is usually expressed in monetary terms ($) or numbers (#).

2. *Competitive measures*: these are expressed as a percentage (%) or index. The objective is to compare some part of the company's performance to that of the industry. Competitive indices are used for benchmark purposes.
3. *Comparative measures*: comparative measures include two company-based variables, and they give information about company dynamics.
4. *Combined measures*: this metric represents a hybrid quotient either in monetary terms or as a ratio that combines more than two company-based variables. The combined measures are the source for the provision of unexpected new perspectives for an organization.

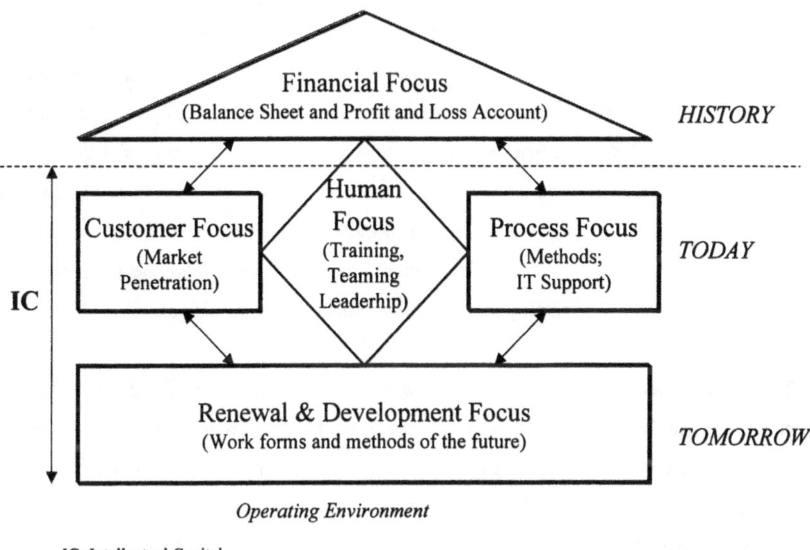

Figure 11: SKANDIA Navigator

The ***financial focus*** resembles the traditional component of the company, and it is history-oriented. The financial report is not independent of the value of intellectual capital. In the long run, all company intellectual capital must convert to some monetary term, or it will not contribute to a value-added view. The role of the IC reporting has changed the assessment of a company to include factors beyond the traditional information included in a company report.

To understand the position of the company in the marketplace in conjunction with its intellectual capital position, ***customer focus*** is a key requirement. An IC report might look at the types of customers for each of the company's products as well as at additional aggregate data such as overall market share and market coverage. The metrics identified by Skandia try to capture the relationship between the company and potential new customers, and it can be categorized into five indictor groups: (1) customer type; (2) customer duration; (3) customer role; (4) customer support; and (5) customer success. The ideal situation for an excellent company-customer relationship is a good rating in all five categories.

The ***process focus*** deals with the company's infrastructure, and the successful application of a technology is a key element of the process focus. By implementing a new technology, the key measure behind it should be the value contribution to the corporate productivity. The ***renewal and development focus*** is concerned with the capacity of a company to respond to future trends and events. One aspect of it is the identification of the company position in the marketplace, e.g., a change in the customer base or a change in consumer demands. A second aspect covers the readiness of a company to respond to change. This might include employee training in connection with anticipated changes.

The ***human focus*** is the most dynamic, and, in many respects, it is the most important element of the Navigator. Measuring the human capital of a company is a task made even more complex by a social shift, such as the move towards part-time work, telecommuting, and outsourcing. The human focus tries to visualize the general knowledge creation process of the company, and it also tries to measure employee satisfaction with their work, a satisfaction which leads to satisfied customers and then to improved company's sales results.

The various intellectual capital indicators can be consolidated into a measurement that can describe the intellectual capital and its development over time [EdMa97, pp. 173], and it can be described as follows:

$$\text{Organizational Intellectual Capital} = iC$$

where

i = Organization's coefficient of efficiency in using that Intellectual Capital;

C = Value of Intellectual Capital in monetary terms.

This indicator makes it possible to compare changes in intellectual capital with changes in the market value, and, therefore, it is an instrument to prognosticate a future value. The Navigator tries to balance past, present, and future measures to give more insight into the value of an organization. Table "Skandia Measures" lists the major indices assigned to each of the five foci [EdMa97, pp. 179].

Focus	Measures/Indices	
Financial	• Total Assets ($) • Revenues/Total Assets (%) • Customer Time/Employee attendance (%) • Profits/Employee ($) • Revenues/Employee ($)	• Market Value ($) • Return on Assets Value (%) • Value Added/Employee ($) • Value Added/IT-Employee ($) • Investments in IT ($) • Value Added/Customer ($)
Customer	• Market Share (%) • Number of Customers (#) • Customers lost (#) • Days spent visiting customers (#)	• Ratio of sales contracts to sales closed (%) • IT investments/salesperson ($) • Support expense/customer ($)
Process	• Administrative expense/total revenue (#) • PC/Laptop/employee (#) • Network capability/employee (#)	• Change in IT inventory ($) • IT capacity (CPU) (#) • IT performance/employee (#) • IT expense/employee ($)
Renewal	• Satisfied Employee Index (#) • Share of training hours (%) • R&D Expense/administrative expense (%) • IT development expense/IT expense (%)	• Educational investment/ customer ($) • Value of EDI system ($) • Patent pending (#)
Human	• Leadership Index (%) • Motivation Index (%) • Empowerment Index (%) • Employee turnover (%) • IT literacy of staff (#) • Number of managers (#) • Number of woman managers (#)	• Average age of employee (#) • Time in training (days/year) (#) • Number of manager with advanced degrees in - Business - Science and Engineering - Liberal Arts

Table 4: Skandia Measures

2.2.5.2 Balanced Scorecard

2.2.5.2.1 General Framework

Kaplan and Norton [KaNo92; KaNo01] first introduced the concept of the Balanced Scorecard (BSC) in 1992. Historically, most organizations have implemented a performance measurement system that focuses on financial performance. The disadvantages of this concept include: backward looking financial measures, short-term oriented measurement, and financial measures that cannot communicate organizational vision and strategy. In the future, organizations need a different performance measurement system, one that supports a long-term, forward looking and strategic view across the entire organization. In recent years, organizations made several attempts to transform themselves into successful competitive companies by using a variety of improvement initiatives such as: Total Quality Management (TQM), Just-in-Time (JIT) Production, Time-Based Competition, Lean Production, Activity-Based Cost Management, Employee Empowerment, and Reengineering Processes.

For Kaplan and Norton, each of these improvement strategies are fragmented, and they did not bring the expected improvement because most of the performance programs are not linked to the organization's strategy and because they focus on monitoring and controlling financial measures of past performances. The Balanced Scorecard is a system that complements the financial measures of past performances with measures of future drivers. The Balanced Scorecard not only is a measurement system but it also is a management system. Kaplan and Norton define the Balanced Scorecard and its objectives as follows [KaNo96, p. 8]:

> *"The objectives and measures of the scorecard are derived from an organization's vision and strategy. ... The Balanced Scorecard expands the set of business unit objectives beyond summary financial measures. ... The Balanced Scorecard captures the critical value-creation activities created by skilled, motivated organizational participants. ... The Balanced Scorecard emphasizes that financial and nonfinancial measures must be part of the information system for employees at all levels of the organization."*

From this one can conclude that the Balanced Scorecard methodology is an analysis technique designed to translate an organization's mission statement and overall business strategy into specific, quantifiable goals and to monitor the organization's performance in achieving these goals. The basic framework is visualized in Figure "Balanced Scorecard Methodology" [KaNo96, p. 9] which shows a company's vision and strategy translated into a set of performance measures.

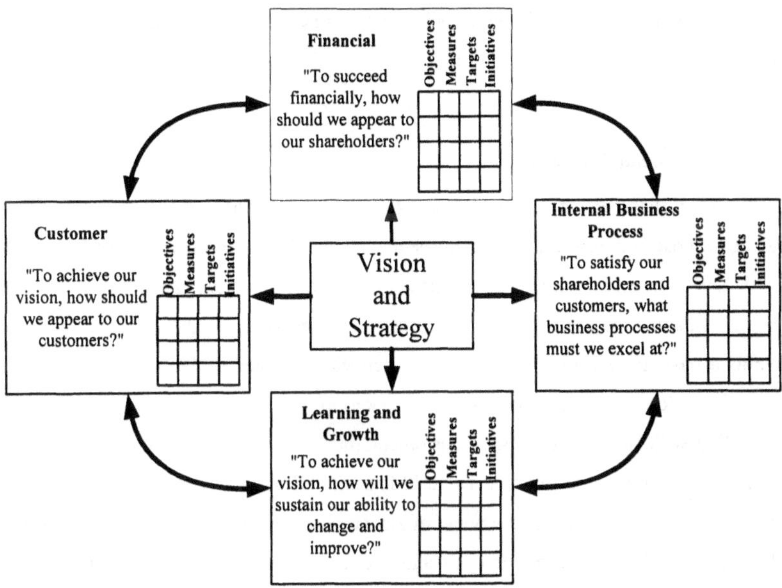

Figure 12: Balanced Scorecard Methodology

The Balanced Scorecard methodology is a comprehensive approach to analyze an organization's overall performance based on the idea that performance assessment through financial returns provides information about how well the organization did prior to the assessment to predict future performance and future proper actions. As a structure, Balanced Scorecard methodology breaks broad goals down into vision, strategies, tactical activities, and metrics. For example, an organization might include a goal of maintaining employee satisfaction in its mission statement, this represents the organization's vision. Strategies for achieving that vision might include approaches such as increased employee-management communication. Tactical activities undertaken to implement the strategy could include regularly scheduled meetings with employees. Finally, metrics could include the quantification of employee suggestions or employee surveys. The measurement must be linked to strategy and vision, and observations on achievement must feed back to strategy. The positive feedback loop is a cornerstone of the Balanced Scorecard concept.

The Balanced Scorecard can be broken down into four different performance indicators, or perspectives [KaNo96, pp. 25] which will be explained in more detail in the following chapters.

2.2.5.2.2 Financial Perspective

The *financial perspective* [KaNo96, pp. 47] monitors traditional monetary measures familiar to most organizations. These measures include, for example, profitability, revenue growth, and shareholder value. The Balanced Scorecard should give managers the ability to link their financial objectives to corporate strategy. The financial performance indicators serve as a basis for all other scorecard perspectives. This means, that the strategy should start with the long-term financial objectives linked to a sequence of actions to be taken in conjunction with financial processes, customers, internal processes, and employees to gain long-term economic performance. Table "Measuring Strategic Financial Themes in the Balanced Scorecard" gives an overview of financial measurement indicators [KaNo96, p. 52] and is a 3x3-Matrix for the life-cycle and financial strategies of business units.

Kaplan and Norton identify different financial objectives for each stage of a business life-cycle. The three life-cycle stages are [KaNo96, pp. 48]:

1. *Growth:* this first stage of the life-cycle is characterized by the fact that products and services have significant growing potential. A business in this stage actually may operate with a negative cash flow and low current return on invested capital.
2. *Sustain*: the second life-cycle stage is focused on a sustained strategy meaning that the business units still attract investments and reinvestments, but they earn excellent returns on investment.
3. *Harvest*: business units in the last life-cycle stage have reached a mature level, and companies want to harvest the investments made during earlier stages. The main goal is to maximize cash flow.

Besides the three life-cycle stages, there are three financial themes that drive the identified business strategy:

1. *Revenue Growth and Mix*: the objectives are to expand the product and service offerings, reach new customers and markets, and change the product and service mix to attain a higher value added in the company.
2. *Cost Reduction/Productivity Improvement*: the objective of this financial strategy are to lower the direct costs of products and services, reduce indirect costs, and share common resources with other business units.
3. *Asset Utilization/Investment Strategy*: managers pursuing this strategy try to reduce the working capital levels required to support a given volume and business mix. Furthermore, companies want to identify the specific drivers they will use to increase asset intensity.

<table>
<tr><th colspan="2"></th><th colspan="3">Strategic Themes</th></tr>
<tr><th colspan="2"></th><th>Revenue Growth and Mix</th><th>Cost Reduction/ Productivity Improvement</th><th>Asset Utilization</th></tr>
<tr><th rowspan="3">Business Unit Strategy</th><th>Growth</th><td>Sales Growth rate by segment; Percentage revenue for new products, services, and customers</td><td>Revenue/Employee</td><td>Investment (percentage of sales); R&D (percentage of sales)</td></tr>
<tr><th>Sustain</th><td>Share of targeted customers and accounts; Cross-selling; Percentage Revenue from new applications; Customer and Product line profitability</td><td>Cost versus competitors' cost reduction rates; Indirect expenses (percentages of sales)</td><td>Working Capital ratios (cash-to-cash cycle); Asset utilizations rates</td></tr>
<tr><th>Harvest</th><td>Customer and Product Line Profitability; Percentage Unprofitable Customers</td><td>Unit Costs (Per unit of output, per transaction)</td><td>Payback; Throughput</td></tr>
</table>

Table 5: Measuring Strategic Financial Themes in the Balanced Scorecard

2.2.5.2.3 Customer Perspective

The *customer perspective* [KaNo96, pp. 63] looks at an organization through the eyes of its customers. Business unit managers identify the customer and market segments in which the unit will compete. The identified segments are the revenue components needed to achieve the financial objectives. Kaplan and Norton [KaNo96, pp. 67] note five core measurements for the customer perspective which apply to all types of organizations:

- *Market Share* reflects the proportion of business unit sales in a given market. To estimate the total market size, it is useful to look at industry groups, trade associations, government statistics, and other public sources.
- *Customer Retention* tracks the rate at which a business unit retains or maintains ongoing relationships with its customers in relative or absolute terms. Another measure in this category is the customer loyalty.
- *Customer Acquisition* measures the rate at which a business unit attracts or wins new customers or businesses in absolute or relative terms. Measurements in this group, for example, are the rate at which a business unit attracts new customers or the total sales to new customer in a segment.
- *Customer Satisfaction* assesses the satisfaction level of customers along specific performance criteria within the value proposition. In recent years, customer satisfaction measures have gained high levels of importance in companies. In order to guarantee a high customer satisfaction rate, companies are doing customer surveys though the mail, by telephone, or in personal interviews.
- *Customer Profitability* measures the net profit of a customer, or a market segment, after allowing for the unique expenses required to support that customer. Even if a company is doing very well in customer retention, acquisition, and satisfaction measures, it does not necessary guarantee a profitable customer. A company should find a balance between the four customer measures and the customer profitability measure.

2.2.5.2.4 Internal-Business-Process Perspective

The *Internal-Business-Process Perspective* [KaNo96, pp.92] assesses the efficiency of internal processes and procedures. This means, that managers must identify critical processes for which they want to gain competitive advantages and follow the shareholder objectives and the targeted customer segments. In contrast to traditional performance measures which focus on past or existing process, the BSC is oriented to identifying new processes. Furthermore, the BSC enables managers to formulate short-term and long-term innovation objectives for the business unit. Kaplan and Norton [KaNo96, pp. 96] have developed a value chain model for the Internal-Business-Process Perspective which has three principal business processes (see Figure "The Internal-Business-Process Perspective - the Value Chain Model" [KaNo96, p. 96]):

- *Innovation Process*: In the BSC, research and development process is part of the internal innovation process. It is essential for companies to know new markets and customers. The first component of the innovation process is concerned with identifying new customer markets. During this stage, managers should initiate market surveys to get more information about forthcoming markets and customers. The second component is concerned with service for the product. For example, BSC measures used by AMD for basic and applied research include: percentage of sales from new products, percentage of sales from proprietary products, new product introduction versus competitors, and the time to develop next generation products. Another measurement group in the innovation process are those for product development.
- *Operation Process*: This process is more short-term oriented, and it starts with the receipt of customer orders and ends with the delivery of the product to the customer. Measures in this group include labor efficiency, machine efficiency, and purchase price variances. During the Total Quality Movement of leading Japanese manufacturers, measurements such as operating process quality, and cycle time were important.
- *Postsales Service Process*: This process is concerned with aftersales service such as warranty and repair activities, treatment of defects and returns, or credit card administration. Measures for the postsales service focus a time, quality, and cost metrics.

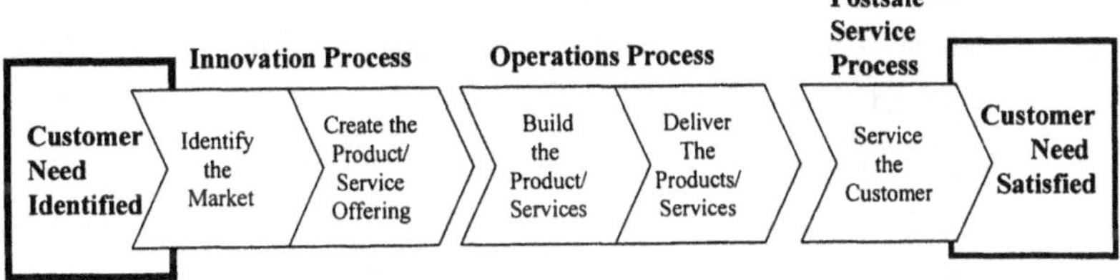

Figure 13: The Internal-Business-Process Perspective – the Value Chain Model

2.2.5.2.5 Learning and Growth Perspective

The *Learning and Growth Perspective* [KaNo96, pp.126] deals with employee issues. The objective of the learning and growth perspective is the provision of an infrastructure which enables the company to achieve the objectives of the four perspectives. This infrastructure includes the development of employee capabilities, investments in information systems capabilities, and, finally, the management of motivation, empowerment, and alignment. The BSC measurement should include the following areas:

1. *Employee Capabilities*: in a BSC, the shift from the very narrowly defined traditional workplace of the industrial age to the new information and knowledge age is apparent. The new employees must be reskilled into creative and innovative employees who help satisfy customer needs and to rebuild internal processes to achieve the company's objectives. For this goal, the measurement process encompasses three major areas:
    a. *Employee Satisfaction*: employee morale and satisfaction in companies becomes a key measurement area. Companies have recognized that satisfied employees have a higher productivity rate, responsiveness, quality, and customer satisfaction. The measurement tool for employee satisfaction is an annual survey in which employees are asked questions about topics such as: involvement in decisions, recognition for doing the job, or the overall satisfaction with the company. The Balanced Scorecard contains an aggregated index of the employee satisfaction.
    b. *Employee Retention*: the company objective is to retain the best-qualified employees. If an excellent employee leaves the company and takes the knowledge with him, then the damage for the company can be very high. Therefore, the measurement in this group should concern metrics of investments made in the most valuable employees. A general measurement is the percentage of key staff turnover.
    c. *Employee productivity*: for Kaplan and Norton, employee productivity measures the output produced by employees in relationship to the number of employees used to produce that output. The most commonly used metric for employee productivity is revenue per employee.

The measures for employee capabilities are the basic measures for the growth and learning perspective. However, in a Balanced Scorecard, the situation-specific drivers also should be identified, e.g., reskilling the work force, information system capabilities, motivation, empowerment and alignment:

2. *Reskilling the Work Force*: if companies are building a Balanced Scorecard, they are undergoing a period of change. Therefore, they must reskill their employees depending on their competencies. An important metric is the strategic job coverage ratio which measures the number of employees qualified for specific strategic jobs relative to anticipated organizational needs.
3. *Information Systems Capabilities*: in the workplace today, employees need excellent information about customers, internal process, and the financial consequences of their decisions. A good information system is the presupposition for being competitive. Kaplan and Norton [KaNo96, p. 136] suggest the strategic information coverage ratio as a metric which measures the current availability of information relative to anticipated needs.
4. *Motivation, empowerment, and alignment*: the third enabler for being successful is to motivate employees and to give them some degree of freedom for decision making. Some examples are (a detailed list of measures can be found in [KaNo96, pp. 136]):
   - Number of suggestions per employee;
   - Half-cycle metric which measures the length of time required for process performance to improve by 50%;
   - Percentage of managers/staff employees exposed to the BSC;
   - Team performance measures such as the percentage of business plans developed by teams and the percentage of customers acquiring shares.

The Balanced Scorecard has the objective of achieving a balance of measures across these four perspectives. However, the measures that make up a BSC do not exist in isolation to each other. They relate to a set of objectives that are linked, the final link usually relating to a financial result of one form or another. Measurement with respect to the BSC is not a control but a communication tool. It resembles a language that gives clarity to vague concepts and the process of building a scorecard. It develops consensus and teamwork throughout the organization. Therefore, a BSC should include four features [KaNo96, pp.

148]: (1) Cause and Effect Relationships (every objective selected should be part of a chain of causes and effects that represent the strategy); (2) Linkage to Financials (every measure selected can ultimately be related to financial results); (3) Performance Drivers (a balance of outcome measures and performance drivers should be given); and (4) Measures that Create Change (some measures that cause the organization to change its behavior or its processes).

The traditional Balanced Scorecard articulated by Kaplan and Norton [KaNo96] has been modified in many ways. Walker and MacDonald [WaMa01] discuss the Human Resource Scorecard which focuses on measures related to workforce issues. Scheibeler [Sche01] discusses specific modifications for the implementation of a BSC in small and medium-sized companies. The implementation of a BSC in small companies is difficult because often the strategic planning process, the definition of objectives, and openness to new concepts and methods are missing. In order to achieve the objectives of the BSC in small and medium-sized companies, the strategy must be written down and be broken down further into operable objectives. Furthermore, Bean and Jarnagin [BeJa02] discuss the integration of the scorecard approach in financial reports.

The American Institute of Certified Public Accountants (AICPA) has proposed a model where the current financial reporting system not only includes financial but also includes non-financial and forward-looking information [BeJa02]. Since more and more companies are using the BSC, it is important to understand its impact and its utilization in company annual reports. The AICPA Committee recommended that reports should include: (1) financial and nonfinancial information; (2) management analysis of both financial and nonfinancial information; (3) forward-looking information; (4) management and shareholder information; and (5) company background. This detailed information is very valuable for decision-making rather than the use of historical financial information. Furthermore, the stakeholders would be able to understand the performance measures the company is using to make decisions. Bean and Jarnagin [BeJa02, p. 61] point out that even if the BSC is a good communication tool for the company performance, some problems should be avoided such as the commitment of top-management to the BSC approach, "balanced" scorecard information, measurement of correct issues, or the flexibility of the measurement to allow changes.

2.2.5.3 Intangible Asset Monitor (IAM)

The last of the SC methods was proposed by Sveiby [Svei97], and it is called the Intangible Asset Monitor (IAM). Sveiby criticizes the old financial measurement systems because they are not able to measure the intangible assets of a company. For Sveiby, any measurement system is limited by uncertainty; Sveiby [Svei97, pp. 155] argues that

> *"There exist no objective measures. The main reasons why financial measures seem more objective or 'real' are that they are founded on implicit concepts of what a company is and have been around for so long that they are guided by definitions and standards. ... Still, there exists no comprehensive system for measuring intangible assets that uses money as the common dominator and at the same time is practical and useful for managers. Depending on the purpose for measuring, I do not think such a system is necessary, either. Knowledge flows and intangible assets are essentially nonfinancial. We need new proxies."*

The major problem with measuring intangible assets is not the design of indicators but rather the interpretation of the results. The IAM uses measures selected from a two-dimensional matrix. The first dimension deals with three categories: growth and renewal, stability, and efficiency. The second dimension looks at the three intangible assets of a company: external structure, internal structure, and employee competence. In general, IAM is a method for measuring intangible assets, and it also is a presentation format that displays the relevant indicators. In order to have a good overview of the intangible assets, IAM should not exceed one page with supplemented comments. The detailed IAM theoretical framework [Svei97, p. 165; http://www.sveiby.com, Date 2003-02-13] and the corresponding question framework are visualized in Table "IAM Measurement Matrix" and in Table "Intangible Assets Monitor Indicators Matrix", where the detailed key indicators for each dimension are listed. The three intangible assets build the basic framework for IAM.

The ***competence of the employees*** is the source for internal and external structure. The experts or also called professionals are the most valuable employees in the organization. They are the ones that create unique solutions for customers and generate new knowledge. The term *competence* refers to the ability of the professionals to act in various situations, and it includes skills, experience, values, and social skills. For Sveiby [Svei97, pp. 65], people are the only source for value creation because all assets, whether tangible or intangible, and structures in an organization are the result of action from human behavior. The competence owner can only be a person who posses the experience gained over the years. The competence of an employee should be included in a balance sheet because an organization cannot be competitive without its people. Especially in knowledge organizations, there is little machinery, so the only business driver is expert's skills. The *growth and renewal* level within the competence dimension focuses on the idea how a person in a company has gained and maintains their skills and experience. The indications that constitute the *competence of the growth and renewal level* are for example [Svei97, pp. 168]:

- Number of years in the profession is an indicator of the skills and experience of a company's experts;
- Level of education is an indicator on what knowledge a company is relying on;
- Training and education costs indicate how much effort is put into upgrading of the employees knowledge;
- Turnover rate is a ratio that gives information of how much competence a company has left and how much joined the company.

The next measurement group covers the indicator of *competence efficiency* such as:

- The leverage effect measurement shows how the ability of professionals to generate revenue is and can be calculated by the following formula [Svei97, p. 171]:

$$\text{Profit per professional} = \frac{\text{Profit}}{\text{Revenue}} \times \frac{\text{Revenue}}{\text{Number of employees + freelancers}} \times \frac{\text{Number of employees + freelancers}}{\text{Number of professionals}}$$

General efficiency indicator	**Sales efficiency indicator**	**Personnel efficiency indicator**	**Leverage indicator**

- Proportion of professionals in a company is a ratio that describes the quotient of experts divided by the total number of employees. The ratio is an indicator of how important the professionals are for a company, and, furthermore, the possibility of making a benchmark with other companies in that industry.

- Value added per professional is an indicator about how much value an expert is producing in the company. The measure of value added per professional, according to Sveiby, is an excellent measure of the ability to produce economic value.

On the *stability level* of the *competence* dimension are indicators such as: average age of the employees; seniority indicator giving information about how long an employee has worked for the company; and professional turnover rate.

The second intangible asset is the ***internal structure*** [Svei97, pp. 78 and pp. 174] which includes the patents, concepts, models, and computer and administrative systems in a company. In contrast to the characteristics of the competence of the employee level, the internal structure belongs to the organization itself. Through interaction and knowledge transfer, employees create the company. This dimension covers all internal processes, and it also focuses on the company culture.

The ***external structure*** [Svei97, pp. 108 and pp. 177] consists of the company knowledge flow with customers and suppliers. It also consists of brand names, trademarks, and the company's reputation and image. For a knowledge organization, it is essential to follow a *knowledge-focused strategy* [Svei97, pp. 118] which earns revenue from intangible assets which are professionals with their individual knowledge and their ability to turn their knowledge into revenue. A knowledge-focused strategy is characterized by a high degree of customization and by selling problem solutions to customers. The value of the external structure lies in how well a customer problem is solved, and this measurement always is determined by uncertainty [Svei97, p. 11].

The Intangible Asset Monitor shows indicators that measure change and knowledge flows. For each company the suggested indicators (see Table "IAM Measurement Matrix", and Table "Intangible Asset Monitor Indicators Matrix") must be adjusted to the reality of a company. The IAM can be used to design a management information system or to make an audit. The IAM and the Balanced Scorecard have the similarity that both concepts attempt to measure the intangible assets of a company and the financial indicators, and, furthermore, they are not a new control instrument but rather an approach for improvement, change, and learning. The IAM was already developed widely used in 1986-1987 in Sweden, while the BSC was developed and used primarily in the U.S. around 1990. Sveiby points out that there are four differences between the BSC and IAM [Svei02b]:

1. The IAM makes the assumption that all human action in a company is converted into tangible and intangible knowledge structures, therefore into internal and external knowledge. The BSC does not have this assumption.
2. The IAM is a stock-flow theory comparable to traditional accounting theory. The IAM uses the three intangible assets as "real" assets, and it focuses on the flow between the assets. This is the reason why indicators measure the change in assets (growth, renewal, stability, efficiency). In contrast, the BSC has the objective of balancing the traditional financial perspective and adding three other nonfinancial perspectives.
3. The external structure dimension of the IAM covers all company partners, beginning with the customer, to the supplier, and to other stakeholders. However, the BSC sees the external structure only under the customer-oriented perspective, and it is much more narrow that the IAM.
4. The BSC derives its measures form the strategy and vision of a company while the IAM goes one step further by demanding the strategy change to a more knowledge-oriented view. The IAM puts the change perspective more in the center of consideration than the BSC.

A knowledge company is competing for two valuable resources: customers and professionals meaning that management has to formulate strategies for attracting customers and for attracting and keeping excellent employees. Therefore, a key concern of contemporary companies should be the development of a knowledge-focused strategy i.e., selling the professional skills of the employees to solve problems. In contrast, an information-focused strategy is primarily oriented to technological development, and it is characterized by a low degree of customization, knowledge is sold as a derivative and people are seen as a cost rather than an asset. A knowledge-focused strategy only can be implemented successfully if measures can be found and developed for the flow of money and for the flow affecting intellectual assets.

INTANGIBLE ASSET MONITOR			
The Business Unit (Total Business Value)			
TANGIBLE ASSETS (Financial Value)	**INTANGIBLE ASSETS**		
	External Structure (Customer Value)	***Internal Structure (Organizational Value)***	***Competence of the People (Competence Value)***
Business Unit What are our key owners? What are the key owners goals? What is our key tangible equipment for serving the customers? What are our key fixed assets?	***Business Unit*** Who are our customers? What is the best metric to measure our output? Can we measure the impact of outcome on the customer's business? Should we also consider suppliers and other partners?	***Business Unit*** Who are our administrative staff? Which are our key tools and processes for serving customers? Which are our key internal tools and processes? Which are our legally protected intangible assets?	***Business Unit*** Who are our key professionals? Which are our key professional competencies? Which are our key social competencies?
Growth Are our tangible Assets growing? Is our shareholder capital growing?	***Growth*** Is the existing customer base growing in value? Who are our image customers?	***Growth*** Are the supportive staff and administrative management improving their competence?	***Growth*** Is the competence of our professionals growing?
Renewal Are our tangible assets being renewed? Are we attracting new shareholders?	***Renewal*** Is the customer base being renewed? Are we attracting new customers?	***Renewal*** Are our products/service tools/processes being renewed? Are we attracting new managers? Is Administration Competence renewed?	***Renewal*** Is our professional competence being renewed? Are we attracting new professionals? staff?
Efficiency Is our financial capital utilized efficiently? Are our tangible assets utilized efficiently?	***Efficiency*** Is the customer base efficient? How profitable is the customer base for us?	***Efficiency*** Are the tools and processes utilized efficiently? Are Administrative Managers and staff efficient	***Efficiency*** Is our professional competence utilized efficiently? Are our professionals utilized efficiently?
Stability Are we financially stable?	***Stability*** What are the attitudes of supportive/administrative managers? What is the legal protection for our processes?	***Stability*** What are the attitudes of our professionals? What is the risk of losing our competence?	***Stability*** What are the attitudes of our professionals? What is the risk of losing our competence?

Table 6: IAM Measurement Matrix

External Structure Indicators	Internal Structure Indicators	Competence Indicators
Indicators of Growth Organic Growth	**Indicators of Growth** Investment in IT; Investments in Internal Structure	**Indicators of Growth** Competence Index; Number of Years in the Profession; Level of Education; Competence Turnover
Indicators of Renewal/Innovation Image Enhancing Customers; Sales to new customers	**Indicators of Renewal/Innovation** Organization enhancing customers; Proportion of new products/services; New processes implemented	**Indicators of Renewal/Innovation** Competence-Enhancing Customers; Training and Education Costs; Diversity
Indicators of Efficiency/Utilization Profitability per Customer; Sales per Customer; Win/Loss Index	**Indicators of Efficiency/Utilization** Proportion of Support Staff	**Indicators of Efficiency/Utilization** Proportion of Professional; Leverage Effect; Value Added per Employee; Value Added per Professional; Profit per Employee; Profit per Professional
Indicators of Risk/Stability Satisfied Customer Index; Proportion of Big Customers; Age Structure; Devoted Customer Ratio; Frequency of Repeat Orders	**Indicators of Risk/Stability** Values/Attitudes Index; Age of the Organization; Support Staff Turnover; Rookie Ratio; Seniority	**Indicators of Risk/Stability** Professional Turnover; Relative Pay; Seniority

Table 7: Intangible Asset Monitor Indicators Matrix[7]

[7] http://www.sveiby.com/articles/Company/Monitor.htm, Date 2002-11-24

3 The Knowledge Potential View

"The essence is that the understanding of the sociology of the new generation of employees is very important in recruiting, training, and getting optimal performance from them for all organizations. Nevertheless, it is especially important for knowledge organizations."

(A. D. Amar)

The objective of this chapter is to discuss and analyze the knowledge measurement approaches presented in Chapter 2. The cognitive science approach will be evaluated and the knowledge measurement methods will be discussed second. Reflection on the measurement approaches leads to the derivation of the knowledge potential view which will be explained, and it will form the basic idea for the knowledge measurement process discussed in Chapter 5.

As an interdisciplinary study of the mind ***cognitive science*** has attracted many representatives from different research fields investigating human intelligence and knowledge. The discipline of philosophy, especially representatives concerned with the philosophy of mind, has tried to find relationships between the mind and knowledge. Also, logical reasoning research is a long established domain for the abstract study of intelligence. Thus, philosophy gives one a general understanding about logic and mind. Recently new developments in reasoning under conditions of uncertainty were established, and they exert strong influence on the field of psychology. This discipline investigates how humans are perceiving, learning, memorizing, speaking, and reasoning, and it gives one a basic insight into the human reasoning process under uncertainty, and it is relevant for knowledge workers who make decisions and solve problems under uncertain conditions. Neuroscience research makes an essential contribution to knowledge, especially because it focuses on concepts of information processing. The field of computational intelligence pursues the objective of developing intelligent computers. Probability theory, the Bayesian approach to uncertainty, and belief networks especially contribute to an overall comprehension of how humans act in a probabilistic and uncertain environment, showing how an expert can be influenced by reasoning processes under uncertain conditions. Linguistics has focused on internal processes by which humans understand, produce, and communicate language. Language itself enables humans, and by extension knowledge workers, to express their tacit knowledge and transfer it to other professionals who have the ability to learn from other experiences. Finally the discipline of culture and cognition is involved with respect to the influence of cultural aspects on cognition. Several aspects of the cognitive science field has focused on identifying issues concerning the reasoning process under conditions of uncertainty and on an overall understanding on how humans gain cognition. The discussion of cognitive science disciplines must be seen in the light of how people behave and act.

Each of the described ***management measurement methods*** have advantages and disadvantages, and each method fulfills a different purpose depending on the target group and the situational context [Svei02a]. The Market Capitalization methods (MCM) and the Return on Assets methods (ROA) primarily offer a $-valuation on the organizational level. These sets of methods build on the traditional accounting rules. Therefore, they easily can be communicated and accepted by managers and CEOs, but they are not very relevant for middle management. The disadvantages of these methods are that they try to translate each concept, action, and intellectual capital into monetary terms and they, especially the ROA methods, depend on interest rate assumptions. The criticism is that the traditional financial performance measures were working well for the industrial era, but they do not apply to the knowledge oriented economy because they do not master the skills and experiences of the company employees.

In recent years there has been a mindset shift in the sense that many accounting systems lack relevance to today's new knowledge economy. Many organizations have inward looking management and controlling systems based on the valuation of physical assets. The knowledge economy needs new evaluation models that rely on a much broader view and that take the valuation of intellectual capital into consideration. Hence, companies need to develop measurement systems that evaluate physical and intellectual capital. This means that the employee intelligence, skills, and experience give a company its distinctive character. The objective is to achieve a balance between the measurement of tangible and intangible assets.

The Direct Intellectual Capital (DIC) and the Scorecard (SC) methods have the advantage that they measure the intellectual capital of the company on the component level and therefore, give a more detailed insight into the company's value. They measure internal departments or specific processes rather than the whole organization. Their major advantage is that they depend on the overall value of intellectual capital rather than financial metrics. A disadvantage of the DIC and SC methods is that they use indicators that are very contextual and customized for each company and each purpose, making a comparison between companies very difficult. Furthermore, the use of these methods is not accepted by managers as the traditional accounting methods and financial perspective. Kaplan and Norton [KaNo01, pp. 360] for example, see one failure in its implementation of a good Balanced Scorecard in the use of too few measures for each perspective and its lack of a balance for all perspectives. However, the major causes for its failures are poor organizational processes such as:

1. Lack of senior management commitment;
2. Too few individuals involved;
3. Keeping the scorecard at the top;
4. Too long of a development process, viewing the BSC as a one time measurement system;
5. Treating the BSC as a systems project;
6. Hiring inexperienced consultants;
7. Introducing the BSC only for compensation.

In general three different measurement groups can be distinguished. The first which includes the MCM and ROA methods view intellectual capital in monetary terms. Their primarily objective is the measurement of the intellectual capital of a company in monetary units. The representatives of this group renounce a detailed description of the different dimensions of intellectual capital. The term intellectual capital is not defined in-depth nor described. The value of the intellectual capital is transferred to a financial measurable unit. The second consists of the agents of the DIC methods. Unlike the first, DIC methods decompose the intellectual capital into different dimensions, but they also aim to measure the value in monetary terms. The SC methods have a similar mental approach but they use indicators to measure the intellectual capital. The intellectual capital is divided into different components measured with these indicators. All three SC methods – Balanced

Scorecard, Skandia Navigator, and Intangible Asset Monitor – use metrics that can be divided into four categories:

- Monetary terms ($, €);
- Number (#);
- Percentage (%) or index; and
- Combination of the above.

This means, that the objective of the measurement procedure lies in the representation of intellectual capital in form of the above measurement indicators. The SC methods are an indicator system for measuring intellectual capital. Even if Kaplan and Norton [KaNo01, pp. 1] claim that their approach is a management system and that the BSC should be derived from the company's strategy and vision, the key measures focus on financial terms, percentages, numbers or indices. Also Sveiby [Svei02a] points out that the Intangible Asset Monitor is built on the stock-flow theory, and it has a close relationship with the traditional accounting systems.

The major criticism of all management measurement approaches and models is that they make no statements about the individual value of the skills and experiences of the knowledge worker. Even if the human capital perspective is included in all SC methods as part of the overall measurement procedure, the value of the employee is still measured, for example, in terms of employee turnover rate, number of managers, average age of the employees, level of education, training and education costs, profit per employee, seniority, and employee satisfaction. In short the value of a professional is measured in monetary terms, percentages, numbers, and a combination of them. But all methods do not take circumstances into consideration to measure the skills, experience, and know-how of the individual employee. This means that all approaches do not put the knowledge worker in the center of their measurement models. The discussed metrics can be seen as an additional information pool for the overall performance of the company, but they do not give the management information about the knowledge potential of the employees. For example, the indicator "sales per customer" of the efficiency component of the external structure in the Sveiby model (see Figure "IAM Measurement Matrix" and Figure "Intangible Asset Monitor Indicators Matrix") does not give further information about the individual value of the employees because cultural difference in dealing with customers are not taken into consideration. All three SC methods offer an indicator system for measuring intellectual capital in four categories [Skyr00, p. 317]:

- Customer capital;
- Human capital;
- Internal (external) structural capital; and
- Impact of each of the components to the financial performance of the company (Figure "Traditional Intellectual Capital Measurement View" adapted from [Skyr98, p. 59]).

However, these methods do not give any information about the individual value of the knowledge worker concerning his skills, experience, and knowledge and the impact of the action knowledge on the success and competitive advantage of the company. Even if the Skandia Navigator (see Chapter 2.2.5.1) has the human focus in middle of the measurement framework, it does not provide management with information about the knowledge value of the employees.

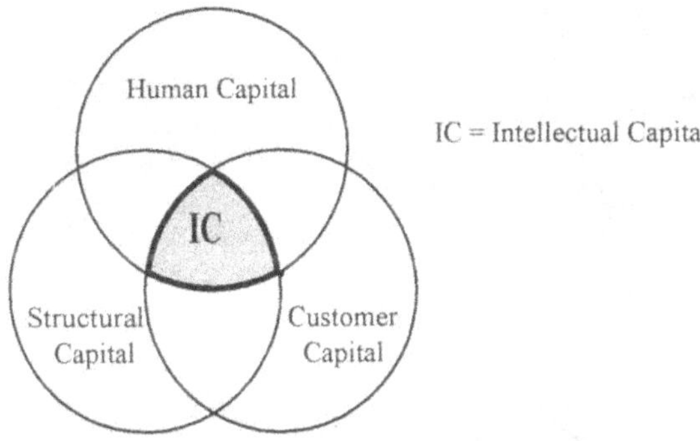

Figure 14: Traditional Intellectual Capital Measurement View

The described objections against the existing measurement systems for intellectual capital led to the formulation of the **knowledge potential view** which puts the knowledge worker with his skills, experience and expert knowledge in the center of the measurement process. Other components such as customers, structural capital, and renewal processes influence and affect his action, therefore, they contribute to his ability to renew his knowledge. The existing SC methods pursue a different objective because they focus on the development of an indicator system for measuring intellectual capital, and, from there, they either balance each perspective/focus or they even try to transfer the results into financial performances.

In the following chapters, a knowledge potential view will be described that puts the knowledge worker in the middle of the measurement process and views all other dimensions as a system influencing the actions, skills, and experiences of the employees. Figure "Knowledge Potential Measurement Framework" illustrates the general applied knowledge potential view which is determined by nine knowledge variables that influence the process of problem solving for each knowledge worker.

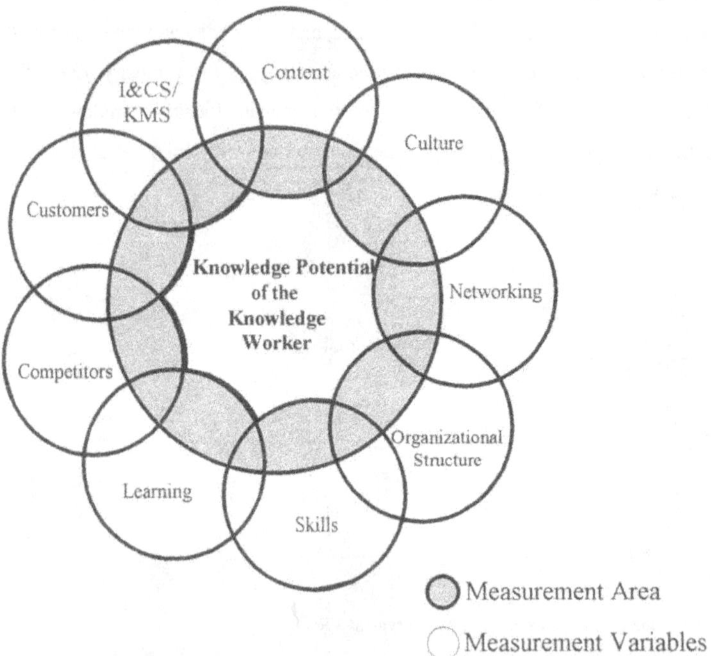

Figure 15: Knowledge Potential Measurement Framework

Human capital represents the major value and source for a successful company. Therefore, it is necessary for management of all levels in the company to get information about the knowledge potential of its employees. The three scorecard methods - Balanced Scorecard,

Skandia Navigator, and Intangible Asset Monitor – build the theoretical background for the derivation of the influencing dimensions. Based on the three scorecard methods, nine identified dimensions have an impact on the acquisition and renewal of the knowledge and skills of the knowledge worker. The knowledge potential of a knowledge worker can be divided into nine categories:

1. Content;
2. Culture;
3. Networking;
4. Organizational structure;
5. Knowledge worker skills;
6. Learning;
7. Customers;
8. Competitors;
9. Information and Communication Systems (I&CS) and Knowledge Management Systems (KMS).

The nine dimensions build a comprehensive system that influences the actions of the knowledge worker. In regard to the measurement process for the knowledge potential of employees, those aspects aligned with the acquisition and renewal of skills and experience are taken into consideration rather than all aspects of each dimension. The red area in Figure „Knowledge Potential Measurement Framework" represents the measurement area. The advantage of this measurement model is its flexibility because it can be

- applied to the organizational level as well as to the component level;
- customized to fit different organizational structures; and
- adjusted to different industries (e.g., consulting company, software company, market research company, and R&D company).

The visualized knowledge measurement view describes a broad measurement system that can be customized and adjusted to all kinds of contexts. The criticisms of the described measurement methods (see Chapter 2) are that they are not measuring the most important resource, the knowledge potential of each individual employee who represent the key success factor of the company. Furthermore, if the value of the knowledge potential can be measured, it is possible to make statements about the:

- future learning and training investments for each employee in order to transform him into an excellent expert;
- knowledge transfer inside and outside the company between experts;
- market success of the company regarding its knowledge worker value; and
- benchmark situation with another companies in the same industry.

A different knowledge measurement system to accomplish the statements, illustrated in Figure "Knowledge Potential Measurement Framework", was developed. In the knowledge economy, companies build on the creativity and expertise of their employees. The measurement of the company knowledge potential ensures its future competitiveness. Each of the nine dimensions must be integrated and balanced to ensure benefit and success. Each of the nine dimensions are overlapping, and they are connected to each other. This means, that each dimension has a relationship to all other dimensions. Obviously, if all nine dimensions are brought into alignment, the company's success grows. The best way to increase the mutual overlapping (red area) is to bring all nine dimensions into balance. Koulopoulos and Frappaolo [KoFr00, p. 419] make the point that

> *"Knowledge management implores you to look at informal networks and protocols, any and all approaches to sharing experiences and know-how, as well as any and all cultural, technological and personal elements that spur creativity and innovation in response to changing stimuli. In order to manage knowledge, it must first be measured. But how? Knowledge is a moving target."*

A successful knowledge measurement process provides management with an analysis of the knowledge potential of its experts and an overview of the impact of the nine knowledge dimensions on the success of the company and, therefore, on its competitive advantages.

4 Quantum Mechanics

"Those who are not shocked when they first come across quantum theory cannot possibly have understood it."

(Niels Bohr)

The objective of Chapter 4 is to give an overview of the basic concepts of quantum mechanics and their interpretation. Thus this chapter functions as a theoretical preparation for a better understanding of the quantum world and of the knowledge measurement process. First, the terminology of the word "quantum" and its impact on the derivation of the term "knowledge quantum" is explained in Chapter 4.1. Then, the discussion moves to the historical development of quantum mechanics. The key issues and current research field for quantum theory will be given in an overview. The following chapters show some insights into key quantum mechanical concepts such as slit-experiments, wave-particle duality, the Copenhagener interpretation, and quantum probability. Chapter 4 closes with an explanation of the Uncertainty Principle of Werner Heisenberg, especially since the Uncertainty Principle is used to derive the knowledge measurement process through the method of analogical reasoning.

4.1 Quantum Definition and Knowledge Quantum

"Quantum" [BiCK92, Omnè94] is a Latin word meaning some quantity of some definite amount of something. A quantum can be defined as the smallest unit of which all matter is composed. Experiments have confirmed the existence of atoms, and scientists have learned to subdivide atoms into something even smaller. That smaller unit, called a quantum, is a general term, and it can be applied to such units as electrons, photons, protons and so on. Even with contemporary technology, it is not possible to see quanta. Quantum theory uses mathematical expressions to describe how these invisible quanta behave in nature. Moreover, it is possible to observe phenomena that are affected by quanta through experiments. By observing such phenomena, physics tries to describe and understand these invisible quanta.

Quanta were born in 1900 with the theory of black-body radiation [Kroe94] put forward by *Max Planck* (1858-1947). Black-body radiation is the electromagnetic radiation emitted by a body in thermodynamical equilibrium, or the radiation contained in a cavity when its walls are at a uniform temperature. By letting radiation escape through a small aperture, one can measure its spectrum and its energy density. Planck assumed that the relationship between the energy and frequency of the quantum transferred from atom to radiation was given by the following formula:

$$E = h * v$$

Energy, E, equals a constant (denoted by the letter *h*) times the frequency (denoted by *v*); h is the Planck constant, and its actual number is $6.63 * 10^{-34}$ Joule seconds (Js). Planck assumed that the emission and absorption of radiant energy could only take place in the form of discrete packets which he called quanta. This theory led to the modern theory between matter and radiation known as quantum mechanics.

The word "knowledge" has characteristics similar to a quantum. Knowledge is referred to as being implicit, tacit, in the people's head, or invisible. Knowledge cannot be seen directly, so it is necessary to find a way to describe something that is invisible like quanta. There are certain similarities between the words quantum and knowledge. Even when something is invisible, it is still possible to manipulate it and then to observe the resulting phenomena. We can observe phenomena that are affected by knowledge through experiments, i.e., an employee is solving a specific and complicated customer problem using knowledge gained over many years of experience in the field of customer relations. The general knowledge of a person or a company must be subdivided into smaller and smaller parts to describe these phenomena. The unit, knowledge, itself is too big to be measured as a whole, so tacit knowledge has to be broken down into small measurable units. **Knowledge quanta** can be defined as the smallest possible unit of knowledge. This means, the overall knowledge of a person is the sum of all his knowledge quanta. To be able to measure a certain amount of a person's knowledge, it must be divided into sub-units (see Figure "Knowledge Quantum). Figure "Knowledge Quantum" illustrates the general measurement process and the use of knowledge quanta. The knowledge potential view defines nine knowledge quanta which will be measured.

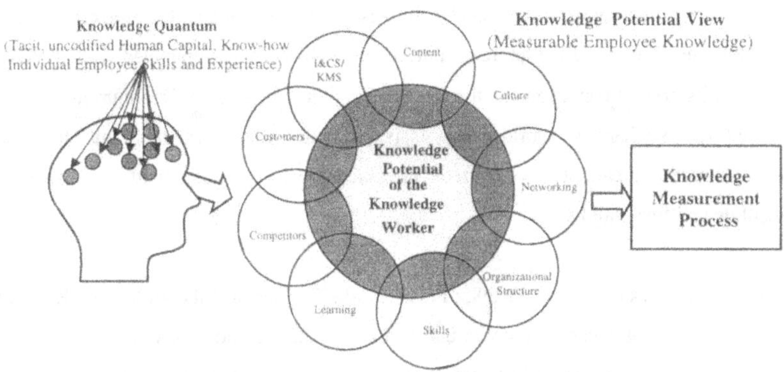

Figure 16: Knowledge Quantum

The objective is to measure the impact of these sub-units on the action knowledge of an expert (knowledge potential view). How much do knowledge quanta affect the action process of a knowledge worker. Since knowledge is action oriented, the individual knowledge quanta are influencing action-oriented processes. Knowledge quanta are a reference of the knowledge potential view where some principles of the quantum world will be applied. It is possible to receive information about the knowledge sub-units through the measurement process. Before dealing with the impact of the Uncertainty Principle on knowledge management, a discussion of the key issues of quantum mechanics is in order.

4.2 History of Quantum Theory

"I think of my lifetime in physics as divided into three periods.
In the first period ... I was in the grip of the idea that Everything is Particles. ...
I call my second period Everything is Fields. ...
Now I am in the grip of a new vision, that Everything is Information."

(John Archibald Wheeler)

The mechanistic view of nature is based on Newtonian mechanics [Scho89]. Two features are essential for Newton's mechanics: the elements of the world (which move in an absolute space and an absolute time) are small, solid, and indestructible objects, always identical in mass and shape. And second, it is causal and deterministic. Definite causes give rise to definite effects, and the future of a mechanical object can be predicted with absolute certainty if its present condition and the forces acting on it are known. Quantum reality has destroyed the mechanistic world view. It is rationally comprehensible, but, like the Newtonian reality, it cannot be visualized. Newtonian mechanics was regarded as a scheme of absolute and final validity.

Quantum mechanics [DaMe86; EiRe85; Fraa91; LaLi77; Land98; Libo80; Mill90; Robi97] is the branch of mathematical physics that deals with atomic and subatomic systems and their interaction with radiation in terms of observable quantities. It is an outgrowth of the concept that all forms of energy are released in discrete units or bundles called quanta. Quantum mechanics is concerned with phenomena that are so small-scale that they cannot be described in classical terms. Throughout the 1800s, most physicists regarded Isaac Newton's dynamic laws as sacrosanct, but it became increasingly clear during the early years of the 20th century that many phenomena, especially those associated with radiation, defy explanation by Newtonian physics. It has come to be recognized that the principles of quantum mechanics, rather than those of classical mechanics, must be applied when dealing with the behavior of electrons and nuclei within atoms and molecules. Although conventional quantum mechanics makes no pretense of completely describing what occurs inside the atomic nucleus, it has helped scientists better understand many processes such as the emission of alpha particles and photodisintegration. Moreover, the field theory of quantum mechanics has provided insight into the properties of mesons and other subatomic particles associated with nuclear phenomena.

In quantum mechanics equations, Max Planck's constant of action $h = 6.626\ 10^{-34}$ Joule seconds (Js) plays a central role. This constant, one of the most important in all of physics, has the dimensions energy time. The term "small-scale" used to delineate the domain of quantum mechanics should not be interpreted literally as relating to extend in space. A more precise criterion related to whether quantum modifications of Newtonian laws are important is whether or not the phenomenon in question is characterized by an "action" (i.e., time integral of kinetic energy) that is large compared to Planck's constant. Accordingly, the notion that there is a discrete, indivisible quantum unit loses significance if a great many quanta are involved. This fact explains why ordinary physical processes appear to be so fully in accord with the laws of Newton. The laws of quantum mechanics, unlike Newton's deterministic laws, lead to a probabilistic description of nature. As a consequence, one of quantum mechanics' most important philosophical implications concerns the apparent breakdown, or a drastic reinterpretation, of the causality principle in atomic phenomena.

The history of quantum mechanics is divided into three main periods. The first began with *Planck's theory of black-body radiation* in 1900, and it is described as the period in which the validity of Planck's constant was demonstrated but its real meaning was not fully understood. Black-body radiation is the electromagnetic radiation emitted by a body in thermodynamic equilibrium. By letting radiation escape through a small aparature, one can measure its spectrum and its energy density. The second period began with the quantum theory of *atomic structure and spectra proposed by Niels Bohr* in 1913. Bohr's ideas gave an accurate formula for the frequency of spectral lines, and they were an enormous help in the codification and understanding of spectra. Nonetheless, they did not represent a consistent, unified theory. Rather, they were a sort of patchwork affair in which classical mechanics was subjected to a somewhat extraneous set of so-called quantum conditions that restricted the constants of integration to particular values. True *quantum mechanics appeared in 1926*, and it reached fruition nearly simultaneously in a variety of forms namely, the matrix theory of Max Born and Werner Heisenberg, the wave mechanics of Louis V. de Broglie and Erwin Schrödinger, and the transformation theory of P.A.M. Dirac and Pascual Jordan. These different formulations were in no sense alternative theories; rather, they were different aspects of a consistent body of physical law.

The following basic steps in the development of quantum theory were important [Scho89, pp. 39]:

- Planck's interpretation of the experimentally determined blackbody radiation implies that energy exchange is quantified. The formula E (Energy) = hv became one of the basic elements in a new picture of reality.
- Einstein made the second step in the discovery of quantum theory. He took the ideas of Planck, and he used them in his 1905 paper on the photoelectric effect in which he explained that light consists of particles, or photons, each one having energy, hv, and movement at the velocity of light. He interpreted the waves of light as a

microscopic feature and the photons (particles) as the microscopic foundation for light waves.

- In 1911 Ernest Rutherford showed that an atom consists of electrons located around a small positively charged heavy nucleus.
- Bohr used the planetary model of Rutherford, and applied the quantum theories of Einstein and Planck to the problem of atomic structure. According to Bohr's theory, electrons emit light when they undergo a transition from one orbit to another [TrCo00, p. 115].
- In 1923 de Broglie (1892-1987) postulated that not only light, but also matter has a wave nature.
- Between 1925 and 1926 the complete mathematical formalism of quantum theory was constructed. In 1926 de Broglie's wave hypothesis was given a precise formulation by Erwin Schrödinger. His contribution was the discovery of an explicit equation for defining the wave function ("Schrödinger equation"). In 1925 Heisenberg discovered the matrix mechanism.
- Also in 1996, Born proposed the interpretation of Schrödinger's wave function as a probability wave. Like a particle, an electron exists in only one spot. This expresses the probability of that electron's position. Born's probability interpretation marks the end of determinism.
- Born's ideas are consistent with Heisenberg's Uncertainty Principle stating that one cannot know with perfect precision both position and momentum or energy and time.

The historical development of quantum theory is described in detail in six volumes by Mehra and Rechenberg: Volume 1/Part 1 [MeRe82a] deals with the quantum theory of Planck, Einstein, Bohr and Sommerfeld, covering the years 1900-1925; Volume 1/Part 2 [MeRe82b] is a continuation of the early years of quantum theory; Volume 2 [MeRe82c] explains the discovery of quantum mechanics, and it covers the year 1925; Volume 3 [MeRe82d] is focused on the years 1925-1926 and the foundation of matrix mechanics and its modification; Volume 4 [MeRe82e] examines the fundamental equations of quantum mechanics and the reception of the new quantum mechanics (1925-1926); Volume 5/Part 1 [MeRe87a] is focused on Erwin Schrödinger and the rise of wave mechanism as well as Schrödinger's years in Vienna and Zurich (1887-1925); Volume 5/Part 2 [MeRe87b] discusses the creation of wave mechanics and its early applications; Volume 6/Part 1 [MeRe00] deals with probability interpretation and the statistical transformation theory which are the physical interpretation and the empirical and mathematical foundations of quantum mechanics (1926-1932).

Although the basic mathematical foundations in quantum mechanics were made in the mid-1920s, quantum theory is still a very active research field. New fields include: *quantum algorithm*, *quantum cryptography*, and *quantum computing*. More recently, from the beginning of the 1990, the field of *quantum information theory* [Gree00, StRi00] was established and rapidly expanded. *Quantum entanglement* began to be seen not only as a puzzle, but also as a resource for communication. Quantum entanglement [Mese99] is a quantum mechanics phenomenon in which a particle or a system does not have a definite state, rather it exists as an intermediate form of two "entangled" states. Imagine the following situation [StRi00, p. 40]: Alice and Bob are given coins, and they play with their coins individually. The coins behave normally, giving random results when they are tossed. However, after a short time, we notice that every time Alice's coin lands heads, so does Bob's and *vice versa*. There is no possible communication between the coins. Physics, on the other hand, has seen such correlation between atoms. Objects correlated this way are called *quantum mechanically entangled.*

Lets look at this phenomenon a little closer [HeVe01]. In the day-to-day world that is described by classical physics, we often observe correlations. Imagine observing a bank robbery. The bank robber is pointing a gun at a terrified teller. By looking at the teller, you can tell whether the gun has gone off or not. If the teller is alive and unharmed, you can be sure the gun has not fired. If the teller is lying dead on the floor from a gun-shot wound, you know the gun has fired. On the other hand, by examining the gun to see whether it has fired, you can find out whether the teller is alive or dead. We could say that there is a direct correlation between the state of the gun and the state of the teller. "Gun fired" means "teller dead", and "gun not-fired" means "teller alive". We assume that the robber only shoots to kill and he never misses.

In the world of microscopic objects described by quantum mechanics, things are not always so simple. Imagine whether or not an atom which might undergo a radioactive decay in a certain time. We might expect that there are only two possible states here: "decayed", and "not decayed", just as we had the two states "fired" and "not fired" for the gun or "alive" and "dead" for the teller. However, in the quantum mechanical world, it is also possible for the atom to be in a combined state "decayed-not decayed", one in which it is neither one nor the other but somewhere in between. This is called a "superposition" of the two states, and it is not something we normally expect of classical objects like guns or tellers. Two atoms may be correlated so that if the first has decayed, the second also will have decayed; and if the first atom has not decayed, the second has not either. This is a 100% correlation. But the quantum mechanical atoms also may be correlated so that if the first is in the superposition "decayed-not decayed", the second also will be in the superposition. Quantum mechanically there is more correlation between the atoms than we would expect classically. This kind of quantum "super-correlation" is called "entanglement". Entanglement, in fact, originally was named in German, "Verschränkung", by Schrödinger who was one of the first people to realize how strange it was. Imagine if it is not the robber but the atom which determines whether the gun fires. If the atom decays, it sets off a hair trigger which fires the gun. If it does not decay, the gun does not fire. But what does it mean if the atom is in the superposition state "decayed-not decayed"? Then can it be correlated to the gun in a superposition state "fired-not fired"? And what about the poor teller who is now dead and alive at the same time? Schrödinger was worried by a similar situation where the victim of a quantum entanglement was a cat in a box where the decaying atom could trigger the release of a lethal chemical. The problem is that we are not used to seeing anything like a "dead-live" cat, or a "dead-live" teller in the everyday world. But such strange states should be possible, if we expect quantum mechanics to be a complete theory describing every level of our experience.

The problem was brought into focus by a 1935 famous paper by Einstein, Podolsky and Rosen [AfSe99; EiPR35], who argued that the strange behavior of entanglement meant that quantum mechanics was an incomplete theory and that there must be what came to be known as not yet discovered "hidden variables". The ideas also are called ERP-Paradox, because they highlight the non-local nature of quantum reality. Einstein, Podolsky and Rosen gave the following formulation of the idea [EiPR35, p. 138]:

"If, without in any way disturbing a system, we can predict with certainty (i.e., with probability equal to unity) the value of a physical quantity, then there exists an element of physical reality corresponding to this physical quantity."

The ERP-Paradox [EiPR35] produced a famous debate between Einstein and Niels Bohr, who argued that quantum mechanics was complete and that Einstein's problems arose because he tried to interpret the theory too literally. However in 1964, John Bell pointed out that the classical hidden variable theories made different predictions from quantum mechanics for certain experiments. In fact, he published a theorem which quantified just how much more highly quantum particles were correlated than would be expected classically, even if hidden variables were taken into account. This made it possible to test whether quantum mechanics could be accounted for by hidden variables. A number of experiments were performed, and the results are accepted almost universally to be consistent with quantum mechanics. Therefore, there can be no "easy" explanation for the entangled correlations. The only kind of hidden variables not ruled out by the Bell tests would be "non-local" [GrRo99], meaning they would be able to act instantaneously across a distance.

The term "non-locality" [NaKa99] describes the way in which the behavior of a quantum entity (such as an electron) is affected by what is going on at one point (locality of the electron), but it also is what is going on at other places. The quantum entities, in principle, can be far away in the Universe. The non-local influences occur instantaneously. Einstein referred to the phenomenon as "spooky action at a distance"; it is as if the quantum entities remain tangled up with one another forever, so that one twitches, instantaneously, no matter how far they are apart when the other is probed [Grib95, pp. 24]. In the case of photons, at the moment the wave function of the photon collapses into one state, the wave function of the other photon also must collapse into the other state. This means, the measurement that is made on one photon has an instantaneous effect on the nature of the other photon [Grib84, pp. 3]. Other ways in which entanglement can be used as an information resource also have been discovered, e.g., dense coding, cryptography, and applications to communication complexity. Entanglement was found to be a manipulable resource. Under certain conditions, states of low entanglement could be transformed into more entangled states by acting locally, and states of higher entanglement could be "diluted" to give larger numbers of less entangled states.

4.3 Quantum Mechanical Concepts

"It's always fun to learn something new about quantum mechanics."
(Benjamin Schumacher)

4.3.1 Slit Experiments

In 1807 the English physicist Thomas Young (1773-1829) performed the slit experiment [Smit95]. The phenomenon being studied was, what will happen if monochromatic light strike the wall after passing through the slits. Young used the knowledge of how waves move across the surface of a pond a single pebble is dropped into the water. The waves form a series of ripples, moving outward in a circle from the point where the pebble dropped. If waves like this arrive at a barrier which has two holes in it, then the waves spread out on the other side of the barrier in two semicircles centred on the two holes. The same pattern can be observed when light passes through. To examine the result [Polk84], three different cases are shown to explain the slit experiment. In the first one (*slit #1 experiment*), a wave strikes the wall after passing through slit #1, then the intensity is greatest at point A which is directly opposite slit#1. As the distance from slit #1 increases, the waves become weaker. The second experiment (*slit #2 experiment*) is similar to the first one with time light passing through slit #2. The intensity is greatest at point B. Figure "Slit #1 and Slit #2 Experiments" [TrCo00, p. 31] visualizes the pattern that emerges by adding together the patterns when each of the holes is open on its own.

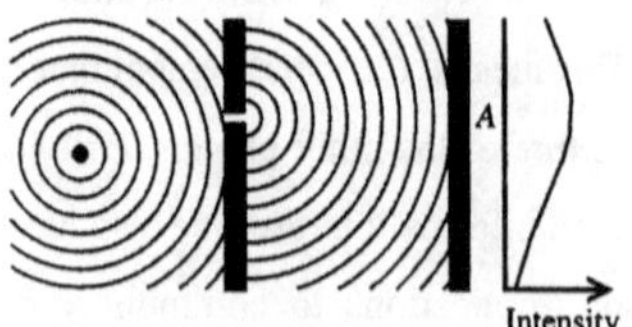

Figure 17: Slit #1 and Slit #2 Experiments

The third case is called the *double-slit experiment* which also can be explained with the analogy of water. Figure "Double-Slit-Experiment" [Grib84, p. 16] illustrates that phenomenon.

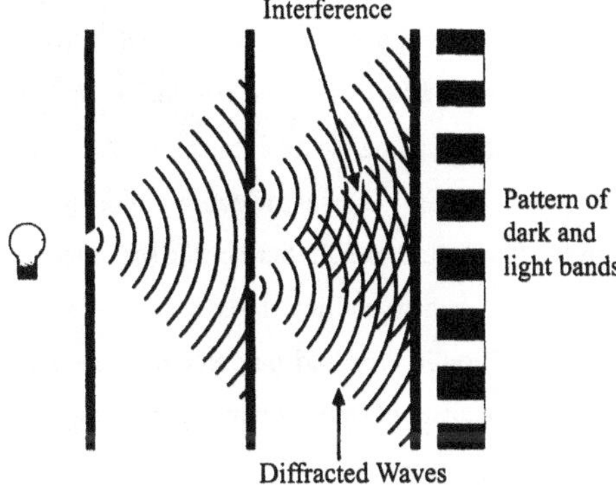

Figure 18: Double-Slit-Experiment

Waves come to a barrier, but this time it has two slits. If one drops two pebbles onto the water, there are two sets of ripples spreading out on the water producing a more complicated pattern of ripples on the surface. If the equivalent experiment is done with light, a similar interference can be seen. When light is shown through two narrow slits, it spreads out with an interference pattern in the area of overlap. The interference pattern shows a pattern of light and dark formed by the alternation of "constructive interference" (an oxymoron meaning the summing of intensity for waves that arrive crest to crest) and "destructive interference" (the cancellation of waves arriving with a crest and partially or completely filling the troughs). So the double-slit- experiment is not the sum of the two single-slit patterns. The double-slit-experiment brings out the wave aspect of a photon or an electron.

4.3.2 Wave-Particle Dualism

Classical mechanics and electromagnetism were based on two kinds of entity: matter and fields. In classical physics, matter consists of particles, and waves are oscillations on a field. Modern physics acknowledges that the universe is made up of entities that exhibit a wave-particle duality [Rae92; Sing97]. The wave-particle dualism [Boro67] is the possession of both wavelike and particle-like characteristics by physical entities (such as light and electrons). On the basis of experimental evidence, Albert Einstein first showed (1905) that light, which had been considered a form of electromagnetic wave, must also be thought of as particle-like. During that time, it was accepted that light travelled in waves, but Einstein used the photoelectric effect to show that a light wave has the nature of a particle, called photon. Light has a dual nature, depending on the experiment it behaves like a wave or like a photon. The Black-body radiation effect, the photoelectric effect, and the Compton effect can be used to explain the photon picture of light but not the wave picture. However, experiments such as the double-slit-experiment and interference need the wave picture. In 1924, the French physicist Louis de Broglie proposed that electrons and other discrete bits of matter, which until then were conceived of only as material particles, also have wave properties such as wavelengths and frequencies.

The mathematical formula for waves was first discovered (1926) by Erwin Schrödinger, and it has been referred to as the wave equation since. The equation [TrCo00, p. 305] for electron wave motion can be written as follows:

$$\nabla^2\Psi + \left(\frac{2\pi v}{u}\right)^2 \Psi = 0$$

where

∇^2 it will determine the amount of spatial change at a given location;

Ψ describes the form of the wave;

π circumference ratio;

v frequency;

u wave speed.

The interpretation of electron waves can be seen as probability waves. The implication is that taking wave-particle duality into consideration, nothing in nature is absolutely certain, meaning we have to specify the probability of finding the electron at a particular point. The Copenhagener Interpretation developed this idea.

4.3.3 Copenhagener Interpretation

The Copenhagener Interpretation [Grib99, Hugh89, Omnè94] is the standard explanation of what will go on in the quantum world. The name derives from Niels Bohr who worked in Copenhagen. The following ideas are the basic foundations of the Copenhagener Interpretation: uncertainty, complementarity, probability, and collapse of the wave function when an observer disturbs the system. Bohr noted that all we know is what we measure with our instruments, and the answers depend on the questions we ask. So according to the Copenhagener Interpretation, it is meaningless to ask what other quantum entities are doing when we are not looking at them. According to Bohr, all we can do is calculate the probability that a particular experiment will come up with a particular result. According to the Copenhagener Interpretation, the act of measurement forces the quantum entity into one state, giving us a unique answer to the question posed by the experiment. But the moment the measurement is made, the quantum entity begins to dissolve in a superposition of states. The Copenhagener Interpretation can be explained by Figure "Copenhagener Interpretation".

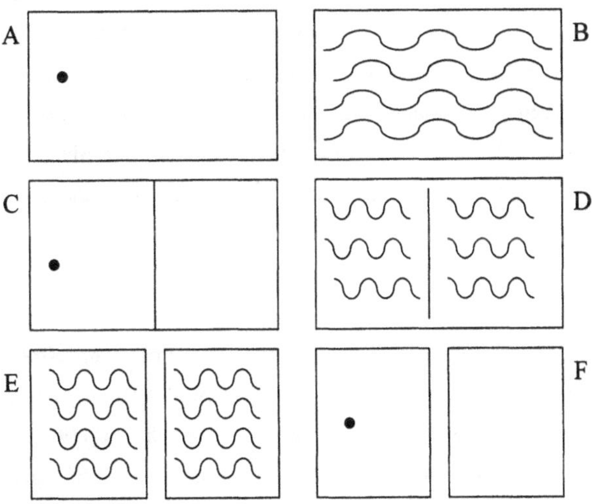

Figure 19: Copenhagener Interpretation

Specifically [Grib99, p. 89]: while common sense would say the electron has a definite location in the box even if we do not look at it, the Copenhagener Interpretation says the electron exists as a wave filling box (B), and it could be anywhere inside the box. At the moment we look in the box, the wave function collapses at location (A). Common sense says that the electron must be in half of the box (C) if we slide a partition onto the box without looking. The Copenhagener Interpretation says the electron wave still occupies both halves of the box (D) as long as we do not look at it, and it only collapses on one side of the barrier when we look inside (C). The wave still fills both boxes (E) as long as we do not look at it even if we move the two halves of the box far apart. Even if the boxes are light years apart, the electron wave function collapses, instantaneously, only when we look into either one, and the electron "decides" which box it is in (F).

The Copenhagener Interpretation also is based on Bohr's notion of *"complementarity"*. Bohr felt that the classical and quantum mechanical models were two complementary ways of dealing with physics *both* of which were necessary. Bohr felt that an experimental observation collapsed or ruptured (his term) the wave function to make its future evolution consistent with what we observe experimentally. Bohr understood there was no precise way to define the exact point at which collapse occurred, and any attempt to do so would yield a different theory rather than an interpretation of the existing theory. Nonetheless, he felt it was connected to conscious observation because it was the ultimate criterion by which we know the occurrence of a specific observation. The idea of "complementarity" means that a certain pair of variables cannot have precise values at the same time. According to the Heisenberg Uncertainty Principle, one of the most classic examples is the pair of complementary properties of position and momentum.

Besides the Copenhagener Interpretation, there are several alternatives to the interpretation of quantum theory. One of the measurement theories is called the "many-worlds-theory" after DeWitt. The originator of the theory [http://plato.Stanford.edu/entries/qm-everett, Date 2003-02-17] was Hugh Everett who called it "relative-state metatheory" (1957). The "many-worlds-theory" was a quantum mechanics reformulation designed to eliminate the need not only of classical observation devices or extraneous observers but also of an *apriori* operational formulation of its formalism [Jamm74, pp. 507]. According to the theory, mathematical formalism defines its own interpretation. Measurement itself plays no fundamental role in the theory. The "many-worlds-theory" is a return to the classical, pre-quantum, view of the universe in which all the mathematical entities of a physical theory are real [Pric95]. In Everett's view, the collapse of the wave function does not occur. This approach to quantum theory has become popular in recent years among quantum cosmologists [Isha95, pp. 156] who welcome the absence of any fundamental structural role for acts of measurement. Albert and Loewer [Barr99, p. 186] understood the "many-worlds-theory" to describe the states of different minds rather than different worlds. They called their approach *"single-mind-theory"* and *"many-minds-theory"*. Another interpretation is the *"hidden variables"* approach, meaning that the standard quantum formalism is incomplete and that the probabilistic nature of the usual results arises from the existence of "hidden variables" [Isah95, p. 160]. Further approaches are *"quantum logic"* and the *"transactional model"* [Pric95]. The Copenhagener Interpretation is the most common one, and it will be used as the standard interpretation. The other alternatives represent different views, however they are not commonly accepted.

4.3.4 Probability

In physics, probability [Grib99, pp. 290; Wu86] means exactly what it means in everyday life or in the casino. The term probability means it is the chance - the likelihood - that a particular event will happen. If a coin is tossed fairly, there is an exact fifty-fifty chance that it will come down heads, and a fifty-fifty chance that it will come down tails. The probability for each outcome is therefore 0.5. Probability lies at the heart of quantum reality because the quantum world obeys strict probabilistic rules. Quantum probabilities are very different from classical physics. In classical physics, probabilities express some lack of information concerning the details about of a given situation [Omnè94, pp. 10]. If a bullet is fired from a gun and if it hits a target at random, then this is just because one does not know exactly, for instances, how much the human hand is shaking. Quantum probabilities are very different because they assume, as a matter of principle, that a more precise knowledge is impossible at the atomic level. It is not the case that there will be a prediction of what will happen in a statistical way when having a large number of quantum events happing at the same time, like the prediction that there will be an 8% raise of tourism next year in the city of Innsbruck. A consequence of these probabilistic considerations is the Uncertainty Principle. Quantum mechanic events are governed by probabilities. In 1935, a thought experiment ("the cat in the box experiment") was introduced by Erwin Schrödinger [Schr83, p. 152] to illustrate the quantum mechanics paradox. Schrödinger postulated a sealed vessel containing a live cat and a device triggered by a quantum event such as the radioactive decay of the nucleus. If the quantum event occurs, cyanide is released and the cat dies; if the event does not occur, the cat lives. In the everyday word, there is a fifty-fifty chance that the cat is killed without looking inside the box. The view is different in the world of quantum mechanics. The cat only could be said to be alive or dead when the box has been opened and the situation inside has been observed. In other words, nothing is real until it is observed. This experiment lead Einstein to his famous words "God does not play dice" [Smit95, pp. 85], meaning that one can opt for a neo-classical or quantum model.

4.4 The Uncertainty Principle

"The more precisely the position is determined, the less precisely the momentum is known in this instant, and vice versa."

(Werner Heisenberg)

In 1927 Heisenberg articulated the so called Heisenberg Uncertainty Principle or Indeterminacy Principle [Gree00, HoKP87, Mill90, PiCh77, Wick95]. According to the Uncertainty Principle, the position and the velocity of an object cannot both be measured exactly at the same time. Any attempt to measure the velocity of a subatomic particle, such as an electron, precisely is unpredictable, so a simultaneous measurement of its position has no validity. This result has nothing to do with inadequacies in the measuring instruments, the technique, or the observer; it arises from the intimate connection in nature between particles and waves in the subatomic realm.

There are four properties which are important to the Uncertainty Principle: the position of the electron, its momentum (which is the electron's mass times its velocity), its energy, and the time. These properties appear as "variables" in equations that describe the electron's motion. Uncertainty relationships have to do with the measurement of these four properties; in particular, they have to do with the precision with which these properties can be measured. Until the advent of quantum mechanics, everyone thought the precision of any measurement was limited only by the accuracy of the measurement instruments used. Heisenberg showed that regardless of the accuracy of the instruments used, quantum mechanics limits precision when two properties are measured at the same time. These are not just any two properties; they are the two represented by variables that have a special relationship in the equations. The technical term is "canonically conjugate" variables. For the moving electron, the canonically conjugate variables are in two pairs: momentum and position in one pair, and energy and time in the other. Roughly speaking, the relationship between momentum and position is like the relationship between energy and time. The Uncertainty Principle can be expressed in words as follows: the simultaneous measurement of two conjugate variables (such as the momentum and position or the energy and time for a moving particle) is a limitation on the precision (standard deviation) of each measurement. Namely, the more precise the measurement of position is, the more imprecise the measurement of momentum is, and *vice versa*. In the most extreme case, absolute precision of one variable would entail absolute imprecision regarding the other. Heisenberg stated in his 1927 uncertainty paper: "The more precisely the position is determined, the less precisely the momentum is known in this instant, and vice versa" [http://www.aip.org/history/heisenberg/, Date 2003-02-23]. The derivation of the Uncertainty Principle for position and momentum can be found in Appendix C.

The uncertainty relationship can be written more precisely by using mathematical symbols. First, the basic symbols have to be defined:

Δ x is the uncertainty in the position measurement;

Δ p is the uncertainty in the momentum measurement;

Δ E is the uncertainty in the energy measurement;

Δ t is the uncertainty in the time measurement;

h is a constant known from quantum theory known as Planck's constant;

π is pi.

Putting these symbols together, the two **uncertainty relationships** look like the following [Gerj93, p. 1490]:

$$\Delta p \Delta x \geq \frac{h}{4\pi}$$

and

$$\Delta E \Delta t \geq \frac{h}{4\pi}$$

Assume that it is possible to measure the position of a moving electron with such great accuracy that Δx is very small. What happens to the precision of momentum Δp, measured at the same instant? From the first relationship, the following formula can be calculated:

$$\Delta p \geq \frac{h}{4\pi} \Delta x$$

It can be seen that the uncertainty in the momentum measurement, Δp, is very large because Δx in the denominator is very small. In fact, if the precision of the position measurement gets so great that the uncertainty Δx gets so small that it approaches zero, then Δp gets so large that it approaches infinity or it becomes completely undefined. The uncertainty relationship for energy is stated as giving an estimate for ΔE in the energy that is found when measuring it in an experiment lasting at most a time Δt. Considering the two equations above, a quite accurate measurement of one variable involves a relatively large uncertainty in the measurement of the other.

Quantum theory measurement is needed in a *microscopic world* because the measurement interaction disturbs the object. The classical theory of measurement is adequate for the macroscopic world because the measurement interaction does not significantly disturb the object. Band describes the major difference between the classical and the quantum theoretical perspective as follows [Band81, p. 825]:

> *"In classical physics we accept the hypothesis that every individual object possesses observables with unique and precise numerical values, and measurement techniques are designed to discover these hypothetical values. In quantum theory we have no need of this hypothesis, and accept the measurement results themselves as the only irrefutable body of scientific truth. In classical theory the physical laws refer to the hypothetical behavior of the hypothetical precise numerical values of observables. In quantum theory the physical laws refer only to the measurement results."*

The Uncertainty Principle of Heisenberg is the theoretical framework for the derivation of the knowledge potential measurement model by applying analogical reasoning.

5 Knowledge Potential Measurement and Uncertainty

"While it is difficult to change a company that is struggling, it is next to impossible to change a company that is showing all the outward signs of success. Without the spur of a crisis or a period of great stress, most organizations – like most people – are incapable of changing the habits and attitudes of a lifetime."

(John F. McDonnell)

In Chapter 5 the knowledge potential measurement model is presented and explained. First, the process of analogical reasoning by transforming the Uncertainty Principle of Heisenberg into the knowledge potential view will be introduced, and the differences between the physical measurement process and the knowledge measurement model will be explained. Then, the knowledge architecture, which is the basic framework for the measurement process, is presented. Then nine knowledge variables will be discussed in detail. Finally, the general and the specific measurement processes are presented and explained. This chapter is the key one for the measurement model and for the derivation of the uncertainty factors associated with the measurement process.

5.1 Analogical Reasoning

The Uncertainty Principle of Heisenberg is the basic theoretical framework for the knowledge measurement procedure. The concept of the Uncertainty Principle occurs during the measurement of two knowledge fields:

1. For the knowledge potential of each knowledge worker;
2. For the uncertainty for each knowledge-engineers.

However, it is not possible to take the equations from Heisenberg and to transfer them to the knowledge potential approach without changes. The Uncertainty Principle functions as a reference-model for the knowledge approach because it is not a physical environment. The theoretical explanation for taking the physical approach and using it in the knowledge context is accomplished by **analogical reasoning** [McIn68]. By definition, analogy is [Gent99, p. 17]

"(1) similarity in which the same relations hold between different domains or systems; (2) inference that if two things agree in certain respects then they probably agree in others. ... The central focus of analogy research is on the mapping process by which people understand one situation in terms of another."

Reasoning by analogy generally involves abstracting details from a set of problems and resolving structural similarities between previously distinct problems. Analogical reasoning refers to this recognition process, and the application of the solution from the known problem to the new problem. Analogical learning generally involves the development of a set of mappings between features of two problems. In other words, analogical reasoning is the ability of people to understand new situations by analogy to old ones and their ability to solve problems based on previously solved problems. Analogical reasoning has great relevance for Artificial Intelligence [Keda88, pp. 65]. Kedar-Cabelli [Keda88] states that the ability of exploiting past experiences to solve current problems in expert systems is a bottleneck to truly robust and intelligent artificial expertise. Furthermore, analogical reasoning is needed for an understanding of natural language, machine learning, and the creation of computers with commonsense reasoning. Thagard [Thag88, pp. 105] also focuses on the computational investigations of analogy which can be organized into four dimensions:

1. *Representation.* Representation of analogy must have syntactic, semantic, and pragmatic components.
2. *Retrieval.* Retrieval focuses on different kinds of mechanisms for finding potentially relevant analogues.
3. *Exploitation.* After a potential analogy has been retrieved, is must be used. Most of the Artificial Intelligence research tries to set up mapping between the source and the target. Also, a justification should be implemented; this means that the validity of mapped target attributes, relationships and causal chains, must be justified.
4. *Learning.* Learning should be an important component in Artificial Intelligence.

Keane [Kean88] sees the analogical reasoning process highly linked to creativity. Creative solutions are achieved when a number of remote concepts are co-present in consciousness.

Anderson [Ande93, pp. 79] has introduced a four step conception of problem solving by analogy to a *prior* example:

1. Find an example that had a similar goal;
2. Map the goal structure of the example to problem;
3. Apply the mapping to the response structure of example to get a response structure for the current goal;
4. Check preconditions.

By analogy to the Heisenberg Uncertainty Principle, the knowledge measurement procedure will be derived (see Figure "Analogous Problem Solving Procedure"). On the left side, the Anderson analogous problem-solving operator is compared with the Heisenberg Uncertainty Principle on the right side which illustrates the analogous problem solving process for measuring the knowledge of a person.

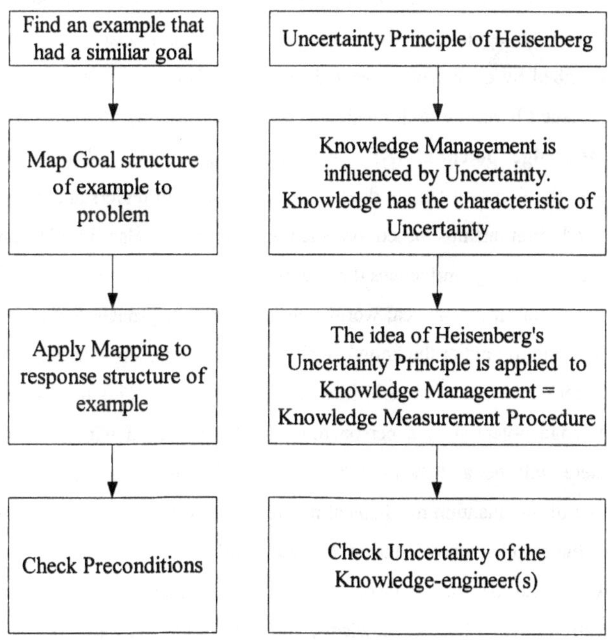

Figure 20: Analogous Problem Solving Procedure

Gentner [Gent89, p. 201] uses the term "structure-mapping" that is defined as "a mapping of knowledge from one domain (the base) into another (the target), which conveys that a system of relations that holds among the base objects also holds among the target objects". In our case, this means the Heisenberg Uncertainty Principle functions as the base and it is mapped to the target in the knowledge management approach. The linking relationship is that uncertainty is the major characteristic of knowledge as well as a physic phenomenon. The measurement procedure of the knowledge worker is greatly influenced by uncertain decisions. The match between the two ideas is the concept of uncertainty. During the analogical mapping process, moreover, the existing structure of the Uncertainty Principle is imported into the new knowledge measurement approach.

Physicists have defined many quantities, and two quantities, momentum and position, are subject to the Heisenberg Uncertainty Principle. The major adjustment is that the physical[8] constant h is not valid for knowledge management. Since h is a fundamental constant of quantum physics, it cannot be applied to the world of knowledge management. An individual cannot be described by a constant measured in the unit Js or in any other unit. As a consequence, the constant h will be re-defined, and it is represented by the letters KP which describe the **knowledge potential (KP)** of a knowledge worker. Within the knowledge potential view, the focus on people does more than imply an understanding of knowledge exchanges and relationships based on such exchanges. It also implies an understanding of how such knowledge influences the action or the potential action based on such exchanges. Like the quantum mechanical world, the knowledge approach deals with uncertainties. It is not possible to predict the knowledge potential of a person with a 100% certainty. We only can speak in terms of probabilities and *indeterminism*. This means, for example, that the knowledge potential of a person only can be measured with an 80% probability and that there will be a 20% probability that tacit knowledge cannot be measured. A consequence of the quantum mechanical nature of the world is that it will not be possible to measure the implicit knowledge of a person with 100% certainty. In the quantum mechanical world, the idea that it is possible to measure things exactly breaks down. The same implication is valid for the knowledge approach in the sense that it is not possible to measure the precise knowledge potential of knowledge worker. The problem of

---

[8] For a detailed description of the constant h, see Chapter 4.1.

measurement in the knowledge approach arises from the fact that several principles of the quantum world appear to be in conflict with the knowledge approach and that, in contrast to quantum measurement, the knowledge approach is influenced by the individual abilities of a person. This is the reason why knowledge management has three **basic assumptions** for the uncertainty measurement:

1. The constant h will not be used; it is substituted for the knowledge potential (KP) of a knowledge worker. KP is not a constant; it is the result of a mathematical equation; there are no constant values in the knowledge world.
2. The measurement procedure is not a physical one. Thus, characteristics of a human resource based approach must be taken into consideration. A basic physical definition has to be re-interpreted and put into a knowledge context by using the analogical reasoning process.
3. The theoretical implication of Heisenberg's measurement is that the more precisely the position is determined, the less precisely the momentum is known in this instant, and *vice versa*. This physical phenomenon is difficult to explain for the knowledge measurement process, hence, the case studies discussed in Chapter 6 show first implications of this phenomenon.

It must be pointed out again that the procedure of measurement in the case of knowledge is not a traditional one in the sense of a physical measurement. Rather it is a measurement in psychology. Michell [Mich99, p. 15; see also MeRa73] points out that there is a difference in measuring in the natural sciences and in a psychological context. Michell, acknowledging Stevens, defines: "measurement is the process of assigning numerals to objects or events according to rules". In the natural sciences numbers are not assigned to anything; they are measured like they are in physics. The difference is that numbers are assigned to objects in psychological measurement. In the knowledge measurement procedure, each knowledge worker is assigned a number, his personal knowledge potential. Also Schoeninger and Insko [ScIn71] discuss measurement in behavioral sciences, and they state that "measurement consists of the assignment of observations to classes or categories (subsets) according to a rule" [ScIn71, p. 2]. In situations where measurement classes have a quantitative meaning, observations are assigned to the number classes. The particular number assigned to an observation is the score for that observation. Whitla [Whit68], for example, defines applied areas of measurement in behavioral sciences, areas such as the structure of intelligence, the measurement of aptitude and achievement, the measurement of personality, the measurement of creativity, the measurement of interest, the measurement of analysis in anthropology, or the measurement for guidance.

5.2 Knowledge Architecture

"Knowledge is the true organ of sight, not the eyes."

(Panchatantra)

The methodical concept for a questionnaire design and the knowledge measurement process follows my know-how-architecture [Fink00a; Fink00b; RoFi97; RoFi98]. Know-how-architecture is an adaptation of the system planning process from Heinrich [Hein94; Hein96], its framework is illustrated in Figure "Knowledge Architecture" [Fink00a, p. 75]. It consists of five stages, and it can be interpreted as a lifecycle model [HeRo98].

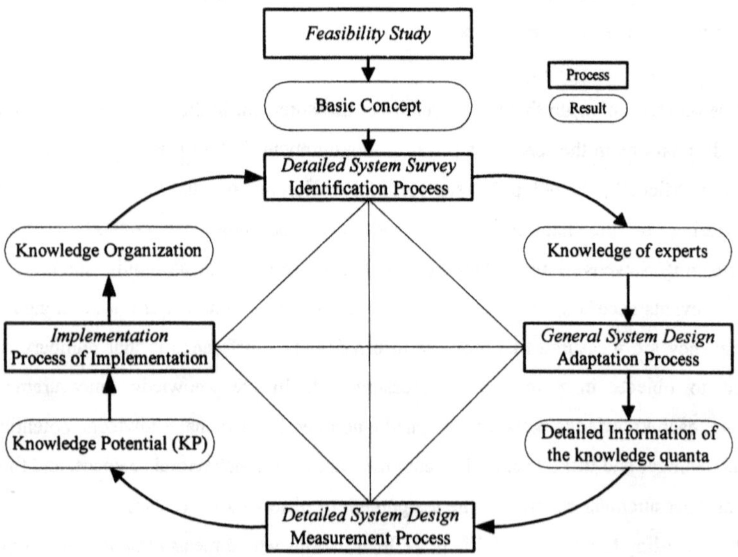

Figure 21: Knowledge Architecture

In the last three years, several changes in the detailed steps of the original know-how-architecture have been made. These changes arise out of several case studies conducted during past studies which made it necessary to modify the architecture. However, the five processes are the same; only the detailed steps within each process were adapted, and the word "knowledge architecture" was utilized instead of using know-how-architecture.

Successful implementation of the knowledge architecture demands a person who is responsible for the achievement of the knowledge potential view, and the position of the so-called **knowledge-engineer** [Fink00a, pp. 100] was created. The term knowledge-engineer was chosen by referring to the information engineering approach [Mart89; Mart90a; Mart90b, Hein99]. A knowledge-engineer is a person who has the social, technological, creative, and methodical skills required for leveraging the knowledge quanta embedded in the minds of knowledge workers in an organization [Fink00a, p. 101]. The tasks of the knowledge-engineer are to identify and network the tacit knowledge of the employees and to reflect about the current knowledge base in order to generate new knowledge quanta. Furthermore, he has to create a culture of trust to have an atmosphere for knowledge sharing. Bontis [Bont01] uses the term Chief Knowledge Officer (CKO) for an evangelist whose job is "to capture that same imagination from all employees while providing a charismatic spark that creates new ideas and innovation. ... Therefore, a CKO oversees all knowledge activities related to human behavior" [Bont01, p. 30]. The job of the CKO and the knowledge-engineer are similar because both terms imply that the objective of this person is to generate as much knowledge as possible from employees to get information about the current and future knowledge base of a company. To be successful, the knowledge-engineer embodies a whole set of functions, and he must be seen as a multi-function person [Bont01, pp. 31]. The **major tasks** of the knowledge-engineer are:

1. *Coordination and implementation of the knowledge architecture processes*. The knowledge-engineer is responsible for the project management of the implementation of the knowledge potential view. He has the task to form a team, which supports him to establish a culture of knowledge sharing.
2. *Interviewer Skills*. Knowledge-engineers are the persons who lead the interviews with the knowledge workers to get information about the defined knowledge quanta. The success of the interviews depends greatly on the skills and experiences a knowledge-engineer brings into the interview technique.

3. *Training Skills.* The knowledge-engineer should work closely with the training and learning staff [Bont01, p. 33] because the knowledge of the experts can be renewed, or leveraged in training programs. Sometimes the knowledge-engineer functions as a personal trainer to the knowledge worker, trying to help by defining future training programs.
4. *Establish a culture of trust and knowledge sharing.* If the knowledge-engineer is working in an environment that lacks trust, the probability that the knowledge workers will share their personal knowledge will decline. This means that the goal is "to make the individual appreciate the consequences of sharing knowledge and appreciate the value of combining disparate perspectives" [Bont01, p. 33].
5. *Multi-skills.* The knowledge-engineer is the person who measures the knowledge potential of each knowledge worker. Hence, he must have a combination of social, methodical, technological, personal, and competent skills. Gupta [Gupt00, p. 371] notes that a person in this position must have several years of experience in the industry, good analytical skills, a keen sense of business, a good understanding of how to deploy technology, and an ability to work with people.
6. *Knowledge Potential Measurement Skills.* The major task of the knowledge-engineer is to measure the knowledge potential of the experts by interviewing them about the nine dimensions representing the knowledge potential view.

The first stage is called the **feasibility study** [Fink00a, pp. 103], and it results in the development of the basic concept that consists of the basic steps for the further procedure. The knowledge-engineer addresses the top and middle management of the company. The feasibility study is oriented towards an analysis of the current situation to derive a future strategy for implementing knowledge management and measurement in the company. Besides analyzing the company information found in written reports, databases, patents, organizational charts, manuals, books, business rules and regulations, the major focus is knowledge about the business that employees gained based on their personal experience, intuition, judgment, and perception. The job of the knowledge-engineer is to give the top and middle management an understanding of the knowledge measurement approach and to communicate it through the implementation of the knowledge potential view so the company decision making will progress and improve its competitive advantages and enhance its customer service. The initial task of the knowledge-engineer is to explain this procedure and the importance of having information about the value of employees. After communicating the objective of implementing a knowledge measurement system, the knowledge-engineer *interviewed the top/middle management* about the defined knowledge quanta. During the process of the feasibility study, the knowledge-engineer talks to the management level. Depending on the company size and type, he can talk with the CEO, members of the board, or the top managers in different departments. However, at this first stage, his interview will be on the management level (see Appendix A which gives the detailed questionnaire for the top management).

Figure "Feasibility Study" gives an overview of the basic steps the knowledge-engineer must make to start the implementation of the knowledge architecture.

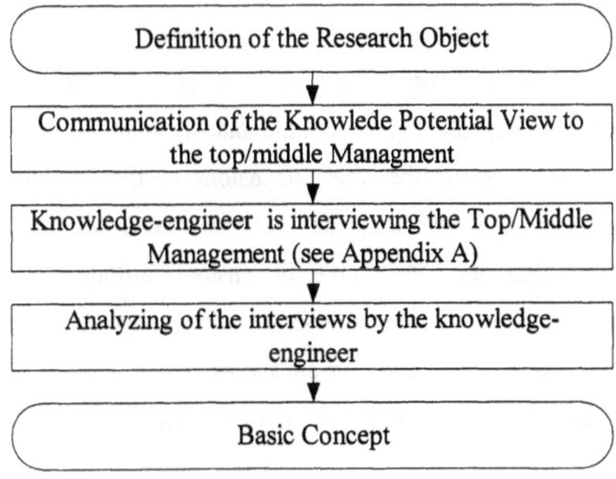

Figure 22: Feasibility Study

The end results of the feasibility study are a commitment from management to implement knowledge measurement in the company and support for management for the future processes. The success depends on the communication to the knowledge worker of the future processes and of the advantages in participating in the interviews. The output of the feasibility study is the basic concept giving information about the general knowledge of the company and about the named knowledge workers by the top or middle management. The objectives of the first stage are:

1. Communication of the knowledge potential view;
2. Definition of the organizational knowledge;
3. Information about the major knowledge workers;
4. Tacit knowledge of the managers.

The second step in the knowledge architecture is the **identification process** [Fink00a, pp, 147] which deals with capturing personal knowledge of each knowledge worker. Probst, Raub and Romhardt [PrRR97, pp. 99] see knowledge identification as a key process of knowledge management. Through knowledge identification, companies gain an overview of their internal skills and knowledge bases. Often management has little information about their internal experts and their skills and experiences collected from many projects. Therefore, it is necessary to make the tacit knowledge of the experts transparent by giving each employee an orientation about the existing knowledge and the use of synergies to build new knowledge. It is the major task of the knowledge-engineer to interview [Fink00a, pp. 158] the experts named by the top or middle management during the feasibility study. The interview process covers the nine dimensions of the knowledge potential view. Through the process of *interviewing* and interview *videotaping*, the knowledge-engineer collects knowledge about the nine dimensions influencing the knowledge potential approach (the detailed questionnaire for the knowledge workers is attached in Appendix B). The objectives of this detailed system survey are:

- Getting information about the current situation about the knowledge and expertise of the knowledge workers;
- Analyzing the data collection and preparing the knowledge measurement process;
- Transcribing the interviews;
- Adapting the basic concept if necessary.

Figure "Knowledge Identification Process" pictures the key steps during the second process. Starbuck [Star97] also uses the interviewing method to gain more insight from the knowledge of experts. Starbuck states [Star97, pp. 154] that

> *"I had only to point to a few issues that interested me, and they would begin to extrapolate – telling me who else I should interview, what issues ought to interest me, where my assumptions seemed wrong, and how their worlds look to them."*

So interviewing the knowledge worker is an adequate method to begin capturing knowledge in the nine knowledge measurement dimensions.

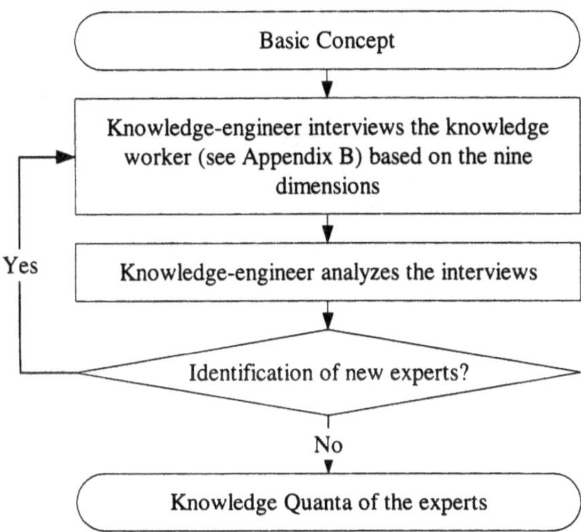

Figure 23: Knowledge Identification Process

The **process of adaptation** [Fink00a, pp. 163] is the third step in knowledge architecture. In this case, because the knowledge workers have not communicated their personal skills and experience in detail, the knowledge-engineer must conduct another *interview* with the experts, the objective being to gather more accurate answers to his questions. This process is identical to the process of identification, and the steps are similar to those visualized in Figure "Knowledge Identification Process".

The **measurement process** is the key stage in the knowledge architecture. Deviating from the original process, called process of networking [Fink00a, pp. 182], the fourth process is the key success factor of the knowledge architecture. During this process, the knowledge potential (KP) for each expert is calculated. The general measurement procedure is described in Figure "Measurement Procedure for the Uncertainty Principle", and it will be explained mathematically in the Chapters 5.4-5.8.

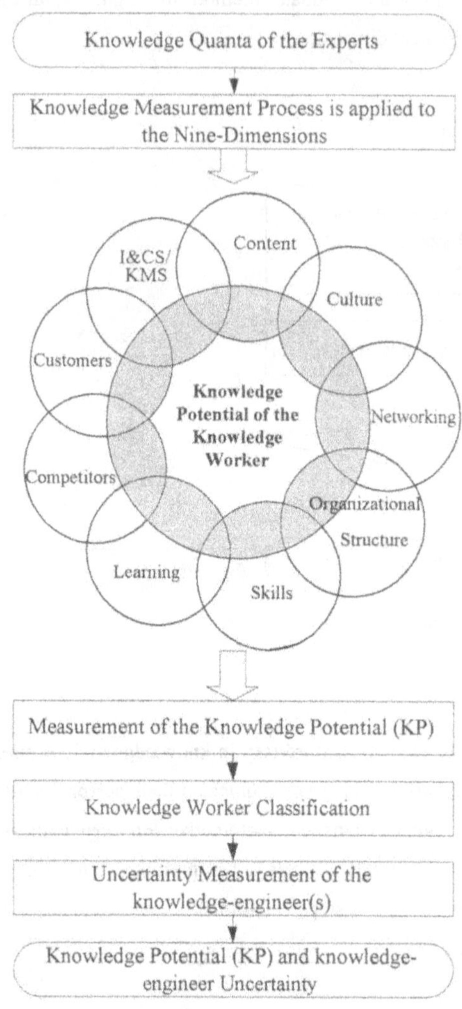

Figure 24: Measurement Procedure for the Uncertainty Principle

The basic framework of the measurement process is the nine-dimension knowledge potential view explained in Chapter 3. The major difficulty is getting information about the general knowledge of the organization, about its existing knowledge workers, and about their tacit knowledge. The questionnaires (see Appendix A and B) are the basis for the data collection and analysis for the measurement of the knowledge potential. Furthermore, the uncertainty measurement must be calculated. As a consequence, measurement error for the knowledge potential must be calculated. Based on the statistical results, a decision support model is developed for the final evaluation of the knowledge workers and their future place in the company. An effective knowledge decision model facilitates a focused evaluation of the company's knowledge management activities and attitudes. Therefore, potential areas of improvement and opportunities must be identified to leverage the knowledge. The result of the measurement procedure identifies the current level of expertise of the knowledge workers, and it also identifies internal and external factors that influence the implementation of a successful knowledge measurement system. Based on the measured knowledge potential, the management must decide how to train and place the expert.

The last process is the **implementation** (see Figure "Implementation Process") of the decisions made by management to deal with knowledge management and to develop and train the knowledge worker to stay competitive and innovative. The major task during the implementation process is for the knowledge-engineers to find a team which will support them by keeping the data collection up-to-date. After the measurement of KP, the knowledge-engineer together with the CKO and his implementation team must analyze the results of the measurement process. It is the task of the knowledge-engineer and his team to communicate the results, explain how the score on the rating scale was evaluated, and to explain the necessary future development and training initiatives to keep the expert on his high level of expertise and to transform good knowledge workers into excellent and experienced employees.

Mr. Haller, CIO of the Bank Austria, once said [RoFi02]: "Seven percent of my employees are excellent and 40 percent of them have potential. Give me the tools and methods to train and educate the 40 percent to become excellent professionals". Furthermore, the measured knowledge potential of each expert must be re-calculated in specific intervals because the knowledge and experiences change over time. If the measurement process is only a single process, the time and money spent to go through the implementation process is worthless. Measuring and updating the current measured KP of each employee is crucial if knowledge management is to be successful.

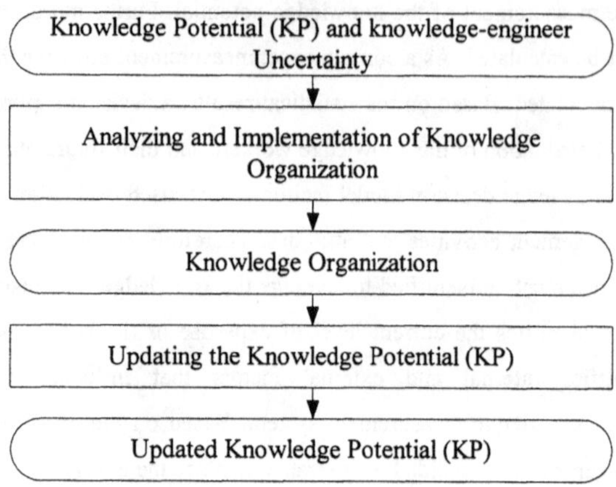

Figure 25: Implementation Process

5.3 Questionnaire Design

"Man is a tool-using animal...
Without tools he is nothing, with tools he is all."
(Thomas Carlyle)

The questionnaire is derived from two sources: (1) a literature search conducted for each of the nine dimensions, the key research findings being expressed in the following chapters, and (2) the Intangible Asset Monitor from Sveiby (explained in Chapter 2.2.5.3 and especially in the two Tables "IAM Measurement Matrix" and "Intangible Asset Monitor Indicators Matrix").

5.3.1 Content (Knowledge)

Before implementing a knowledge-architecture, there must be a common understanding of the term knowledge, its characteristics, and the impact on knowledge management and measurement. The terminology of knowledge reflects the multi-faceted nature of the term itself [KaKK01, pp. 138]. In the past, newspapers, managers, and CEOs often use the slogan "knowledge is our most valuable resource". However, the key question is the impact of this sentence on future knowledge initiatives. The objective of this dimension is the provision of information about the understanding of the term knowledge by both management and knowledge workers. The expertise of the knowledge worker is the resource for networking and organizational structure. Davenport and Prusak [DaPr98] use the term **"knowledge-in-action"** to express the characteristics of the term knowledge in a way it is valuable for the company and to capture it in words because it resists in the minds of the humans and their actions. Davenport and Prusak [DaPr98, pp. 6] identify five key components that describe the term knowledge:

1. The first component is *experience*. Knowledge develops over time, and it builds on the lifelong learning and training practice of an employee. Experience has a historical perspective, and it is based on the skills the knowledge-worker applies to familiar patterns to make connections between these links.
2. The second component of the term knowledge is *"ground truth"* [DaPr98, p. 8] which is a term used by the U.S. Army's Center for Army Lessons Learned (CALL). CALL used the term "ground truth" to express experiences that come from the ground rather than from theories and generalizations. "Ground truth" means that the persons know what works and what does not. CALL experts' take part in real military situations, and they pass their observations to the troops through videotapes or photos. The success of this knowledge management approach lies in "After Action Review" program which tries to cover the gap between what happened during an action and what was supposed to happen. This reflection process helps uncover disparities and differences (see also reflection theory by Schön [Schö82] in Chapter 7).
3. The third component is *complexity*. The skill to solve complex problems and the ability to know how to deal with uncertainties distinguish an expert from a normal employee.
4. A forth characteristic of knowledge is *judgement*. An expert can judge new situations based on experience gained over time. Furthermore, he has the ability to refine them through reflection. Knowledge, in this sense, is a living system that interacts with the environment.
5. Finally, knowledge is about heuristics and *intuition*. An expert acts based on his intuitive knowledge.

Also Sveiby [Svei97, pp. 31] shares an analogous view of the term knowledge. Knowledge is tacit, action-oriented, supported by rules, and it is constantly changing. In its report *The Knowledge Based Economy* OECD [OECD96, p. 12] clusters the term knowledge into four categories:

1. *Know-what* is about knowledge of "facts". It is similar to the term information, and it can be broken down to bits.
2. *Know-why* belongs to the scientific knowledge of the principles and the law of nature. Know-why often is found in research laboratories, universities, and specialized organizations. To have access to this kind of knowledge, companies must make joint ventures to promote the knowledge transfer between these institutions.
3. *Know-how* refers to skills and action knowledge. Know-how resides in the heads of the experts.
4. *Know-who* is a term that refers to the kind of knowledge, a problem solving ability, a person possesses. The acquisition of know-who skills is through social practice and special educational environments. Know-who also develops through the interaction with customers, suppliers, or independent institutions.

I use a similar list of characteristics for the term knowledge [Fink00a, pp. 30]:

1. Knowledge is gained in a learning process; knowledge is process-oriented.
2. Knowledge is based on an individual cognitive approach because knowledge resides in the human mind.
3. Knowledge is action and skill oriented; it is the output of a process of acting and re-acting.
4. Knowledge has an intuitive component because experts act upon past experiences.
5. Knowledge is tacit and implicit. The term implicit knowledge comes from Polanyi [Pola85, p. 14; Pola97] who states that "we can know more than we can tell" [Pola97, p. 136].

Questions concerning this knowledge dimension are developed to get more insight about the use of the term knowledge in a company. This dimension uncovers a gap in the understanding of knowledge management on both the management and on employee levels. A method for getting information about the knowledge of the company is to make a *SWOT*

(*S*trength-*W*eakness-*O*pportunities-*T*hreats) *Analysis*. Hinterhuber [Hint96, pp. 121] uses SWOT-Analysis to identify the core competencies of a company compared to its competitors. Also, Tiwana applies the knowledge-based SWOT-analysis to get more insight into the business strategy and knowledge management system of a company [Tiwa00, p. 192].

5.3.2 Culture

A successful implementation of knowledge management only can be achieved in a culture [Hold02] that supports knowledge sharing and transfer. Nakra [Nakr00] addresses the issue that a knowledge culture is the most important value for the implementation of knowledge management because "one important aspect of knowledge management is having a culture that fosters collaboration and sharing. Organizations often fail to acknowledge that it is the people, not technologies, that are the source of knowledge" [Nakr00, p. 54]. Organizational knowledge resides in the culture, structure, and individuals who make up the organization. Three key processes and systems can be identified [Nakr00, p. 55]:

- *Organizational knowledge* reflected in the corporate mission, objectives, and strategies;
- *Task knowledge* found in corporate functions and processes;
- *Individual knowledge* reflected in organizational structure and individual roles.

The implementation of a knowledge management system depends highly on the corresponding corporate culture and organizational structure. If people want to transfer their experience and expertise, they need an environment that is based on trust and an atmosphere that supports the sharing of creative ideas. Davenport and Prusak identify seven sources that inhibit a knowledge transfer through a culture that does not support a knowledge sharing [DaPr98, pp. 96]:

1. *Lack of trust*. A solution for this friction is the creation of an atmosphere where knowledge is shared through face-to-face meetings.
2. *Different cultures, vocabularies, frames of references*. A major success factor for sharing knowledge is a common level of education, language, teamwork, and job rotation. If a group of experts wants to exchange knowledge, they must have the same level of expertise and talk in the same professional language.

3. *Lack of time and meeting places, narrow idea of productive work.* Sometimes it is necessary to bring knowledge workers together to create new ideas by simply establishing the times and places for knowledge transfer, such as conferences, talk rooms, coffee brakes.
4. *Status and rewards for knowledge owners.* Davenport and Prusak point out that "people judge the information and knowledge they get in significant measure on the basis of who gives it to them" [DaPr98, p. 100].
5. *Lack of absorptive capacity in recipients.* A company should have a culture that educates the knowledge worker for flexibility by providing them with time for learning and education and encouraging them to be open to new ideas.
6. *Belief that knowledge is the prerogative of particular groups, the not-invented-here syndrome.* A knowledge sharing culture is based on a non-hierarchical approach to knowledge; this means that the quality of knowledge is more important than the status of the source.
7. *Intolerance of mistakes and the need for help.* A company must have a culture that allows for and accepts the fact that their employees also can make creative errors and not be punished for doing so.

A company needs a culture that facilitates a knowledge transfer through a more human factor because knowledge workers want to share their knowledge through communication and interaction. A good knowledge worker is characterized by two kinds of skills [DaPr98, p. 110]: "hard" skills such as structured knowledge, technical abilities, and professional experience and "soft" skills which help him communicate the creative ideas. An appropriate organizational culture can empower effective knowledge management and measurement. The organizational culture of a company consists of the shared values or norms which involve common beliefs and feelings, regularities of behavior, and historical processes for transmitting values and norms [StBe02, pp. 647]. A similar definition of the culture is used by Trompenaars and Hampden-Turner [TrHa98, pp. 6] who define culture as a group of people concerned with problem solving processes and reconzilation dilemmas. Culture itself has three different levels. The first, and highest level, is *national culture* or regional society; the second level describes the *organizational culture*, and, finally, the *professional culture* which is focused on the knowledge of specific groups. A fundamental issue that arises out of different cultural settings is individualism versus communitarianism [TrHa98, pp. 51]. Behind this dualism stands the question: does a person see himself as an individual or a part of a group? Self-orientation is an element of modern society and it is taken for granted in many Western countries that individuals create businesses, invent new products, or deserve higher salaries. In a survey conducted by Trompenaars and Hampden-Turner concerning ways of working, participants had to answer the following question [TrHa98, p. 55]:

"Which kind of job is found more frequently in your organization?

A.) Everybody works together and you do not get individual credit.

B.) Everybody is allowed to work individually and individual credit can be received."

The empirical result showed that the answer was highly dependent on national culture. Those interviewed in Egypt, Japan, Mexico, India, and France believed that between 40 and 49 percent of a job is organized for individual credit. In Germany, Canada, Australia, Switzerland, Sweden between 62 and 66 percent of those interviewed believed that the job is done on an individual basis. Those interviewed in the USA, Spain, Finland, Bulgaria, Poland, Russia, and Czech Republic representing a score of about 73 percent, believed that individual credit was received. The authors suggest that there must be a synthesis between the two extreme positions of individualism and communitarianism (see Figure "Reconciling Individualism and Communitarianism" [TrHa98, pp. 59]).

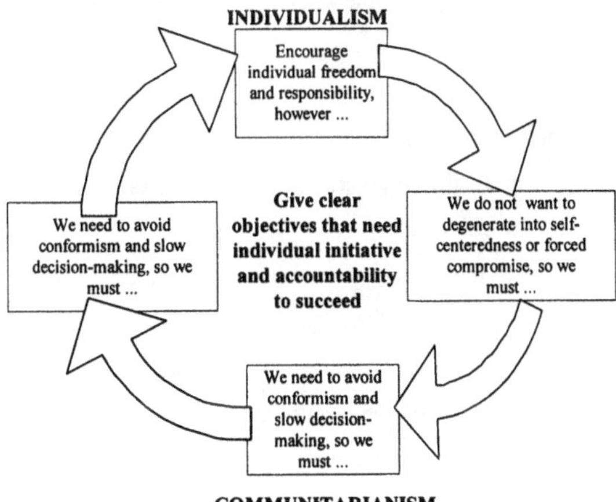

Figure 26: Reconciling Individualism and Communitarianism

Depending upon where one starts, individualism is the end of the development process or a communicative culture is the end of the learning process. The circle is a process, and it tries to balance each extreme position. These general statements about culture apply to every organization or business unit. Depending on their cultural background, employees will be more trained to work as individuals or in group processes. The company culture greatly influences the communication processes inside and outside the organization. The impact of the organizational culture to networking processes is highly significant. The objective of the cultural dimension was to get a general overview of the rules, attitudes, and guiding principles, and both internal and external values. The dimension of knowledge networking is focused on getting more in depth information about knowledge sharing, team working, and network building with partners.

5.3.3 Networking

Personal knowledge and skills are the greatest assets of an employee [Skyr99, pp.125]. The focus of this chapter is the question of what an individual needs to perform to succeed in a networked knowledge organization. In an analysis of high-performing knowledge workers, Kelley and Caplan identify nine recurring characteristics for successful knowledge networking [KeCa93, pp. 128]:

1. Initiative taking: they will act beyond the defined scope of their job.
2. Good networkers: they will directly tap into the knowledge and expertise of their co-workers.
3. Self-management: they have good control over their use of time, making, and meeting commitments and career developments.
4. Effective teamworkers: they coordinate their activities with co-workers, and they assume joint responsibility for the outcomes.
5. Demonstrative leadership: they formulate and state common goals, and they work to achieve a consensus and a commitment to them.
6. Supportive followers: they support the achievement of their leaders their goals through initiative taking rather than waiting for specific instructions.
7. Broad perspective: they see their work in its wider context, and they take the perspectives of other stakeholders on board.
8. Show-and-tell: they present ideas persuasively.

9. Organizational savvy: they are aware of organizational "politics", and they negotiate their way around it to promote co-operation and to get things done.

These listed characteristics show that a successful knowledge networker needs more skills than job specific ones. He must work across organizational boundaries and must be engaged in teamwork and networking. Thus, in a knowledge organization, networking and internal and external communication with other experts is a characteristic that adds value to the company. Skyrme [Skyr99, p. 15] lists two fundamental descriptions of networking:

- Networking organizations are less about organizational structures *per se*, and more about the informal human networking processes.
- The technology of computer networking undergirds and enhances human networking.

Knowledge networking is a dynamic process in which knowledge, experiences, and expertise are shared, developed, and evolved. A knowledge sharing culture can be developed through human interaction supported by information technology to foster new and innovative knowledge. Knowledge networking is connectivity to achieve new levels of interactivity, usability, and understanding across organizations and communities. Badaracco [Bada96, pp. 133] uses the term *knowledge links* for alliances that give organizations access to the skills and capabilities of other organizations, and they sometimes enable them to work with other organizations to create new capabilities. There are two forms of knowledge links: tactical and strategic. The first feature is concerned with the creation of just a single knowledge link that can help the organization build new skills in a limited area of operations. The strategic issue covers knowledge links with a broad array of partners such as customers, suppliers, labor organizations, and universities. A knowledge link that can strengthen each other's competitive advantage and which is more long-term is called a strategic knowledge link. Knowledge links can be described with four characteristics [Bada96, pp. 134]:

- A central objective of an alliance is the acquisition and creation of new knowledge. In a knowledge link, organizations can gain expertise from other companies by combining the special knowledge of each. The aim in a knowledge link is for both organizations to benefit from each other.

- Knowledge links are more intimate than product links. This means, when the two companies are learning embedded knowledge from each other, this relationship claims a close interaction and it is more a situation of a master and apprentice.
- A knowledge link can be formed by a wide range of partners. Badaracco describes the situation as follows [Bada96, p. 135]:

  "company-union alliances often involve extensive training programs, so that workers become 'multiskilled': instead of performing simple, repetitive tasks, workers develop, as individuals and as teams, the broader range of capabilities that a company needs."
- Knowledge links have a high strategic potential because they can help an organization extend or modify its existing basic capabilities and therefore to renew core competencies.

Knowledge links enable an organization to create and renew its expertise, and, by doing so, to improve its knowledge base. *Virtual teams* are microcosms of knowledge networking [Skyr99, p. 113]. Lipnack and Stamps define a virtual team in contrast to a conventional team, as a team that "works across space, time, and organizational boundaries with links strengthened by webs of communication technologies" [LiSt97, p. 7]. In contrast to small groups, a team is distinguished by its task-orientation and results-orientation. Teams set goals, and their task is to carry out the defined objectives. The virtual team distinction lies in the interaction across boundaries. In virtual teams, experts from different organizations work together and form a cross-organizational team. Lipnack and Stamps distinguish four types of teams that mix according to spacetime and organizational boundaries [LiSt97, p. 43]. Table "Varieties of Teams" illustrates the four forms.

Organization / Spacetime	**Same Organization**	**Different Organization**
Same Spacetime	Collected	Collected Cross-Organizational
Different Spacetime	Distributed	Distributed Cross-Organizational

Table 8: Varieties of Teams

In *collected teams* (those in the same space at the same time), people work together side-by-side in the same organization on independent tasks. In a *collected cross-organizational* structure, teams are formed with people from different organizations, but the meeting place is the same. The third variety is the *distributed team*. This is a team formation that works in the same organization but in different places either independently or separately. The final group, called the *distributed cross-organizational* teams, involves experts from different organizations working in different places. This is the classical form of virtual teams.

5.3.4 Organizational Structure

Future organizations are greatly influenced by virtualization. Opportunities through virtualization came through reconfiguring activities in the knowledge areas and processes, time, and structure [Skyr99, p. 98]. In a knowledge-based organization, there are three key structural issues, and they support:

1. A networking structure;
2. A dynamic structure;
3. An object-orientation, such as customer orientation.

As already discussed in Chapter 1, the traditional hierarchical or Newtonian organization does not foster the knowledge sharing and knowledge renewal processes. To deal with the challenge of managing and measuring knowledge in an organization, its structure has to correspond to the knowledge potential view. Experts are highly creative and individual employees who need a structure that enables the creation and innovation of new knowledge and knowledge sharing with other knowledge workers. Teamwork or networking is a structural form for the exchange of capabilities between experts. Kilmann [Kilm01, pp. 154] uses the term quantum organization (analogous to the word knowledge organization) to present a new organizational structure for the self-motioned and self-organizing experts. Kilmann defines the structure of the new organization, opposed to the Newtonian form, as follows [Kilm01, pp. 265]:

> *"A quantum organization must function as a collective brain that has continual access to its declarative and procedural schemas – and can restructure its schemas gradually and radically. Developing a collective mind/brain of shared schemas (including a shared paradigm) thus represents*

the epitome of creating and applying knowledge across all organizational boundaries."

This view is not only focused on the identification of knowledge, it also is focused on the creation of future knowledge areas and processes. In a knowledge organization, there should be a balance between the information about existing products and, more importantly a vision and innovation for new products or services. A knowledge organization must realize that the present allocation of resources, especially those residing in the minds of the knowledge workers, must be leveraged to the future. The view must always point to the future invention of new knowledge products, knowledge services, and knowledge processes. The structural form of this new organization is portrayed by Kilmann in Figure "Quantum Organization" [Kilm01, p. 68; the figure was adapted by the author]

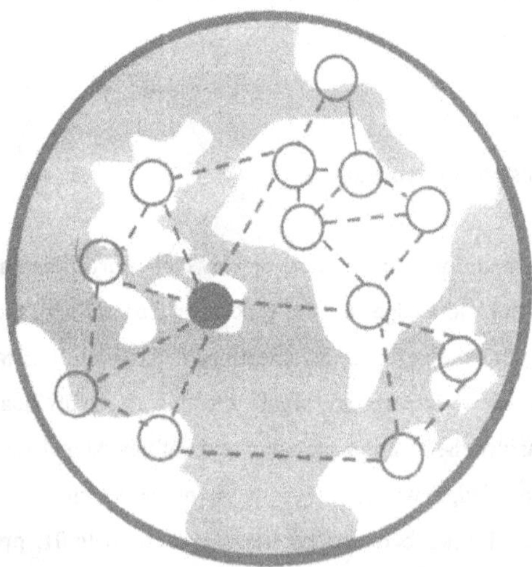

Figure 27: Quantum Organization

The structural form of the new type of organization is characterized by interconnectivity and interrelationships among different kinds of organizations. Knowledge workers share their capabilities and expertise with other professionals to solve problems derived from customer demands. The key objective in the creation of a knowledge network structure is putting the human being at the center of the strategy. Individuals must see a value in the network structure, so they can share existing knowledge for four reasons [HöEd98, p. 81]:

- They require knowledge to answer questions and to solve problems and situations;
- They have a desire to learn new things;
- They want to help one another;
- They see there is something in it for them.

More value is created through the process of knowledge sharing when it is used and transformed into organizational knowledge [HöEd98, p. 82]. Nonaka et al. [NoKT01, pp. 13] view knowledge management not as a static procedure but as a dynamic management of the knowledge creation process from knowledge. The creation of organizational knowledge is a "self-transcending" process because the term knowledge is content-specific, relational, and is created in social interaction. For North [Nort98, pp. 71], organizations only can survive knowledge competition if they manage to balance the issues of stability versus renewal and cooperation versus competition. Too much structural change can lead to an unbalanced organizational system, one which makes it difficult to navigate through an unstable business environment. The successful implementation of knowledge management and measurement is a long-term initiative, and it must be an integral part of a company management system.

5.3.5 Skills of a Knowledge Worker

The dimension of asking questions about the specific skills of the knowledge workers becomes apparent in the feasibility study as well as during the identification process. During the feasibility study, the knowledge-engineer asks the management to identify the key professionals in the company and to identify their specific skills. The objective of these questions is the acquisition of information from the management about their excellent professionals and the kind of knowledge required for innovation and competition. During the second process, identification process, the named knowledge-workers will be asked to describe their knowledge and skills. Furthermore, they should name other knowledge workers who are important for their daily knowledge sharing. As a result, it is possible to see if there is a gap between the views of management and knowledge workers regarding their skills, experience, training, and education. A method for positioning the value of the knowledge workers is the *knowledge portfolio* [Fink00a, pp. 113].

Future Knowledge Potential	low	medium	high
high	Knowledge Selection	Knowledge Development	Knowledge Renewal and Development
medium	Knowledge Analysis	Knowledge Selection	Knowledge Development
low	Knowledge Retrenchment	Knowledge Analysis	Knowledge Selection

Current Knowledge Potential

Figure 28: Knowledge Portfolio

Figure "Knowledge Portfolio" illustrates a 3x3 matrix for the positioning of the knowledge workers. Two dimensions evaluate the knowledge portfolio: (1) current knowledge position which aims to position the skills a knowledge worker has at the time; and (2) the future knowledge potential which tries to determine the skills required to be creative and innovative in the future. There are four company strategies:

1. *Knowledge Retrenchment*: if the current and future knowledge potential of an expert is low, then the management has to think about how to reposition the professional in the company.
2. *Knowledge Analysis*: it is the task of management to look at the development of the knowledge worker in future projects.
3. *Knowledge Selection*: the three fields are difficult to evaluate. Either the knowledge worker is developing into an excellent employee who has to be trained and educated or he will fall into the category of knowledge retrenchment.
4. *Knowledge Renewal and Knowledge Development*: knowledge workers who are positioned in these three fields are the best experts in the company because their current and future knowledge is of high value to the company.

The knowledge portfolio is a tool that enables management to get an overview of the skills of their experts in their current situation and for future problem solving processes. In a knowledge organization, each person or team is building knowledge through learning activities. Leonhard-Barton [Leon95, pp. 8] identifies four activities that create and control current and future knowledge:

1. Shared, creative problem solving;
2. Implementing and integrating new methodologies and tools;
3. Formal and informal experimentation to build capabilities for the future;
4. Pulling expertise in from the outside.

These learning activities are influenced by four core capabilities:

1. *Employee knowledge and skills*, referred to as the most important source of learning, are embodied in the heads of the experts, and it is the dimension most associated with the term core capability.
2. *Physical technical systems* cannot only be found in the heads of the experts, but can be found in the physical system of an organization such in its databases or software programs. The tacit knowledge of the experts is embedded in the development of their products, services, software products, or processes. The expertise of individuals or of teams is preserved in the physical system because it contains the skills necessary for innovation [Leon95, p. 22].
3. *Managerial system* is the channel through which knowledge is accessed and transferred. The knowledge of the experts is monitored and measured in the company's management system by activities such as education, training, learning, rewards, and incentives. Incentive and educational programs or promotional practices can have a high impact on the knowledge of the experts.
4. *Values and norms* form the basis for knowledge building and creation because the organization culture determines a system of rituals of behavior, professional beliefs or status. The organization value system is responsible for the success of the skill acquisition and transfer, of the implementation of the physical and managerial system.

Abell [Abel00, pp. 33] introduces a model that integrates core professional, social, organizational, and knowledge management skills that need to be balanced to achieve a successful knowledge management environment. This view implies that knowledge management and therefore measurement requires not only people skills but also managerial, communication, social, and technical skills. Only the balance among all four views leads to the successful implementation of knowledge management. Table "Skills for Knowledge Management Environments" presents a visualization of the skills needed in each of the four categories and is an adaptation of the model from Abell [Abel00, p. 36].

<table>
<tr><td></td><td>KM enabling Skills and Competencies</td><td></td></tr>
<tr><td></td><td>Business process identification and analysis</td><td></td></tr>
<tr><td></td><td>Understanding the knowledge process within the business process</td><td></td></tr>
<tr><td></td><td>Understanding the value, context, and dynamics of knowledge and information</td><td></td></tr>
<tr><td></td><td>Understanding the knowledge culture</td><td></td></tr>
<tr><td></td><td>Knowledge mapping and flows</td><td></td></tr>
<tr><td></td><td>Change management</td><td></td></tr>
<tr><td></td><td>Knowledge Potential Measurement</td><td></td></tr>
<tr><td rowspan="11">Core Competency building

• Continuing professional and technical education and training

• Business, sector and work experience

• Continuing education and training of knowledge-engineer</td><td>Leveraging ICT to create KM enablers</td><td rowspan="11">Organizational Skills and Competencies

• Communications
• Teamwork
• Negotiation
• Persuasion
• Facilitation
• Coaching
• Mentoring
• Business Processes
• Measurement Skills</td></tr>
<tr><td>An understanding of support and facilitation of communities and teams</td></tr>
<tr><td>Project management</td></tr>
<tr><td>Information structuring and architecture</td></tr>
<tr><td>Document and information management and work flows</td></tr>
<tr><td>An understanding of information management principles</td></tr>
<tr><td>An understanding of publishing processes</td></tr>
<tr><td>An understanding of technological opportunities</td></tr>
<tr><td>An understanding of knowledge measurement processes</td></tr>
<tr><td>An understanding of the knowledge potential view</td></tr>
<tr></tr>
<tr><td colspan="3">Professional, technical and craft skills and education</td></tr>
</table>

Table 9: Skills for Knowledge Management Environments

5.3.6 Learning and Experience

Sveiby sees the competence of the *professional* as a key intangible asset [Svei97, pp. 168]. A group of professionals is different from a group of *supportive staff* [Svei97, pp. 59] who work, for example, in accounting, administration, or reception. Their function in the company is to support and to assist the professionals and managers, but they do not know much about the business idea. However, their role in the company is also important, because they know, for example, how to provide excellent customers service. There also can be exceptions. In a company where the skill of a secretary is an integral part of the business idea, then the secretary belongs to the group of company experts. Supportive staff are often characterized by having modest demands towards the company and only working within their regular office hours.

The professionals are the most valuable persons in the company. They are the experts who focus on finding solutions to a problem. The skills of the professionals depend on their *training and education* [Fine97, pp. 98]. Amar [Amar02, pp. 45] goes one step further and says that the traditional training and learning programs, which were successful for traditional companies, do not apply to knowledge organizations. New concepts such as self-help, self-teach, and support group techniques are much more effective than classroom learning environments. With Roithmayr [FiRo02, pp. 219], I developed a three-dimensional measurement framework for learning environments. We found a demand for a combination of traditional classroom learning and e-learning environments. A survey conducted at the University of Innsbruck's SAP Business School Vienna among MBA students showed that the combination of real and virtual learning environments is a highly appreciated concept by managers in the middle and top management.

Organizations must apply different kinds of learning methods to build their knowledge and to distribute up-to-date knowledge by providing a good education and training system. Learning is a long-term activity. Pucik [Puci96, pp. 159] makes the point that the costs associated with learning are immediate, but the benefits are accrued over time. Therefore, short-term measures for learning possibilities may have a negative impact on the performance measures. So managers are sometimes forced to economize the costs because the pay-off of the learning process is long-term. Senge [Seng90] uses the term learning organization which is influenced by five disciplines: (1) system thinking; (2) personal mastery; (3) mental models; (4) building shared vision; and (5) team learning. Learning comes from experience, people are learning through the process of "trial and error" by taking actions and seeing their consequences. Senge describes the purpose of the learning organizations as follows [Seng90, p. 139]: "Organizations learn only through individuals who learn. Individual learning does not guarantee organizational learning. But without it no organizational learning occurs".

Rowley [Rowl00, pp. 8] describes the process of learning and knowledge creation as follows: information is seen as an input for organizations that conceptualize it to make it consistent with its norms, cognitive framework, context, and cultures. This conceptualization process is referred to as learning which leads to the building of knowledge. Knowledge is the basis for the decision-making processes, behavior, and actions. This final process stage requires feedback from those actions, which may generate new information which may initiate new learning, and so on. Sometimes it also can be necessary to have intermediate feedback loops between the individual stages (information, learning, knowledge, action).

Training is a form of knowledge dissemination, and it should not be neglected in the knowledge management program [KlSL01, pp. 131]. There are two forms of training:

- Training by in-house experts who can help to multiply internal best practices;
- Training by external instructors who provide employees with new outside perspectives and views that may complete with existing knowledge.

Both training forms help to reinforce the embedded knowledge of the experts. In a knowledge organization, training should be part of the life of the knowledge workers because new knowledge is built. Furthermore, motivation is crucial for a successful knowledge management initiative. For Sveiby [Svei97, pp. 68], *motivation* is not only based on monetary rewards, but it also is based on intangible rewards such as peer recognition, participating in learning programs, opportunities for independence, and so on. Professionals also can be motivated by money as a symbol for their prestige and wealth. On the other hand, it is the task of managers to motivate their experts to share their knowledge, sometimes only done when these professionals see a benefit from sharing their skills [BuWi00, pp. 167].

5.3.7 Customer Knowledge

The measurement of the customer dimension for Sveiby is one of the most important variables in the measurement process because the professionals spend most of their time on knowledge conversion for the customers [Svei97, pp. 177]. The customers are valuable assets for the company because they can provide employee training or they can act as a reference for the company and its image potential. Furthermore, they can encourage a company to develop new products or services [http://www.sveiby.com/articles/IntangibleRevenues.html, Date 2003-01-22]. In the Intangible Asset Monitor from Sveiby, customer measurement belongs to the external structure[9]. The first step in the measurement process is the categorization of the customers. For example, the Danish consulting firm PLS-Consult categorizes its customers into three groups:

- Customers who contribute to the image, references, and/or new assignments. These customers are either opinion leaders in the industry or they are satisfied with the service of PLS-consult.
- Customers who have projects to contribute to the company's internal structure. These kinds of customers yield opportunities to develop new methods and products. Davidow and Malone [DaMa92, pp. 3] refer to the term "virtual product" which is defined as a product that is customized and fulfils the customers' demands. These products exist mainly before they are produced because they are already conceptualized in the minds of the professionals.
- Customers who improve the individual competence of the experts.

After categorizing the different types of customers, the company measures the impact of the customer dimension in the sub-categories growth/renewal, efficiency, and stability [Svei97]. The customer dimensions measures the knowledge transfer between the experts and the customers. Companies that have experienced a rapid growth are those with a strategy that values the customer, and it is not only focused on cost reduction. Blosch [Blos00] identifies two types of customers: (1) *ad hoc* who are only interested in the product or service; and (2) *sophisticated* who interact with the company in many ways such as price negotiation, ordering, customer service inquires, technical support, and invoice payment. In the case of the sophisticated customer, the company must understand the

[9] For a detailed description of the Intangible Asset Monitor see Chapter 2.2.5.3.

various forms of interaction to transfer knowledge to the customers. The interactions also are a basis for gathering customer knowledge. Blosch [Blos00] sees two directions for innovations processes: from the customer to the company by analyzing how these interactions are facilitated and how they can be improved; and from the company to the customer by the improvement of business processes and the provision of better access and add more value to the customer. Customer knowledge is a key success factor, and it is "perhaps the most important aspect of the knowledge base in that it shows how the organization's knowledge is used by its customers, who are, after all, the object of its activities" [Blos00, p. 268]. The dimension of measuring customer knowledge refers to the understanding of the customers, their needs, wants, and aims, and it aligns it to the company's processes, products and services to build a good customer relationship. Some companies do have parts of their customer knowledge either stored in information systems or stored only in the minds of its experts, but in a fragmented form that is difficult to analyze and share. The aim of building strong body customer relationships is that the company can share its knowledge with the customers and to develop good customer relationships.

Tiwana [Tiwa01] points out that the customers have to be clustered before measuring the customer knowledge; Sveiby, as discussed above, also suggested this process. Awareness and understanding of customer knowledge is a basis for planning and implementing a customer relationship management aligned with its business strategy. Customer knowledge is not only information in customer records or databases, but it primarily is tacit knowledge about customer needs, rituals, processes, structures, and people. Tiwana [Tiwa01, pp. 132] clusters customers into three groups:

- Most valuable customers (MVCs);
- Most growable customers in the near future (MGCs); and
- Customers with zero or negative value to the business (BZCs).

After clustering the different kind of customers, one can begin an auditing process. One source of customer knowledge is available in electronic format (e.g., warranty records, invoicing systems, or complaint handling systems). The second can be retrieved with diagnostic questions [Tiwa01, pp. 138] from the four processes in the Customer Relationship Management (CRM) program: identification, differentiation, interaction, and transferring. The term CRM can be defined as "the infrastructure that enables the delineation of and increase in customer value, and the correct means by which to motivate valuable customers to remain loyal – indeed, to buy again" [Dych02, p. 4]. Tiwana understands *knowledge-enabled customer relationship management* (KCRM) as knowledge management approaches applied to e-business management. [Tiwa01, pp. 43]. KCRM arises out of the combination of knowledge management, e-business management, and collaborative management. Table "Sample Diagnostic Questions [Tiwa01, pp. 138] gives on overview of some questions designed to measure customer knowledge (for a detailed list of questions, see [TiWa01, pp. 138]).

Identification
• Do you have mechanisms for identifying each customer individually? • Do you use any other sources for customer-identifying mechanisms? • How much information about each customer do you collect? • Does each business unit in your business have its own customer records?
Differentiation
• Do you currently have criteria for identifying MVCs, MGCs, and BZCs, even if your do not actually use those terms to describe those customers? • Do you currently use any measures or predictors of customer loyalty? • Do you track the number of business units, divisions, and related concerns of your customer organizations? • Do you measure or evaluate expectations about future loyalty and attrition rates from newly acquired customers?
Interaction
• What interaction channels do your customers use? • Is knowledge of past interactions and individual differences applied in future interactions? • If the customer interacts with one division of your business, is this knowledge accessible across the enterprise, and in other unrelated interactions? • Can the customer interact with other customers who share similar profiles or interests (e.g., Amazon.com)?
Customization and Customer Knowledge Management
• How does transferring delivery add value to your product or service's design modularity? • How does your business match customer needs and transferring? • Are customer knowledge management processes adequately rewarded? • What does your company reward – team performance or individual performance?

Table 10 : Sample Diagnostic Questions

At the end of the process, each of the values is rated on a scale. These sample questions are used for evaluating customer knowledge assets. The rating is based on the knowledge growth framework from Bohn [Tiwa01, pp. 279] a method for measuring the capability process, and technological knowledge; it was developed for evaluating goods and services. Tiwana applied this method to the evaluation of e-business KCRM domains. The knowledge growth framework is divided into eight stages:

1. *Complete Ignorance*. This kind of knowledge does not exist.
2. *Awareness*. This kind of knowledge is primarily tacit.
3. *Measure*. This kind of knowledge is primarily in written form (pretechnological).
4. *Control of the Mean*. This kind of knowledge is written down and embodied in methodological routines.
5. *Process Capability*. This kind of knowledge is found in local recipes and operating manuals.
6. P*rocess Characterization*. This kind of knowledge is in empirical equations such as cost-reducing tradeoffs.
7. *Know why*. This kind of knowledge is found in procedures, methodologies and algorithms.
8. *Complete Knowledge*. This is a form of knowledge that can never be reached; it is called the knowledge nirvana.

The more the KCRM moves up the stages, it is easier to build a solid customer relationship and to react to customer demands. The Knowledge Growth Framework helps a company audit its relationship to its customers. For example, if a customer cancels his order and never places another order, then the audit must document this process in order to use other measures to improve future customer relationships. In a knowledge-intensive company, the integration of customer knowledge becomes a key success factor. The collaboration and integration of customers to the business is essential, especially in the age of e-commerce and e-business.

5.3.8 Competitors

Whether you are in business, manufacturing, the sciences, or the public service sector, you have a critical need for knowledge about issues, regulations, competitors, organizations, people, and trends. Your success depends upon how well you understand the myriad factors that could potentially affect your company. Sveiby sees knowledge about competitors as a valuable source for the evaluation of the external structure [Svei97]. Sample questions are [http://www.sveiby.com/articles/questions.html, Date 2003-01-22]:

- How can we create learning opportunities with the competitors?
- How can we construct a research project with the competitors or suppliers?

Benchmarking [Nort98, p. 243] is a practical tool for improving performance by learning from best practices [Nort98, p. 242] and the processes by which they are achieved [APQC99]. Benchmarking involves looking outward (outside your own company, organization, industry, region or country) to examine how others achieve their performance levels and to understand the processes they use. In this way, benchmarking helps explain the processes behind excellent performance. When the lessons learned from a benchmarking exercise are applied appropriately, they facilitate improved performance in critical functions within an organisation or in key areas of the business environment.

Best Practice is a technique used by successful companies around the world in all business sectors (both manufacturing and service) to help them become as good as or better than the best in the world in the most important aspects of their operations. For the American Productivity and Quality Center (APQC), benchmarking "focuses on how to improve any given business by exploiting 'best practice' rather than merely measuring the best performance. Best practices are the cause of best performance. Studying best practices provides the greatest opportunity for gaining a strategic, operational, and financial advantage" [APQC99]. Gibbert and Krause [GiKr00] discuss the establishment of a best practice marketplace at Siemens Medical Engineering Group. Siemens implemented a best practice sharing networking within its "top^{+} program" that is a corporate-wide business improvement program. The exchange of best practice was implemented through a Best Practice Marketplace which contained documented knowledge and pinpointed topic-related bearers of knowledge in the company. The person who is offering a practice is required to describe the problem, the problem-solving approach, the solution process, critical success factors, expenses involved, and the result. Another employee is now able to find a practice and the person who posted the practice to exchange their experiences. In 1998/99, Siemens implemented a pilot project which was called "Recruiting Network". This network enabled participants to share their experiences with other colleagues to learn from the other's knowledge. In addition, facilitators support the implementation process because they have the task of coordinating and promoting the Best Practice Sharing project. The support and he success of the project relies on the commitment of the managers by stressing their importance and showing their involvement. The success of the sharing program depended on the willingness of employees to share their knowledge and to receive an excellent technical support [GiKr00, pp. 82]. Another example of the best practice method is Texas Instruments Europe [ZaWh00]. Texas Instruments Europe uses best practice in a very broad sense because it covers any process, technique, or tool that will improve a situation. Best practice sharing at Texas Instruments Europe can be exemplary described as follows [ZaWh00, pp. 71]:

- Best practice is part of the Texas Instruments Strategy;
- Launch of total quality initiatives;
- Continuous improvement;
- Linking best practice to organizational objectives;
- Using the internal knowledge base.

Another example of best practice sharing is British Aerospace [HeVo01, pp. 138] which is perusing the idea that if someone in the company has an excellent practice or concept that has worked successfully, it should be shared with other experts in the company. The atmosphere of trust and sharing enables the exchange of information and knowledge among staff members, professionals, business units, external partners, and departments. To facilitate best practice web sites, electronic forms, search engines, agents, workshops, and the publication of the best practice are offered on the Intranet. At British Aerospace, tacit knowledge is shared in workshop sessions while explicit knowledge is communicated and published in the Intranet. Kluge et al. [KlSL01, pp. 91] see benchmarking not only as an internal process, but they also stress that an external benchmark can bring an additional and innovative knowledge gain. The objective is transfer knowledge from competitors to their own product or service.

5.3.9 Information and Communication Systems (I&CS)

The objective for knowledge management technology is the creation of a connected environment for the exchange of knowledge [Duff00; Gall01, p. 61; MeAY01, pp. 94; NaKr01]. These new software products facilitate communication and interaction among people as well as among people and systems. Mentzas et al. discuss two key components that are required to support the sharing of information and knowledge [MeAY01, p. 95]:

1. *Collaboration facilities* for knowledge workers is mainly the domain of groupware products such as Lotus Notes, Microsoft Exchange, and Novel's GroupWise. Other technology examples in this group are email systems, workflow automation, discussion groups, document management, shared databases, scheduling and calendar functions.
2. *Discovery facilities* are required for searching and retrieval purposes. Knowledge workers are in constant need of finding and accessing information and knowledge from other experts. A wide variety of information sources support the finding of expertise, and they include the Internet, corporate Intranets, legacy systems, corporate LAN.

Österle [Öste00] highlights the fact that multimedia applications and networking make it possible to access existing knowledge, and they enable new forms of knowledge representation, searching, and utilization. The examples given are similar to Mentzas et al., and they are groupware systems, search engines, expert maps, and discussion groups. Knowledge management systems structure, process, edit, and store multimedia documents, and it is referred to as weakly structured data [ÖsFA00, pp. 28]. Multimedia documents are text files, spreadsheets, presentation graphics, images, video, and audio files. Bach [Bach00, pp. 71] lists six instruments for business knowledge management:

1. Expertise Directories that support the company-wide search for contact persons.
2. Skill planning tools that evaluate the qualifications of the employees in the categories low, medium, and high. The result is a skill matrix that shows the existing qualifications.
3. Content Management [Kmuc00; KoJO01] is the management of organizational information (content) and it covers four major components: generation, organization, distribution, and usage.
4. Communities of Practice show the information flow in projects, and it visualizes informal networks.
5. Knowledge Desk that enables an employee to search in external databases and provides project results in a database.

6. Knowledge Network that connects communities for the development of knowledge with knowledge outside the communities.

The knowledge architecture, which was explained in Chapter 5.2 must be supported by information and communication systems (IC&S) in order to successfully implement a knowledge organization. According to Skyrme [Skyr99, pp. 72] five criteria are necessary for the implementation of knowledge architecture, and they are complemented by the knowledge measurement criteria:

1. Knowledge inputs cover the process of data collection for project, the organizational and tacit knowledge of knowledge workers, and internal and external knowledge; e.g., techniques are creativity tools or mind mapping which assist in the creation of knowledge. Furthermore, tools that enhance knowledge discovery are data mining, text mining, and visualization tools.
2. Knowledge processing enhances the retrieval of case histories, and examples of tools are case-based reasoning and expert systems.
3. Knowledge repositories are central for the storage of explicit knowledge, and examples are the Internet, data warehouses, document management systems, and databases. A further example is the implementation of a thesaurus management system.
4. Knowledge flows are supported by workflow management software systems.
5. Knowledge use and renewal are enhanced through technologies that support the creative thinking and decision-making processes.
6. Knowledge measurement must be supported by systems that facilitate the knowledge measurement processes conducted by the knowledge-engineers.

The six perspectives enhance the knowledge potential view, and implementation of the knowledge architecture. Borghoff and Pareschi [BoPa98] also suggest that the management of knowledge has to be supported by different kinds of technological components. The authors introduce a Knowledge Management Architecture composed of four components:

1. The flow of knowledge is the most central component because it glues the other three together. The flow of knowledge supports the interaction among the tacit knowledge that it is transferred among the communities of knowledge workers, with the explicit knowledge that is contained in the knowledge repositories in form of

libraries and document archives, and with the explicit meta-knowledge through which an organization maps its own territory.

2. Knowledge cartography covers knowledge navigation, mapping, and simulation. Organizational knowledge needs to be described in a variety of ways to serve a number of user interests. The challenge is to map and categorized available organizational knowledge in all different kinds of ways such as from core competencies to individual expertise, from communities of practice and interest to the customer databases. To some extent, most of these representations already exist in organizations in the form of process maps, or organizational charts, but what is needed is a way to capture the variety of these representations.
3. Communities of knowledge workers: a great amount of knowledge generation takes place through the informal exchange of tacit knowledge between knowledge workers and colleagues. In global organizations, it is necessary to support the flow of knowledge by information technology to overcome the physical distance and to create conditions of a face-to-face communication.
4. Knowledge repositories and libraries: electronic libraries are becoming increasingly relevant for organizations because they handle the large amount of stored explicit knowledge found in electronic or paper form.

For example, CommonKADS is a methodology designed for the development of knowledge based systems analogous to methods of software engineering. The development of these methods was funded by the European Community's ESPRIT program between 1983 and 1994. A good overview of CommonKADS can be found in Schreiber et al. [ScAA00]. CommonKADS supports most aspects of a knowledge based system development project, including project management, organizational analysis, knowledge acquisition, conceptual modelling, user interaction, system integration, and design.

Knowledge management is more than the technological solutions provided to give people acccess to better and more relevant information [WaPl02, pp. 113]. It is important that the design of the knowledge management systems reflect the mindset of the knowledge workers and their way of offering highly qualitative knowledge solutions with quick (high velocity) solution processes. An effective knowledge management system must integrate people, processes, technology and the organizational structure. Table "Overview of the

Basic Knowledge Management Technologies" is provided by Hoffmann, and each tool required for knowledge management solution is briefly described [Hoff01, pp. 78] below:

Knowledge Management Solution	*Description*
Intranet technology	Intranets and Extranets are technologies that can be used to build a knowledge management system. The unified surface and access to various sources of information make this technology transfer perfect for the distribution of knowledge throughout a company.
Groupware	Groupware offers a platform for communication within a firm and for cooperation among employees.
Electronic document management	Documents are a central means of storing and spreading knowledge. Procedures for using and maintaining such documents, such as a check whether an update is overdue can be easily implemented for KMS.
Information Retrieval Tools	Information Retrieval offers a solution to tasks from text searches to the automatic categorization and summation of documents. Advanced search algorithms use thesauri and text mining to discover contexts that could not be found with simple queries. Semantically text analyzes also can be implemented.
Workflow management system	The business processes of a company contain a great deal of knowledge. In addition, the integration of knowledge management into business processes is an important factor for success.
Data Analysis	Pattern recognition, classification, and forecasting are the techniques used for data analysis. Data analysis is a possible method for generating new knowledge.
Data Warehousing	A modern database is where data and information is stored. Connections that are not readily apparent can be uncovered with the use of data mining and OLAP. These techniques are part of data analysis.
Agent technology	Software agents based on the essentials of artificial intelligence enable the user to search independently for information according to a personal profile and to use various sources and other agents.
Help Desks	Help desks are an important application area for case-based reasoning technology based on individual cases. Case knowledge can be put into use quickly in this way.
Machine Learning	This technology from the field of artificial intelligence allows new knowledge to generate automatically and processes can be automatically optimized with little necessity for human intervention.
Computer based training	This technology is used to pass on knowledge to colleagues. This spread of implicit knowledge is possible with multi-media applications.

Table 11: Overview of the Basic Knowledge Management Technologies

5.4 Defining Momentum, Position, and Velocity

From the physical point of view, *momentum* [Schm93, p. 812; WeWW01] is the product of mass times velocity. Momentum can be defined by the following equation:

$$p = m * v$$

where

p = Position;

m = Mass;

v = Velocity.

Schmidt [Schm93, p. 812] notes that linear momentum is the product of a scalar and a vector quantity and that it is a vector, hence it has both magnitude and direction. *Mass* is a quantity representing the amount of matter in a particle or an object [Nede93, pp. 767]. The standard unit of mass in the International System of Units, a scientific method of expressing the magnitudes or quantities of seven important natural phenomena, is the kilogram (kg) [Weil93, p. 1495]. Mass is measured by determining the extent to which a particle or object resists a change in its direction or speed when a force is applied. Isaac Newton stated that the mass of a body is the measure of the quantity of matter the body contains. Nedelsky [Nede93, p. 767] defines mass as "the quantitative or numerical measure of a body's inertia, that is, of its resistance to being accelerated".

The key question is, how can mass and velocity be interpreted in the knowledge potential approach, meaning how can **knowledge mass ($m^{(K)}$)** be described and defined. What is the mass of an individual, of an employee, of the company experts? Knowledge mass is a quantity representing the amount of expertise, skills, and experience of a knowledge worker. Mass is characterized by an individual dimension, and it is dependent on the personal ability of a knowledge worker to deal with his experience. Mass can be defined as a *person-dependent variable*. The amount of the mass is influenced by variables which depend on the experience of a knowledge worker. The variables concerning individual knowledge acquisition, transfer, and learning experience are assigned to the mass index. The knowledge mass is the sum of the four dimensions of the knowledge potential view: content, networking, skills, and learning information. Therefore, knowledge mass can be defined as follows:

Knowledge Mass ($m^{(K)}$) = {Content, Networking, Skills, Learning}.
The term knowledge mass is defined as the sum of person-dependent variables that influence the knowledge potential of an expert.

Velocity [Rusk93a, pp. 1501] is an expression for the displacement an object or particle undergoes with respect to time. Time is an observed phenomenon by means of which human beings sense and record changes in the environment and in the universe. Velocity then, is the time rate of change of position of a body in a particular direction. So velocity is direction-oriented. When evaluating the velocity of an object, one must monitor the direction. To determine the velocity of an object, one would need to know the speed and direction of the object. *Speed* [Rusk93b, p. 1327] is defined as the time rate of change in the position of a body without regard to direction. The term speed is the numerical magnitude of a velocity, and it is a scalar quantity. Linear speed is measured in units [Weil93, p. 1495] such as meters per second or miles per hour. Consider a car moving at 20 m/s (with respect to the surface) on a highway, travelling northward. If you are driving the car, its velocity relative to your body is zero. If you stand by the side of the road, the velocity of the car relative to you is 20 m/s northward. If you are driving a car at 15 m/s on a road and if you are travelling northward and another car moving at 20 m/s passes you in the same direction, the velocity of the other care relative to you is 5 m/s northward. But, if that other car passes you in the opposite direction, its velocity relative to you is 35 m/s southward.

In terms of the knowledge potential view, **knowledge velocity ($v^{(K)}$)** is the accomplishment of problem solving objectives. How good or bad has a knowledge worker reached his objectives within a certain time? This means, if a person has to solve a problem, quality of the problem solution and length of time to solve a problem are important facts. The quality of the solution process is relevant, but the time it took to solve the problem also is relevant. Velocity is an expression of the quality of the problem solution process for a knowledge worker in a certain time. It is not enough that a knowledge worker solves a problem quickly, but you also need to know the direction of the solution process. Velocity measures the degree to which any knowledge contributes to knowledge potential. An optimal velocity performance is knowledge with a high degree of contribution towards the improvement of the knowledge potential. Tiwana [Tiwa00, p. 36] uses the term *"knowledge velocity"* that successful companies must develop to overcome knowledge sluggishness and to gain competitive advantages. Tiwana notes that knowledge sluggishness is to learn from failures and their analyses to prevent the repetition of past mistakes. It is necessary to integrate a knowledge velocity into the knowledge processes of a company's business processes. Knowledge velocity should allow people to learn from past decisions and to apply this experience to new complex choices and to future decisions. For Amar [Amar02, p. 12], a special characteristic of a knowledge worker is their skill to manipulate time and space. This skill enables the knowledge worker to make connections with past, present, and future occurrences, to search for solutions, and to understand the interactions. This means, "it is the ability to comprehend a myriad of physical and discarnate variables with all possible interrelationships at any point in time and to regress or extrapolate them along the time or space dimension to any other point" [Amar02, p. 12].

Davenport and Prusak point out that a successful and efficient knowledge transfer is influenced by the velocity of the transfer, "the speed with which knowledge moves through an organizations. How quickly and widely is it disseminated? How quickly do the people who need the knowledge become aware of it and get access to it? [DaPr98, p. 102]. For Kluge et al. [KlSL01, p. 147] "speed [velocity] is the only efficient countermeasure against perishability". In times of accelerating innovation cycles, companies must search for the latest solutions even if they have to adjust or even destroy the existing company structure. If a company is only focusing on protecting its existing knowledge, dynamic innovation is prevented, and returns begins to decrease. Furthermore, companies need a "good speed" of decision-making [KlSL01, pp. 150]. In a company, there must be a general acceptance for rapid decision-making and the quick application of knowledge to the development of new products and services. Velocity is an important variable for one to understand how efficiently a company is using its knowledge capital. The term "knowledge velocity" in the knowledge potential view can be defined as follows:

Knowledge Velocity ($v^{(K)}$) = Degree of quality that a knowledge worker uses to solve a problem with respect to the time dimension. Thus, how rapidly can customers receive high quality problem solutions? Knowledge velocity is the implementation speed for good solutions and the quality of the solution to the problem. Knowledge velocity is directed towards the high quality solution of customer problems. Knowledge velocity is the accomplishment of problem solving objectives.

Finally, the term **knowledge position ($x^{(K)}$)** has to be described. The questions behind the knowledge position measurement are: In what environment is a person applying his knowledge? Where does the action take place? What factors influence the application of knowledge? The position variable is system-dependent. The knowledge worker cannot directly influence the position dimensions because they are not dependent on his personal behavior.

Knowledge Position ($x^{(K)}$) = {Culture, Organizational Knowledge, Competitors, Customers, I&CS/KMS}

The term knowledge position covers all system-dependent variables that influence the creation of the knowledge potential of the knowledge worker.

Knowledge position covers all of the influencing variables for knowledge potential, variables that cannot be manipulated and changed directly by the knowledge worker. The action-knowledge is embedded in outputs such as products or services demanded by a customer. Knowledge position consists of what Sveiby[10] refers to as the external and internal structure of a knowledge organization.

5.5 General Measurement Procedure of the Knowledge Potential

The derivation of the equation for knowledge potential (KP) is explained, and the measurement of the knowledge potential of a knowledge worker is determined. The method of analogical reasoning facilitates the derivation of the knowledge measurement process for the experts. First, the variables for knowledge momentum and knowledge position must be defined. The two measured properties are:

- Knowledge momentum (person-dependent variables); and
- Knowledge position (system-dependent variables).

The definition of the two variable groups depends on the company specific structure and on industry-dependent influencing factors. These properties appear as variables in an equation that describes the knowledge potential of a knowledge worker. To make a prediction of the

[10] See for a detailed description of the internal and external structure Chapter 2.2.5.3.

individual knowledge potential, the knowledge-engineer has to rate the knowledge dimensions of each knowledge worker. Each knowledge worker has answered questions concerning the nine dimensions which cover the different knowledge management aspects. These nine dimensions cover the major influencing knowledge fields. The number of dimension also can be enlarged to more than nine or reduced to less than nine dimensions. These specifications depend on the industry and on the specific company setting. The general measurement formulas are presented before more detail is given for the nine-dimension measurement framework. Each variable (knowledge mass, knowledge velocity, knowledge momentum, and knowledge position) is described in mathematical terms. The **general valid knowledge mass equation** can be written as follows:

$$m^{(K)} = \sum_{i=1}^{l} Dim_i$$

where

l = Number of dimensions (variables) for the knowledge mass measurement;

Dim_i = The different types of variables influencing the knowledge mass of a company;

$m^{(K)}$ = The knowledge mass for the number (l) of dimensions (variables) for knowledge mass measurement.

$v^{(K)}$ is the **knowledge velocity** for the problem solving process for each knowledge worker.

The general valid formula for **knowledge momentum** can be derived from the variables $m^{(K)}$ and $v^{(K)}$ as follows:

$$p^{(K)} = m^{(K)} * v^{(K)}$$

Then, the **general valid knowledge position equation** can be defined by the following equation:

$$x^{(K)} = \sum_{j=1}^{r} Dim_j$$

where

r = Number of dimensions for the knowledge position measurement;

Dim_j = Different types of variables influencing the knowledge position of a company;

$x^{(K)}$ = Knowledge position for the number (r) of dimensions (variables) for the knowledge position measurement.

In consideration of the Heisenberg[11] uncertainty equation for the measurement of uncertainty, the following **equation for the measurement of the knowledge potential (KP)** can be derived:

$$p^{(K)} * x^{(K)} = \mathrm{KP}$$

[Knowledge Momentum * Knowledge Position = Knowledge Potential]

and by substituting the knowledge momentum $p^{(K)}$ with $(m^{(K)} * v^{(K)})$, the more detailed equation is:

$$(m^{(K)} * v^{(K)}) * x^{(K)} = \mathrm{KP}$$

[(Knowledge Mass * Knowledge Velocity) * Knowledge Position = KP]

Finally, the sum values are inserted into the equation $(m^{(K)} * v^{(K)}) * (x^{(K)}) = \mathrm{KP}$, and it results in the following formula for the calculation of the **knowledge potential (KP)** for each knowledge worker:

$$(\sum_{i=1}^{l} Dim_i * v^{(K)}) * (\sum_{j=1}^{r} Dim_j) = \mathrm{KP}$$

where

KP = Knowledge Potential;

l = Number of dimensions (variables) for the knowledge mass measurement;

r = Number of dimensions (variables) for the knowledge position measurement;

Dim_i = The different types of variables influencing the knowledge mass of a company;

Dim_j = The different types of variables influencing the knowledge position of a company;

$v^{(K)}$ = Knowledge velocity.

---

[11] See Chapter 4.4.

The multiplication of the momentum value by the position value yields the knowledge potential (KP) of each knowledge worker. Each measured property is determined by a certain number of dimensions explaining and describing the impact of the variables. Therefore, the knowledge potential can be defined as the multiplication of knowledge momentum (person-dependent variables) times knowledge position (system-dependent variables) by the application of the Uncertainty Principle of Heisenberg through the process of analogical reasoning.

5.6 The Specific Measurement of the Knowledge Potential (KP)

In this chapter, the general measurement process is transformed into the specific knowledge measurement procedure, depending on the knowledge potential view. The nine-dimension questionnaire is the basic framework for the measurement procedure of the knowledge potential of each knowledge worker. Therefore, the general equations from the previous chapter must be adapted to the nine dimensions. The equation for **knowledge mass** can be written as follows:

$$m^{(K)} = \sum_{i=1}^{4} Dim_i$$

where

number of dimensions for the knowledge mass = 4 (Content, Networking, Skills, Learning);

$m^{(K)}$ = Knowledge mass for the four person-dependent variables.

The **knowledge velocity** ($v^{(K)}$) is the accomplishment of problem solving objectives.

The formula for **knowledge momentum** ($p^{(K)}$) can be derived from the variables $m^{(K)}$ and $v^{(K)}$:

$$p^{(K)} = m^{(K)} * v^{(K)}$$

The equation for the **knowledge position** ($x^{(K)}$) can be described as follows:

$$x^{(K)} = \sum_{j=1}^{5} Dim_j$$

where

number of dimensions for the knowledge position = 5 (Culture, Organizational Structure, Competitors, Customers, and IC&S/KMS);

$x^{(K)}$ = Knowledge position for the five system-dependent variables.

The equation for **knowledge potential (KP)**, based on the nine-dimension measurement framework, can be written as follows:

$$p^{(K)} * x^{(K)} = \text{KP}$$

then, the more detailed equation is:

$$(m^{(K)} * v^{(K)}) * (x^{(K)}) = \text{KP}$$

If the sum of the knowledge mass and knowledge position for the nine-dimension measurement framework are inserted into the above formula, then the new equation is:

$$(\sum_{i=1}^{4} Dim_i * v^{(K)}) * (\sum_{j=1}^{5} Dim_j) = \mathbf{KP}$$

where

$20 \leq \text{KP} \leq 2500$;

number of dimensions for the knowledge mass = 4;

number of dimensions for the knowledge position = 5;

$m^{(K)}$ = Knowledge mass for the measurement of Dim_i with the four person-dependent variables;

$x^{(K)}$ = Knowledge position for the measurement of Dim_j with the five system-dependent variables;

$v^{(K)}$ = Knowledge velocity.

According to the knowledge architecture, the knowledge-engineer makes interviews with the experts to evaluate each defined dimension. This means, each knowledge-engineer gives a score on the rating scale (see Chapter 5.7.1) based on the questions of interviews for the nine dimensions. Each knowledge-engineer (KE_1, KE_2, ... KE_m) measures each knowledge worker (KW_1, KW_2, ... KW_n) on an ordinal scale in each of the nine dimensions

(Dim_1, Dim_2, ... Dim_9). The final result is the individual knowledge potential (KP) score for each expert, and it is calculated by the above described formula $(m^{(K)} * v^{(K)}) * (x^{(K)}) = KP$. The derivation of the KP for each knowledge worker by the knowledge-engineer is divided into three major measurement processes:

1. Measurement of the knowledge momentum;
2. Measurement of the knowledge position; and
3. Final measurement result (knowledge potential for each knowledge worker).

The first process focuses on the **measurement of the knowledge momentum**. Table "Knowledge Momentum Measurement" illustrates the single values that each knowledge-engineer is giving to each knowledge worker for the four knowledge mass variables and for their knowledge velocity. Table "Knowledge Momentum Measurement" is characterized by the following variable definitions:

KE = Knowledge-Engineer = KE_1, KE_2, ... KE_m;
KW = Knowledge Worker = KW_1, KW_2, ... KW_n;
Dim_l = Dim_1, Dim_2, Dim_3, Dim_4 (knowledge mass variables);
v = Knowledge velocity[12];
p = Knowledge momentum[13];
m = Knowledge mass[14].

The knowledge momentum derivation is characterized by a *multiplication effect* due to the fact that the knowledge mass is multiplied by the knowledge velocity for each knowledge worker. This means, for example, if a knowledge-engineer gives a knowledge worker a very good score, then the knowledge mass is multiplied by a very good rate. On the other hand, if a knowledge-engineer rates the knowledge velocity with a very bad score, then the knowledge mass is multiplied by a very bad score and has a higher impact on the knowledge momentum value.

---

[12] In the following tables $v^{(K)}$ is substituted for simplicity reasons with the letter v.

[13] In the following tables $p^{(K)}$ is substituted for simplicity reasons with the letter p.

[14] In the following tables $m^{(K)}$ is substituted for simplicity reasons with the letter m.

KE \ KW	KW	Knowledge Mass Variables: Content Dim_1	Network Dim_2	Skills Dim_3	Training Dim_4	Knowledge Mass	Knowledge Velocity	KNOWLEDGE MOMENTUM
KE_1	KW_1	p^1_{11}	p^2_{11}	p^3_{11}	p^4_{11}	$m_{11} = \sum_{i=1}^{4} p^i_{11}$	v_{11}	$p_{11} = \sum_{i=1}^{4} p^i_{11} * v_{11}$
	KW_2	p^1_{12}	p^2_{12}	p^3_{12}	p^4_{12}	$m_{12} = \sum_{i=1}^{4} p^i_{12}$	v_{12}	$p_{12} = \sum_{i=1}^{4} p^i_{12} * v_{12}$
	...	...	...	...	...	...	...	...
	KW_n	p^1_{1n}	p^2_{1n}	p^3_{1n}	p^4_{1n}	$m_{1n} = \sum_{i=1}^{4} p^i_{1n}$	v_{1n}	$p_{1n} = \sum_{i=1}^{4} p^i_{1n} * v_{1n}$
...	...	...	...	...	...	...	...	...
KE_m	KW_1	p^1_{m1}	p^2_{m1}	p^3_{m1}	p^4_{m1}	$m_{m1} = \sum_{i=1}^{4} p^i_{m1}$	v_{m1}	$p_{m1} = \sum_{i=1}^{4} p^i_{m1} * v_{m1}$
	KW_2	p^1_{m2}	p^2_{m2}	p^3_{m2}	p^4_{m2}	$m_{m2} = \sum_{i=1}^{4} p^i_{m2}$	v_{m2}	$p_{m2} = \sum_{i=1}^{4} p^i_{m2} * v_{m2}$
	...	...	...	...	...	...	...	...
	KW_n	p^1_{mn}	p^2_{mn}	p^3_{mn}	p^4_{mn}	$m_{mn} = \sum_{i=1}^{4} p^i_{mn}$	v_{mn}	$p_{mn} = \sum_{i=1}^{4} p^i_{mn} * v_{mn}$

Table 12: Knowledge Momentum Measurement

The second measurement process is concerned with the **knowledge position measurement**. Table "Knowledge Position Measurement" illustrates the single values each knowledge-engineer gives each knowledge worker for the five knowledge position variables. Table "Knowledge Position Measurement" is characterized by the following variable definitions:

KE = Knowledge-Engineer = $KE_1, KE_2, \ldots KE_m$;

KW = Knowledge Worker = $KW_1, KW_2, \ldots KW_n$;

Dim_r = Dim_1, Dim_2, Dim_3, Dim_4, Dim_5 (knowledge position variables);

x = Knowledge position[15].

The multiplication effect for the knowledge position measurement does not apply because the five position variables are summed. The multiplication effect is especially valid for

[15] In the following tables $x^{(K)}$ is substituted for simplicity reasons with the letter x.

knowledge momentum because these are the person-dependent variables. The knowledge position consists of the system-dependent variables which influence the indirect problem solving process for each knowledge worker.

KW / KE	KW	Knowledge POSITION Variables Culture Dim_5	Structure Dim_6	Customers Dim_7	Competitors Dim_8	I&CS/KMS Dim_9	KNOWLEDGE POSITION
KE_1	KW_1	x^5_{11}	x^6_{11}	x^7_{11}	x^8_{11}	x^9_{11}	$x_{11}=\sum_{i=5}^{9} x^i_{11}$
	KW_2	x^5_{12}	x^6_{12}	x^7_{12}	x^8_{12}	x^9_{12}	$x_{12}=\sum_{i=5}^{9} x^i_{12}$
	...	...	...	...	...	...	...
	KW_n	x^5_{1n}	x^6_{1n}	x^7_{1n}	x^8_{1n}	x^9_{1n}	$x_{1n}=\sum_{i=5}^{9} x^i_{1n}$
...	...	...	...	...	...	...	...
KE_m	KW_1	x^5_{m1}	x^6_{m1}	x^7_{m1}	x^8_{m1}	x^9_{m1}	$x_{m1}=\sum_{i=5}^{9} x^i_{m1}$
	KW_2	x^5_{m2}	x^6_{m2}	x^7_{m2}	x^8_{m2}	x^9_{m2}	$x_{m2}=\sum_{i=5}^{9} x^i_{m2}$
	...	...	...	...	...	...	...
	KW_n	x^5_{mn}	x^6_{mn}	x^7_{mn}	x^8_{mn}	x^9_{mn}	$x_{mn}=\sum_{i=5}^{9} x^i_{mn}$

Table 13: Knowledge Position Measurement

Table "Knowledge Potential Measurement Matrix" visualizes the derivation of the **knowledge potential measurement** which is the result of the multiplication of knowledge momentum times knowledge position given by a certain knowledge-engineer for each knowledge worker. Table "Knowledge Potential Measurement Matrix" is characterized by the following variable definitions:

KE = Knowledge-Engineer = KE_1, KE_2, ... KE_m;

KW = Knowledge Worker = KW_1, KW_2, ... KW_n;

p = Knowledge momentum;

x = Knowledge position;

KP = Knowledge Potential.

KE \ KW	KW	Knowledge Momentum	Knowledge Position	KNOWLEDGE POTENTIAL (KP)
KE_1	KW_1	$p_{11} = \sum_{i=1}^{4} p_{11}^{i} * v_{11}$	$x_{11} = \sum_{j=5}^{9} x_{11}^{j}$	$KP_{11} = (\sum_{i=1}^{4} p_{11}^{i} * v_{11}) * \sum_{j=5}^{9} x_{11}^{j}$
	KW_2	$p_{12} = \sum_{i=1}^{4} p_{12}^{i} * v_{12}$	$x_{12} = \sum_{j=5}^{9} x_{12}^{j}$	$KP_{12} = (\sum_{i=1}^{4} p_{12}^{i} * v_{12}) * \sum_{j=5}^{9} x_{12}^{j}$
	...	...	...	...
	KW_n	$p_{1n} = \sum_{i=1}^{4} p_{1n}^{i} * v_{1n}$	$x_{1n} = \sum_{j=5}^{9} x_{1n}^{j}$	$KP_{1n} = (\sum_{i=1}^{4} p_{1n}^{i} * v_{1n}) * \sum_{j=5}^{9} x_{1n}^{j}$
...	...	...	...	...
KE_m	KW_1	$p_{m1} = \sum_{i=1}^{4} p_{m1}^{i} * v_{m1}$	$x_{m1} = \sum_{j=5}^{9} x_{m1}^{j}$	$KP_{m1} = (\sum_{i=1}^{4} p_{m1}^{i} * v_{m1}) * \sum_{j=5}^{9} x_{m1}^{j}$
	KW_2	$p_{m2} = \sum_{i=1}^{4} p_{m2}^{i} * v_{m2}$	$x_{m2} = \sum_{j=5}^{9} x_{m2}^{j}$	$KP_{m2} = (\sum_{i=1}^{4} p_{m2}^{i} * v_{m2}) * \sum_{j=5}^{9} x_{m2}^{j}$
	...	...	...	...
	KW_n	$p_{mn} = \sum_{i=1}^{4} p_{mn}^{i} * v_{mn}$	$x_{mn} = \sum_{j=5}^{9} x_{mn}^{j}$	$KP_{mn} = (\sum_{i=1}^{4} p_{mn}^{i} * v_{mn}) * \sum_{j=5}^{9} x_{mn}^{j}$

Table 14: Knowledge Potential Measurement Matrix

The knowledge potential derivation also is characterized by the *multiplication effect* due to the fact that the knowledge position value is multiplied by the knowledge momentum values. This has a reinforcing impact for the knowledge potential of each knowledge worker given by the knowledge-engineer. The quality of the knowledge potential is highly dependent on the interviewer skills of the knowledge-engineer. Consequently, it is necessary to measure the individual uncertainty factors of knowledge momentum and knowledge position for each knowledge-engineer. The measurement process for the uncertainty factors will be described in Chapter 5.8. The evaluation of the knowledge workers is based on an ordinal rating scale. After the interview sessions, the knowledge-engineer rates each knowledge worker on the nine dimensions, and he rates the knowledge velocity on an ordinal scale. Based on this personal judgment and on his interpretation of the video-tapes, the knowledge-engineer gives ordinal scores for each knowledge worker.

5.7 Skill Acquisition and Rating Scale for the Knowledge Worker

5.7.1 Ordinal Scale

A major feature of social science research is classification, meaning that often people or events are classified into different categories. In this case, measurement involves the assignment of objects to numerical categories according to a set of rules. There are different types of measurement. The type used in this research project is an *ordinal measurement* [Cohe96; Dunn83]. A variable can be said to be measured on an ordinal level when the categories can be ordered on some continuum or dimension. For example, four individuals who differ in height are assigned to numbers, from 1 (the tallest individual) to 2 (the next tallest) to 3 (the tallest) and to 4 (the shortest). In this case, the height is measured on an ordinal level, allowing us to order the individuals from tallest to shortest. An ordinal scale assigns numerals to subjects or objects that subsequently are rank ordered with respect to some characteristic or combination of characteristics. An ordinal scale, is then a measurement scale that assigns values to objects based on their ranking with respect to one another. In another example, a doctor might use a scale of 0-10 to indicate degree of improvement in some condition, from 0 (no improvement) to 10 (disappearance of the condition). While one knows that a 4 is better than a 2, there is no implication that a 4 is twice as good as a 2. Nor is the improvement from 2 to 4 necessarily the same "amount" of improvement as that from 6 to 8. Thus, ordinal measurement allows the researcher to classify individuals into different categories that are ordered along a dimension of interest. Descriptive statistics apply to ordinal scales. Other types [Torg58] are nominal, interval, and ratio measurements. Cliff [Clif96] gives three reasons why behavioral researchers use ordinal methods:

1. In behavioral science, it is often argued that data have only ordinal justification. This means that ordinal methods are preferable because of the "possibility that conclusions from a metric analysis of ordinal data could be changed, even reversed, under ordinal transformation of the data, whereas ordinally based conclusions will not" [Clif96, p. 1].
2. The second reason for using ordinal methods is that the questions to be answered by the data are themselves ordinal in substantial fraction of applications. This

means that ordinal scales answer the ordinal research question more directly than does a metric analysis.

3. The most cited and traditional reason for preferring an ordinal method is that ordinal methods have greater statistical robustness.

In the case of the knowledge potential measurement, each variable is measured on an ordinal scale. The knowledge-engineer is measuring the value of each dimension based on the interview session. Each dimension is divided into several questions which cover the nine knowledge dimensions and measure the value of each expert on the specific dimension. The ordinal scale is divided into five categories: 1 = very good (excellent), 2 = good, 3 = medium, 4 = bad, and 5 = very bad.

Furthermore, the knowledge-engineer can evaluate professionals with values between the five categories such as 1.4, 2.6, 3.7, or 4.9. After the interviews, the knowledge-engineer gives his measurement judgment on the ordinal scale. Since each dimension is measured on an ordinal scale, ranging from 1 (very good) to 5 (very bad), the knowledge scale ranges from 20 to 2500 points on an ordinal scale (Table "Knowledge Potential Rating Scale Matrix"). This means, the highest knowledge scale score that a knowledge worker can be assigned to is 2500 points, meaning that he has very bad rating scores in all dimensions. The lowest knowledge score is 20 points, meaning he has all necessary knowledge for solving specific problems. 20 and 2500 are the mathematical minimum and maximum numbers. The higher one goes on the rating scale, the lower is the qualification of the knowledge worker, and the lower one goes on the rating scale, the higher is the expertise of the knowledge worker.

5.7.2 Skill Acquisition Model from Dreyfus

The rating scale (Table "Knowledge Potential Rating Scale Matrix") is sub-divided into five knowledge-rating intervals or stages. These five stages are based on the skill acquisition model of Dreyfus and Dreyfus [DrDr87; DrDr97; Drey02]. The Dreyfus Model of skill acquisition was developed in 1980, and it is a model that can be applied to the learning of any skills. Dreyfus and Dreyfus [DrDr97] criticize Artificial Intelligence workers because they claim it will be possible for machines to make interferences similar to those of humans. Dreyfus takes the position that machines never have a creative component because "human beings seem to be able to form and compare images in a way that cannot be captured by any number of procedures that operate on descriptions" [DrDr97, p. 40]. The **Dreyfus model of skill acquisition** has the basic idea that those persons who master specific skills must pass through five levels of learning: novice, advanced beginner, competency, proficiency, and expertise. The Dreyfus model is the basic theoretical model for clustering the rating scale of the knowledge potential into five areas. There are similarities between the skill acquisition model of Dreyfus and the learning levels of a knowledge worker because the time an expert acquires experiences can be divided into five levels: poor knowledge worker, standard knowledge worker, undefined knowledge worker, good knowledge worker, and excellent knowledge worker.

5.7.2.1 Novice (Poor Knowledge Worker)

The first learning process is the novice level. The teacher deconstructs the task and its environment into features and parts which are free of context and easily recognizable to the novice. The novice internalizes these features. In this stage, the instructor has to decompose the task environment into context-free features which the beginner can recognize without previous experience in the task domain. After this, the beginner gets the rules for determining actions on the basis of these features. For example [DrDr87, p. 44], a social sciences student learns about the theories of cost-benefit-analysis and consumer behavior and relates them to context-free features such as production cost, market share, or demographic data. However, the novice student is not able to see an interference pattern and to make connections between those theories and their meaning for solving business problems. A novice can be compared with a person who learns to drive a car, but he starts and stops the car in a jerking fashion because he does not know how much gas to give the car.

A *poor knowledge worker* is unable to make his own intuitive decision, but he has to follow given rules because he is not able to rely on a large experience repertoire. He is governed by "if … then" rules given by his instructor or mentor. On his way to become an excellent knowledge worker, he has to collect experience and to gain the ability to make intuitive decision. His action is governed by facts, and he has little understanding of the problem as a whole. A poor knowledge worker is a slow employee trying to remember all the rules and their priorities.

5.7.2.2 Advanced Beginner (Standard Knowledge Worker)

As the novice experiences more and more real situations, he moves to the advanced beginner stage. At this level, the advanced beginner notes examples of meaningful experiences. The advanced beginner focuses on rules, but he has begun to rely on previous experiences with the time and experience. Still this person needs guidelines from an instructor to perform at an acceptable level. The advanced beginner is now able to recognize "situational" aspects and to use context-free and situational features. For the car example, the advanced beginner driver now listens to the sound of the engine (situational aspect) and to the speed (nonsituational) and uses this information for his gear-shifting rules. Or the advanced beginner student in the marketing department now uses his experience to determine the competitiveness of his company for a new product. The level of the advanced beginner is comparable to a *standard knowledge worker*, who has learned to combine situational aspects and nonsituational aspects. He is still rule-focused and begins to rely on previous experiences gained in his knowledge environment.

5.7.2.3 Competence (Undefined Knowledge Worker)

As the advanced beginners gain more experience in real situations, they begin their transition to the level of competence. The competent learner takes experience and adopts it to a hierarchical view of decision making. The competent learner internalizes a small set of examples to be relevant. The competent performer is more organized, and he has a plan to become more efficient. However, the competent learner has to develop a feeling for what is important, and, from there, he must develop a plan to determine which elements are important and which can be ignored. The competent learner feels responsible for choosing a plan, but psychological aspects have to be taken into consideration. For example, a competent marketing manager will focus his decision process on the hierarchical order, and he will only pay attention to a few alternatives which influence his decision. Another example is the car driver. A competent car driver who is leaving a freeway on an off-ramp curve takes speed, surface condition, and time into account, and then makes a decision whether the car is moving too fast. After that process, he must choose whether to let up on the accelerator, remove his foot altogether, or step on the brakes. He is finally relieved if he did not have any accident, and he has collected new experiences.

A competent performer in the Dreyfus model is comparable in knowledge potential view with a knowledge worker whose future learning development is unknown *(undefined knowledge worker)*. There are two options, either he brings the skills to transform himself into a good or an excellent knowledge worker with him, or he will stay on the competent level for a while and then even fall back to being a standard knowledge worker.

5.7.2.4 Proficiency (Good Knowledge Worker)

The proficient performer recognizes a certain plan, goal or perspective due to a high level of experiences. A proficient learner is able to learn from previous experiences, and he can modify his response in a given situation. A proficient marketing manager may intuitively realize that he should reposition a product by studying the situation and doing a market analysis. He has learned to recognize a problem, and he tries to find an intuitive solution. The proficient performer "after seeing the goal and the important features of the situation, must still *decide* what to do. To decide, he falls back on detached rule-following" [Drey02, p. 3]. They still have to think about what they need to do. They perform the task almost without a conscious effort. This is also the reason why a proficient performer can be called a *good knowledge worker*. On the rating scale, his evaluation mainly has good ratings scores on all nine variables. The good knowledge worker has gained enough experience to not only follow rules but also to choose between different alternatives. A good knowledge worker makes his decision from experiences because his actions are based on his intuition rather than thinking about each step being performed.

5.7.2.5 Expertise (Excellent Knowledge Worker)

In transition, the proficient performer deconstructs the experiences gained over so many years into various classes and sub-classes that each share the same decision alternatives, either action or plan. The development of an immediate intuitive response marks the transition to the expert level. The expert sees what needs to be done, then they do it, and he does it without applying rules. Dreyfus and Dreyfus [DrDr97, p. 34] describe the expert level as follows:

> *"experts generally know what to do because they have a mature and practiced understanding. When deeply involved in coping with their environment, they do not see problems in some detached way and consciously work at solving them. The skills of the experts have become so much a part of them that they need be no more aware of them than they are of their own bodies."*

The experts with their extensive experience and their ability to see the significance within a contextual whole are very flexible in performing their skills. For example, an athlete develops a feel for the ball, an airline pilot self-corrects the landing process without having to think about each step of the process. The skills and experience are so much a part of the expert that he acts when having to make decision. A person on the expertise level is called an *excellent knowledge worker* which is the highest level of learning. He has "very good" to "good" rating scores on all nine measurement variables, and he is doing the job based on experienced and profound know-how. A knowledge company needs workers equipped with creative and intuitive skills and experiences, meaning importantly that the skills are associated with the intellect of the individual.

A knowledge company must be very careful that the experienced workers do not walk out of the door and take their tacit knowledge with them. Because the knowledge is in their brains and because it is very difficult to articulate, knowledge leaves the company forever. Another threat is the knowledge worker joining a competitor. These professional knowledge workers have to be treated very special even if they demand increased job satisfaction, more freedom, or better working conditions. A knowledge management focus for the excellent knowledge worker demands that a company finds a way to renew and rejuvenate the existing workforce as well as to attract young and fresh people.

Amar identifies six knowledge skills for a knowledge worker in a knowledge organization [Amar02, pp. 10]:

1. *Skill to Refract*. Refractivity is a knowledge skill that enables the knowledge worker to divide a set of identical-looking elements into several sub-sets and to deal with highly complex situations by identifying the difference between similar looking physical and metaphysical variables and their interrelationships.

2. *Skill to Work with the Abstract.* The challenge for knowledge organizations is to teach the individuals the ability to make abstractions; this means that innovative ideas will be generated if the employee can transfer his knowledge from a known field to another one by using his experiences.
3. *Skill to Connect.* The skill of connectivity leads to the revelation of unique scenarios. Even if this technique is used in organizations for many years, it should be emphasized much more. This ability can help one find innovative solutions by looking at interdisciplinary fields such as psychological, sociological, or physiological problems.
4. *Skill to Extend.* A knowledge worker should have the creative ability to take knowledge from one field where it is well known and apply it to other fields where it is unknown.
5. *Skill to Manipulate Time and Space.* This essential skill of an excellent knowledge worker distinguishes him from a standard or poor knowledge worker because he has the ability to make decisions fast, and, therefore, to find excellent problem solutions quickly. This characteristic is an enabling force, and it is represented in the measurement model by the knowledge velocity ($v^{(K)}$) variable.
6. *Skill to Disseminate.* The skill of dissemination deals with the ability to transfer the knowledge from the sender to the receiver and that the receiver is able to understand the "tacit knowledge" from the sender. This means, "a fast, effective, and efficient way to spread thoughts to the precisely targeted audience is achieved through *perception dissemination*, which may or may not need a medium" [Amar02, p. 13]. It requires sender and receiver on both sides with the knowledge skill to understand the meaning of the sending information or know-how.

Nonaka et al. [Nona92; NoTa95; NoRe00] introduce a model for the process of knowledge creation and utilization, one which distinguishes four knowledge modes: socialization, externalization, combination, and internalization. The first two modes focus on the creation of knowledge while the second two modes emphasize the utilization of knowledge. The primary focus of this process is the individual worker whose knowledge and expertise are defined as tacit and explicit. *Explicit knowledge* is formal and systematic, and it is easy to communicate and share. *Tacit knowledge* consists of mental models, beliefs, and perspectives that cannot be articulated and shared easily. It is the movement between these two forms of knowledge that forms the process of creating new knowledge. The authors establish an epistemological foundation that distinguishes tacit and explicit knowledge, explaining that knowledge conversion is the result of interactions between tacit and explicit knowledge. This means, from tacit to tacit (Socialization), from explicit to explicit (Combination), from tacit to explicit (Externalization), and from explicit to tacit (Internalization). *Socialization* is a process of sharing experiences. It occurs in groups and organizational cultures through shared experiences, technical skills, and mental models acquired through apprentice/master relationships, on-the-job training, imitation, observation, and practice. In this case the key success factor is experience; the mere transfer of information is not enough. *Externalization* is a process of articulating what we know into explicit concepts through the use of metaphors, analogies, and models. This process is crucial for knowledge creation because new and explicit concepts can be derived from tacit knowledge. Metaphors link contradictory things and ideas; analogies resolve these contradictions by showing similarities, describing new ideas graphically, and making the knowledge available to the rest of the company. *Combination* is a process in which information is combined, exchanged, published, documented, or discussed at meetings. This existing information can be sorted, added, combined, categorized, etc. for new knowledge. An example is data-mining in large scale databases [NoRe00, p. 90]. *Internalization* is a process of organizational learning related to learning by doing. Knowledge should be verbalized in documents, manuals, or success stories. Dreyfus talks in this context about the competent performer who internalizes the experiences.

Nonaka et al. [NoTa95] emphasize that knowledge always involves individuals who are sharing their knowledge with others. Furthermore, organizational knowledge creation is a spiral process which starts at the individual level, expanding to greater communities of interactions that move across sections, departments, divisions and other organizational boundaries. This dimension is called the ontological dimension, meaning that the level of social interaction and knowledge expands like a spiral.

The "Knowledge Potential Rating Scale Matrix" gives an overview of the possible rating scores each knowledge-engineer can make for the person-dependent and system-dependent variables. The given scores (1.2; 1.4; … 4.8; 5.0) can be interpreted as examples for each knowledge dimension. All scores, ranging from 1.0 to 5.0, can be given depending on the measurement process of the knowledge-engineers. Furthermore, the matrix shows the calculation of knowledge momentum and knowledge position which results in the knowledge potential value. The minimum value for KP is 20, meaning that a knowledge worker receives an excellent score 1.0 on all nine dimensions including the velocity. The maximum value is 2500 meaning that the knowledge worker is receiving on all nine dimensions very bad scores.

The rating scale is not determined by equal intervals due to the fact that increasingly higher scores correspond to increasingly higher KP values, therefore the evaluation of the knowledge workers is becoming worse. In order to get an equal-interval measurement, the knowledge potential rating scale has to be transformed into a linear scale. The basic idea here is that the interval between the numbers on the ordinal scale are becoming equal in size. Up to this measurement point, the intervals for the categorization of the knowledge workers are organized as follows:

- Novice = Poor Knowledge Worker ($1481.8 \leq KP \leq 2500.0$);
- Advanced Beginner = Standard Knowledge Worker ($786.1 \leq KP < 1481.8$);
- Competence = Undefined Knowledge Worker ($351.5 < KP < 786.1$);
- Proficiency = Good Knowledge Worker ($116.6 \leq KP < 351.5$);
- Expertise = Excellent Knowledge Worker ($20.0 \leq KP < 116.6$).

The intervals show that the distance in a knowledge worker classification is not equal, meaning that the interval of a poor knowledge worker is much larger than the one for the excellent knowledge worker. The transformation of the KP rating scale is done by using the cube root which leads to a **linearization of the scale**. The process of linearization causes an interval to have equal distances. Therefore each interval for the knowledge worker classification in the Dreyfus model is based on an equal-interval measurement. The classification for each interval is compared to the original ordinal scale, and it is illustrated in Table "Linearization of the Ordinal Scale".

The *cube root* was selected because of three influencing variables: knowledge mass, knowledge velocity, and knowledge position. The process of linearization transforms the unequal intervals (interval distance in Table "Linearization of the Ordinal Scale") produced by the multiplication of the three variables into equal intervals (linear distance in Table

"Linearization of the Ordinal Scale"), counteracting the multiplication effect. The application of the cube root to interval scale is different from the original Heisenberg Uncertainty Principle equation, hence the linearization process of the knowledge rating scale is distinct from the Heisenberg equation.

Rating	Ordinal Interval	Interval Distance	Linearization	Linear Distance
Poor Knowledge worker	1481.8≤KP≤ 2500.0	1018.2	11.40≤KP<13.57	2.17
Standard Knowledge Worker	786.1≤KP<1481.8	695.7	9.23≤KP<11.40	2.17
Undefined Knowledge Worker	351.5≤KP<786.1	434.6	7.06≤KP<9.23	2.17
Good Knowledge Worker	116.6≤KP<351.5	234.9	4.89≤KP<7.06	2.17
Excellent Knowledge Worker	20.0 ≤KP<116.6	96.6	2.71≤KP<4.89	2.17

Table 15: Linearization of the Ordinal Scale

Table "Knowledge Potential Rating Scale Matrix" describes four major settings:

- The ordinal scale with its possible rating values;
- The minimum and maximum values for KP;
- The linearization of the rating scale by applying the cube root;
- The assignment of experts to knowledge-worker classification schema based on the Dreyfus model of skill acquisition.

Once again, it must be pointed out that the ordinal values used in the Table "Knowledge Potential Rating Scale Matrix" are examples of possible rating scores each knowledge-engineer can give knowledge workers during the measurement process.

Measurement Variables																					
Content	1.0	1.2	1.4	1.6	1.8	2.0	2.2	2.4	2.6	2.8	3.0	3.2	3.4	3.6	3.8	4.0	4.2	4.4	4.6	4.8	5.0
Networking	1.0	1.2	1.4	1.6	1.8	2.0	2.2	2.4	2.6	2.8	3.0	3.2	3.4	3.6	3.8	4.0	4.2	4.4	4.6	4.8	5.0
Skills	1.0	1.2	1.4	1.6	1.8	2.0	2.2	2.4	2.6	2.8	3.0	3.2	3.4	3.6	3.8	4.0	4.2	4.4	4.6	4.8	5.0
Learning	1.0	1.2	1.4	1.6	1.8	2.0	2.2	2.4	2.6	2.8	3.0	3.2	3.4	3.6	3.8	4.0	4.2	4.4	4.6	4.8	5.0
Knowledge Mass ($m^{(K)}$)	**4.0**	**4.8**	**5.6**	**6.4**	**7.2**	**8.0**	**8.8**	**9.6**	**10.4**	**11.2**	**12.0**	**12.8**	**13.6**	**14.4**	**15.2**	**16.0**	**16.8**	**17.6**	**18.4**	**19.2**	**20.0**
Knowledge velocity ($v^{(K)}$)	1.0	1.2	1.4	1.6	1.8	2.0	2.2	2.4	2.6	2.8	3.0	3.2	3.4	3.6	3.8	4.0	4.2	4.4	4.6	4.8	5.0
Knowledge Momentum ($p^{(K)}$)	**4.0**	**5.8**	**7.8**	**10.2**	**13.0**	**16.0**	**19.4**	**23.0**	**27.0**	**31.4**	**36.0**	**41.0**	**46.2**	**51.8**	**57.8**	**64.0**	**70.6**	**77.4**	**84.6**	**92.2**	**100.0**
Culture	1.0	1.2	1.4	1.6	1.8	2.0	2.2	2.4	2.6	2.8	3.0	3.2	3.4	3.6	3.8	4.0	4.2	4.4	4.6	4.8	5.0
Organizational Structure	1.0	1.2	1.4	1.6	1.8	2.0	2.2	2.4	2.6	2.8	3.0	3.2	3.4	3.6	3.8	4.0	4.2	4.4	4.6	4.8	5.0
Customers	1.0	1.2	1.4	1.6	1.8	2.0	2.2	2.4	2.6	2.8	3.0	3.2	3.4	3.6	3.8	4.0	4.2	4.4	4.6	4.8	5.0
Competitors	1.0	1.2	1.4	1.6	1.8	2.0	2.2	2.4	2.6	2.8	3.0	3.2	3.4	3.6	3.8	4.0	4.2	4.4	4.6	4.8	5.0
IC&S/KMS	1.0	1.2	1.4	1.6	1.8	2.0	2.2	2.4	2.6	2.8	3.0	3.2	3.4	3.6	3.8	4.0	4.2	4.4	4.6	4.8	5.0
Knowledge Position ($x^{(K)}$)	**5.0**	**6.0**	**7.0**	**8.0**	**9.0**	**10.0**	**11.0**	**12.0**	**13.0**	**14.0**	**15.0**	**16.0**	**17.0**	**18.0**	**19.0**	**20.0**	**21.0**	**22.0**	**23.0**	**24.0**	**25.0**
Knowledge Potential (KP)	**20.0**	**34.6**	**54.9**	**81.9**	**116.6**	**160.0**	**213.0**	**276.5**	**351.5**	**439.0**	**540.0**	**655.4**	**786.1**	**933.1**	**1097.4**	**1280.0**	**1481.8**	**1703.7**	**1946.7**	**2211.8**	**2500.0**
Cube Root	2.7	3.3	3.8	4.3	4.9	5.4	6.0	6.5	7.1	7.6	8.1	8.7	9.2	9.8	10.3	10.9	11.4	11.9	12.5	13.0	13.6
KP Rating	Excellent Knowledge Worker					Good Knowledge Worker				Undefined Knowledge Worker				Standard Knowledge Worker				Poor Knowledge Worker			
Dreyfus Model	**Expertise**					**Proficiency**				**Competence**				**Advanced Beginner**				**Novice**			

Table 16: Knowledge Potential Rating Scale Matrix

5.8 Measurement of the Uncertainty of the Knowledge-engineer

5.8.1 Measurement Error

The limitations of any measured value involve uncertainty, thus uncertainty should be taken into consideration for any calculated value. For Rones [Rone88, pp. 6], this means that the "limitation of the scientific procedure is represented by the results of any scientific measurements and their analysis. In this sense the measured results are approximate". Rones states, that from a physical viewpoint, all measured values are approximate and any degree of accuracy is subject to the limitations of the Heisenberg Uncertainty Principle in the sense that uncertainty is inherent in physical processes. He further identifies three sources of uncertainty for a system designed to measure a required response [Rone88, p. 7]:

1. One major source of uncertainty derives from the fact that all of the parameters (also known as the input parameters) that determine the response are known with a certain degree of uncertainty.
2. A second field of uncertainty is due to the fact that all the parameters influencing the system are not considered in the analysis. In nature, everything is connected to everything else; therefore we have an infinite number of parameters.
3. The third source of uncertainty is the fact that the phenomenon we are trying to investigate is not completely known and understood. However, there is little we can do about it.

Rones makes the point that the accuracy of physical parameters improves over time, and it reduces uncertainties. This case is demonstrated for the velocity of light in a vacuum [Rone88, p. 8]. However, this basic idea from physics also can be transferred to the knowledge potential view, meaning that the measurement uncertainty can be reduced over time. In our everyday life, decisions are made based on the calculation of numerical values. The quality of the decision is highly dependent on the size of the error associated with those values. A single measurement can be the basis for further actions concerning our safety, health, and environment or, in our case, the company's knowledge value. Therefore, it is important to keep the uncertainties of such measurements small enough that any actions based on the measurement are negligibly affected. For Cameron [Came82, p. 547], error analysis "can be looked upon as the methodology by which one arrives at a numerical value for the 'shadow of doubt' or uncertainty associated with his measurement. The goal is to be able to determine the uncertainty to be attached to an isolated measurement on a possibly transient phenomenon". Variables differ in "how well" they can be measured, i.e., in how much information their measurement scale can provide. There obviously is some measurement error involved in every measurement which determines the amount of information that can be obtained. There are three *different kinds of errors* [Bols89, p. 416]:

1. *Systematic errors* either overestimate or underestimate the results of measurements, and they arise for specific reasons such as the incorrect set-up of the measuring equipment. As a consequence, the measurement process is affected and altered in one direction.
2. *Gross errors* come from miscalculating the data or from the incorrect reading of the measurement equipment. This kind of error is easily to identify because the measurement result differs from other results done before.
3. *Random errors* arise from unforeseen events on the measurement. The theory of errors only is focused on the study of gross and random errors.

The measurement of the nine variables done by the knowledge-engineer includes an uncertainty which affects the system of measurement and, hence, the outcome of that system. This means the calculated knowledge potential (KP) for each knowledge worker is associated with an uncertainty based on the measurement error of the knowledge-engineer. In the knowledge potential approach, the measurement procedure of the knowledge-engineer for each expert is influenced by his personal measurement uncertainty. The key question is: What is the impact of his personal uncertainties on the measurement of the knowledge position and momentum variables, and, therefore, for the knowledge potential (KP)? The accuracy (correctness) and precision (number of significant figures) of his measurement is limited by the degree of refinement of the measurement apparatus used, especially by the skill of the observer (knowledge-engineer). However, the idea exists in our mind that we measure correct values. Cameron [Came82, p. 545] states that we cannot achieve a certain value due to imperfections in our understanding of the quantity being measured (model error) and due to our ability to make measures without error.

Heisenberg (see Chapter 4.4) disproves the classical belief that the precision of any measurement was limited only by the accuracy of the instruments. Uncertainty is a fundamental consequence of the properties of the knowledge world. It becomes overtly visible only when we deal with *the micro-world.* Hence, a particle can be described in terms of probabilities. Classical physics assumes that a real external objective world independent of observers exists. Heisenberg asserted that the distinction between the observer and the observed vanishes in the act of observing atomic processes, and that things cannot have meaning beyond their observed precision. This was contrary to the basic supposition of science. The developments in classical physics since the time of Galileo and Newton led to a deterministic world-view, that there is a law of causality (i.e., every effect is preceded by a cause, and that knowledge of the present would enables us to predict the future). The Uncertainty Principle challenges this notion, by stating that exactitude is impossible; and the most one can have are the probabilities of possible results. Since the present itself cannot be known completely, the future remains even more obscure. The implication of the Heisenberg Uncertainty Principle also applies to the adjusted knowledge potential view. To this point, the uncertainty of the measurement procedure was not part of the calculation of the value of the knowledge worker expressed in the term knowledge potential (KP). The uncertainty of the KP measurement result comes from the uncertainties of momentum and position measurement done by the knowledge-engineer. Uncertainty is a quantitative indication of the quality of the result. It gives an answer to the question, how well does the result represent the value of the quantity being measured? It allows users of the result to assess its reliability.

Gupta [Gupt92] argues that every human is confronted with uncertainties arising from our thinking, cognition, and perception processes. In our learning process, every human is collecting experiences from which useful information is extracted from the uncertainties in our environment, and this information is used for further actions and decision making processes. Gupta describes the phenomenon of uncertainty [Gupt92, p. 3]:

> *"Uncertainty is an inherent phenomenon in our universe and in our lives which stands continuously open to our gaze. To some, it may become a cause of anxiety, but to scientists, it becomes a chapter full of challenges. Scientists attempt to comprehend the language of this uncertainty through mathematical tools, but these mathematical tools are still incomplete."*

Gupta uses the term “cognitive uncertainty” which means uncertainty arises out of human thinking, and perception processes. Cognitive uncertainty has two characteristics: it is relative and context dependent. The knowledge-engineer is affected by *cognitive uncertainty* rather than physical uncertainty. The set of conditions underlying the process of analogical reasoning for the transformation of the Heisenberg Uncertainty Principle to the knowledge potential view assumes that uncertainty is associated with the perceptions of human beings, and it does not arise from physical processes.

The following section explains the basic mathematical terms associated with the calculation of the uncertainty measurement. *Variance* [Cohe96, p. 104; Este91, p. 27] is a measure of how spread out a distribution is. Variance is the mean of the squared deviations from the mean, and is calculated from the formula:

$$\sigma^2 = \frac{\sum(X_i - \mu)^2}{N}$$

where

σ^2 = Variance;

μ = Mean;

N = Total number of scores;

X_i = Sample of scores; i =1,2, ... N.

The *standard deviation* [Cohe96, p. 105; Este91, p. 27; RaRa85, p. 68] is a concept from statistics, and it is a measure of the amount of variation or deviation that might be expected between the actual indicator value and the forecasted value, and it is given in the same units as the indicator. The standard deviation is defined as the square root of the variance, and it is a measure that provides a good description of the variability of a distribution. The standard deviation is symbolized with the Greek letter sigma (σ) and, it can be expressed as follows:

$$\sigma = \sqrt{\sigma^2} = \sqrt{\frac{\sum(X_i - \mu)^2}{N}}$$

where

σ = Standard deviation;

μ = Mean;

N = Total number of scores;

X_i = Sample of scores; i =1,2, … N.

Standard deviation is a statistical term that provides a good indicator for volatility [Buff02]. It measures how widely values (closing prices for instance) are dispersed from the average. Dispersion is the difference between the actual value (closing price) and the average value (mean closing price). The larger the difference between the closing prices and the average price, the higher the standard deviation will be and the higher the volatility will be. The closer the closing prices are to the average price, they will have a lower standard deviation and lower volatility.

The standard deviation is the amount of swing in the performance that the knowledge-engineer can be expected to have during the interview with the knowledge worker. The higher the measured standard deviation is, the greater is the volatility, and, therefore, the greater is the uncertainty. The standard deviation is a statistical term that provides a good indicator for interview volatility for each knowledge-engineer. The objective of taking the standard deviation is to have an indicator for the uncertainty in the measurement of each of the nine knowledge variables. The standard deviation for the knowledge-engineer is an indicator for the uncertainty, one which each knowledge-engineer makes during the interview sessions. So far, the measurement of the knowledge potential (KP) did not take the uncertainty in the measurement into consideration. To take the Δ of the Heisenberg Uncertainty Principle into consideration, the standard deviation of measurements taken during the interviews is interpreted as the uncertainty during the interview measurement. The objective is to measure the individual uncertainty for each knowledge-engineer, one which can be interpreted as an uncertainty arising out of the cognitive processes during the interview session. Each knowledge-engineer has his personal standard deviation which illustrates his measurement error (uncertainty) during the face-to-face interviews with the experts.

5.8.2 Uncertainty Measurement of the Knowledge-Engineer

After the measurement of the knowledge potential (KP), the uncertainty of the measurement derived from the measurement error of the knowledge-engineer has to be computed. The fact that the interviewer (knowledge-engineer) affects some answers of the experts to a significant degree defines the problem for measuring uncertainty. Each knowledge-engineer brings a number of characteristics into the interview sessions with the experts, characteristics that might affect the answers of the respondents. The calculation of the measurement error of the knowledge-engineer is sub-divided into two steps:

1. The calculation of standard scores;
2. The calculation of the standard deviation for each knowledge-engineer based on the measurement of the standardized data.

Standardization is important because it removes the dependence on the individual measurement data. To derive standard scores [Anas76, pp. 80], often referred to as z scores, the difference between the individual's raw score and the mean of the normative group is calculated and the difference is divided by standard deviation of the normative group. In the knowledge potential view this means that the standard score is the difference between the individual score each knowledge-engineer has made for a given knowledge worker and the mean of all scores made by all other knowledge-engineers. The standardized values can be computed in mathematical notation as [ScIn71, pp. 55]:

$$z = \frac{x - \bar{x}}{s}$$

where

z = Standard score;

x = Individual score;

$\bar{x}$ = Mean of all scores;

s = Standard deviation.

Schoeninger and Insko [ScIn71, pp. 55] note that z scores have two characteristics:

1. The mean of a distribution of z scores, $\bar{z}$, is always equal to zero. This means in mathematical terms: $\bar{z} = 0$.
2. The variance and standard deviation of a distribution of z scores are always equal to one which means expressed mathematically: $s_z = 1$.

Standardization produces a new dataset containing the standardized values. The objective for calculating z scores is to make the scores on different interviews comparable. The standard scores are the bases for the measurement of the uncertainty for each knowledge-engineer. These new values form the basis for calculating the uncertainty of momentum and position for each knowledge-engineer. The basic matrix for the calculation of the standard scores is visualized in Table "Accumulated Momentum Values" and Table "Accumulated Position Values". The values of the two matrixes are taken from the Tables "Knowledge Momentum Measurement" and "Knowledge Position Measurement".

KW / KE	1	2	...	j	...	n	Sums of values	Mean	Standard Deviation
1	p_{11}	p_{12}	...	p_{1j}	...	p_{1n}	$p_{1.}$	$\overline{p}_{1.}$	$s_{1.}$
2	p_{21}	p_{22}	...	p_{2j}	...	p_{2n}	$p_{2.}$	$\overline{p}_{2.}$	$s_{2.}$
...	...	...	...	...	...	...	...	...	...
i	p_{i1}	p_{i2}	...	p_{ij}	...	p_{in}	$p_{i.}$	$\overline{p}_{i.}$	$s_{i.}$
...	...	...	...	...	...	...	...	...	...
m	p_{m1}	p_{m2}	...	p_{mj}	...	p_{mn}	$p_{m.}$	$\overline{p}_{m.}$	$s_{m.}$
Sums of values	$p_{.1}$	$p_{.2}$	...	$p_{.j}$	...	$p_{.n}$			
Mean	$\overline{p}_{.1}$	$\overline{p}_{.2}$	...	$\overline{p}_{.j}$	...	$\overline{p}_{.n}$			
Standard Deviation	$s_{.1}$	$s_{.2}$	...	$s_{.j}$	...	$s_{.n}$			

Table 17: Accumulated Momentum Values

The calculation of the **standard score for knowledge momentum** (z_p) can be expressed mathematically:

$$z_p = \frac{p - \overline{p}}{s_p}$$

or

$$z_{p_{ij}} = \frac{p_{ij} - \overline{p}_{.j}}{s_{p_j}}$$

where

$z_{p_{ij}}$ = Standard score given by the knowledge-engineer for the knowledge momentum for each knowledge worker;

P_{ij} = Knowledge momentum value for each knowledge worker;

$\bar{p}_{.j}$ = Mean of the momentum values of the j-th knowledge worker;

s_{p_j} = Standard deviation for knowledge momentum for the j-th knowledge worker.

KE \ KW	1	2	...	j	...	n	Sums of values	Mean	Standard Deviation
1	x_{11}	x_{12}	...	x_{1j}	...	x_{1n}	$x_{1.}$	$\bar{x}_{1.}$	$s_{1.}$
2	x_{21}	x_{2}	...	x_{2j}	...	x_{2n}	$x_{2.}$	$\bar{x}_{2.}$	$s_{2.}$
...	...	...	...	...	...	...	...	...	...
i	x_{i1}	x_{i2}	...	x_{ij}	...	x_{in}	$x_{i.}$	$\bar{x}_{i.}$	$s_{i.}$
...	...	...	...	...	...	...	...	...	...
m	x_{m1}	x_{m2}	...	x_{mj}	...	x_{mn}	$x_{m.}$	$\bar{x}_{m.}$	$s_{m.}$
Sums of values	$x_{.1}$	$x_{.2}$	...	$x_{.j}$	...	$x_{.n}$			
Mean	$\bar{x}_{.1}$	$\bar{x}_{.2}$	...	$\bar{x}_{.j}$	...	$\bar{x}_{.n}$			
Standard Deviation	$s_{.1}$	$s_{.2}$	...	$s_{.j}$	...	$s_{.n}$			

Table 18: Accumulated Position Values

The calculation of the **standard scores for knowledge position** (z_x) can be expressed mathematically as follows:

$$z_x = \frac{x - \bar{x}}{s_x}$$

or

$$z_{x_{ij}} = \frac{x_{ij} - \bar{x}_{.j}}{s_{x_j}}$$

where

$z_{x_{ij}}$ = Standard score for the knowledge position for each knowledge worker given by the knowledge-engineer;

x_{ij} = Knowledge position value for each knowledge worker;

$\bar{x}_{.j}$ = Mean of the position values of the j-th knowledge worker;

s_{x_j} = Standard deviation for knowledge position for the j-th knowledge worker.

After the calculation of standard scores for the knowledge position and knowledge momentum for each knowledge-engineer and each knowledge worker, one must consider the uncertainty for each knowledge-engineer. The standard deviation is the measure for the uncertainty for the knowledge position and knowledge momentum of each knowledge-engineer. This means that the standard deviation or uncertainty for each knowledge-engineer arises out from the fact that the knowledge-engineer has an uncertainty in his rating during the measurement of the KP of the experts. The z-scores – knowledge momentum and knowledge position – for the knowledge-engineer are shown in Table "Standard Scores for Knowledge Momentum" and Table "Standard Scores for Knowledge Position" which form the basic matrix for the further derivation of the uncertainty for each knowledge-engineer.

KE \ KW	1	2	...	j	...	n	
1	$z_{p,11}$	$z_{p,12}$	...	$z_{p,1j}$	...	$z_{p,1n}$	$\bar{z}_{p,1}$
2	$z_{p,21}$	$z_{p,22}$	...	$z_{p,2j}$	...	$z_{p,2n}$	$\bar{z}_{p,2}$
...	...	...	...	...	...	...	...
i	$z_{p,i1}$	$z_{p,i2}$	...	$z_{p,ij}$	...	$z_{p,in}$	$\bar{z}_{p,i}$
...	...	...	...	...	...	...	...
m	$z_{p,m1}$	$z_{p,m2}$	...	$z_{p,mj}$	...	$z_{p,mn}$	$\bar{z}_{p,m}$

Table 19: Standard Scores for Knowledge Momentum

KE \ KW	1	2	...	j	...	n	
1	$z_{x,11}$	$z_{x,12}$	...	$z_{x,1j}$	...	$z_{x,1n}$	$\bar{z}_{x,1}$
2	$z_{x,21}$	$z_{x,22}$	...	$z_{x,2j}$	...	$z_{x,2n}$	$\bar{z}_{x,2}$
...	...	...	...	...	...	...	...
i	$z_{x,i1}$	$z_{x,i2}$	...	$z_{x,ij}$	...	$z_{x,in}$	$\bar{z}_{x,i}$
...	...	...	...	...	...	...	...
m	$z_{x,m1}$	$z_{x,m2}$	...	$z_{x,mj}$	...	$z_{x,mn}$	$\bar{z}_{x,m}$

Table 20: Standard Scores for Knowledge Position

The **uncertainty for knowledge momentum measurement** for i-th knowledge-engineers is expressed by the following mathematical equation:

$$s_{p,i} = \sqrt{\frac{\sum_{j=1}^{n} (z_{p,ij} - \bar{z}_{p,i})^2}{n}}$$

where

$s_{p,i}$ = Momentum uncertainty for the i-th knowledge-engineer;

$z_{p,ij}$ = Knowledge momentum standard score of the i-th knowledge-engineer for the j-th knowledge worker;

$\bar{z}_{p,i}$ = Mean of the knowledge momentum standard score for the i-th knowledge-engineer;

n = Number of knowledge workers evaluated by i knowledge-engineers, i = 1, … m.

The **uncertainty for knowledge position measurement** for i-th knowledge-engineers can be calculated as follows:

$$s_{x,i} = \sqrt{\frac{\sum_{j=1}^{n} (z_{x,ij} - \bar{z}_{x,i})^2}{n}}$$

where

$s_{x,i}$ = Position uncertainty for the i-th knowledge-engineer;

$z_{x,ij}$ = Knowledge position standard score of the i-th knowledge-engineer for the j-th knowledge worker;

$\bar{z}_{x,i}$ = Mean of the knowledge position standard score for the i-th knowledge-engineer;

n = Number of knowledge workers evaluated by i knowledge-engineers, i = 1, … m.

From these two formulas the **uncertainty for the knowledge-engineer** can be obtained:

$$s_{p,i} * s_{x,i} = U_{KEi}$$

[Uncertainty Momentum * Uncertainty Position = Uncertainty knowledge-engineer]

More precisely, the uncertainty factor for the knowledge-engineer can be written as follows:

$$\sqrt{\frac{\sum_{j=1}^{n}(z_{p,ij} - \bar{z}_{p,i})^2}{n}} * \sqrt{\frac{\sum_{j=1}^{n}(z_{x,ij} - \bar{z}_{x,i})^2}{n}} = U_{KEi}$$

where

U_{KEi} = Uncertainty of i-th knowledge-engineers.

The result of the measurement is a value which indicates the uncertainty measurement of each knowledge-engineer. The higher the standard deviation is, the more uncertain is the measurement for the knowledge potential of each knowledge-worker. The interview situation is highly dependent on the measurement quality of the knowledge-engineer. One must take into consideration the fact that the multiplication of the uncertainties has a reinforcing impact of the uncertainty measurement. During the face-to-face interview process, the knowledge-engineer (the interviewer) impacts the responses from the knowledge worker through their performance. Each knowledge-engineer has his own way of asking questions, his own way of recording the information, and his own way of interacting with the respondents. The data gathering during the interview process is affected by the personality and behavioral traits which manifest themselves in the interview setting [LyKa91, pp. 240]. Lyberg and Kasprzyk [LyKa91] note that surveys often underestimate the impact of the measurement error. They identify two methods of dealing with this source of error: (1) reduction and (2) measurement. Measurement error through reduction is addressed by standardizing the interviewer performances. Reduction is possible reached through training, observation, and program monitoring. The second error measures interviewer error that can occur through sample designs that permit the calculation of the variance attributed to interviewers. Similar to Lyberg and Kasprzyk [LyKa91], Fowler [Fowl91] identifies five ways to reduce the effect of interviewer-related error on survey data [Fowl91, pp. 263]:

1. The interviewer should have a procedure which he can follow to minimize the extent to which he will influence respondent answers. There are four rules which should be kept in mind at the beginning of an interview session:
   a. The interviewer should read the questions exactly as they are written down;
   b. If the respondent fails to answer the questions adequately in response to the original question, the interviewer should conduct nondirective follow-up probes and questions;
   c. Each respondent answer should be recorded without interviewer interpretation or editing;
   d. Interviewers should have a neutral relationship with the respondent.

   Following these four rules helps to minimize interviewer-related errors, and it helps to obtain a high quality interview.
2. To reduce the interviewer error, the interviewer should have training sessions, and supervision. Fowler [Fowl91, pp. 270] found that a training program lasting about two days improves the interviewer skills, and a training program lasting more than ten days does not necessarily minimize the interviewer error. The only exception is the probing of open ended questions because they are the most difficult task for interviewers.
3. The interviewer selection process should guarantee that only interviewers at least likely to affect the answers are chosen. The third way for error reduction lies in the method of choosing interviewers. Error can be minimized if the interviewer demographics are associated with the respondent's demographic data; e.g., whites selected to interview whites.
4. The administration of the questions should be consistent. The fourth and the most critical area for errors is the questionnaire design. Fowler [Fowl91, p. 275] found out that questions which require an interviewer probe to obtain an adequate answer are the questions mostly affected by errors. The training and supervision of the interviewers is a way to reduce interviewer bias, especially if survey questions are greatly affected by interviewers. Fowler suggests the use of standardized questions to minimize interviewer-related errors.
5. The reduction of the interviewer assignments will reduce the impact of error generated by interviewers on the total error of survey estimates. The fifth possibility

of reducing interviewer-related errors is the reduction of the number of interviews made by interviewers during a survey. Therefore, interviewer fatigue will be minimized.

The interviewer-related errors discussed above also apply to the knowledge-engineer who makes the face-to-face interviews with knowledge workers. This is the reason to compute uncertainties for knowledge momentum and position. The result, U_{KEi}, is the estimated interviewer error. Higher U_{KEi} values indicate a higher interviewer-related error. Since U_{KEi} is the result of the multiplication of the standard deviation for knowledge momentum and the standard deviation for knowledge position, it produces a multiplication effect. Four **knowledge uncertainty cases** can be differentiated:

1. If $s_{p,i}$ and $s_{x,i}$ are high, then the uncertainty measurement of the knowledge-engineer for both variables also is high. In this case, the performance of the knowledge-engineer is poor, and it calls for the reconsideration of his task of interviewing knowledge workers because the measurement error for knowledge momentum and position does not fit the skills of a knowledge-engineer.
2. If $s_{p,i}$ and $s_{x,i}$ are low, then the knowledge-engineer error is lower. This is a sign that the knowledge-engineer has excellent interviewer skills and that he has an excellent performance for all five rules stated by Fowler.
3. If $s_{p,i}$ is high $s_{x,i}$ is low, then the knowledge-engineer should receive training to improve his questions regarding knowledge momentum.
4. If $s_{p,i}$ is low $s_{x,i}$ is high, then the knowledge-engineer should receive training to improve his interviewer skills on the dimensions of the knowledge position. High values of $s_{p,i}$ indicate questions with interviewer impact on the person-dependent variables, and the amount of interviewer-related errors is correspondingly higher than lower values of $s_{x,i}$. High values of $s_{x,i}$ indicate uncertainties on system-dependent variables.

The success and the quality of the interviews with knowledge workers are dependent on the skills and experiences of the knowledge-engineer. Interviewer bias arises from the interviewer behavior. The interviewer error of the knowledge-engineer is the result of a lack of thorough training and interviewing experience. Effective interviewer training and control mechanisms during interviews are the best defenses against interviewer error.

6 Case Studies for Knowledge Measurement

"Selection, appraisal, development, and interpersonal interaction are key processes in organizations, and human resource experts design systematic methods to ensure reliability and validity of these processes."

(Manuel London)

The objective of this chapter is an evaluation of the knowledge potential measurement model. For this reason, three case studies were conducted to test the measurement model and to make statements about the validity of the knowledge measurement process. The case study design is described in detail, covering the pre-test study, the development of the measurement framework, the interview concept, and the companies for the case studies. The chapter concludes with a data analysis of the case studies.

6.1 Case Study Design

6.1.1 Pre-test Case Study

A questionnaire was developed in summer 1999 from a literature research about knowledge management. Once agreement was reached about the questionnaire design, a pre-test was administered on a market research company in Linz, Austria [RoFi99a; RoFi99b; RoFi99c]. The two major objectives of the pre-test were to test the questionnaire and to train knowledge-engineers (interviewers) for the interview process. According to the knowledge architecture, the interview procedure was divided into two phases:

- Interview with the company market research CEO (feasibility study), and
- Interviews with the knowledge workers named by the CEO of the market research company (the process of identification and adaptation).

The questionnaire pre-test was the proving ground for open ended versus closed responses, question wording, question sequence, and administration convenience. Another important goal was the evaluation of the time required to administer the interview. The pre-test revealed three weaknesses:

- The interview time was too long, lasting more than 100 minutes in some cases.

- The structure of the questions needed improvement because some questions were too broad and because the respondents had difficulty understanding the intention of the questions.
- The interviews were not recorded on videotape, depriving the investigator of a richer data analysis.

The strength of the pre-test was the training of the two knowledge-engineers to improve their interviewer skills and to refine the administration of the interview. The pilot test at the research company was used to discover and correct problems for the case study research. The lessons learned from the pre-test resulted in an improved nine-dimension questionnaire design for the knowledge measurement process (see Appendix A for the feasibility study questionnaire and Appendix B for the identification process questionnaire).

6.1.2 Case Selection and Description

To investigate the knowledge potential approach, especially its measurement procedure, the *case study* method was chosen because it excels at the development of an understanding of a complex issue or object. Case studies emphasize detailed contextual analysis of a limited number of events or conditions and their relationships. Social scientists, in particular, have made wide use of this qualitative research method for examining contemporary real-life situations and for providing the basis for the application of ideas and the extension of methods. Gillham [Gill00, p. 1] defines the case study research method as:

- "an unit of human activity embedded in the real world;
- which can only be studied or understood in context;
- which exists in the here and now;
- that mergers in with its context so that precise boundaries are difficult to draw."

The studies were conducted at three U.S. companies in the New Orleans, Louisiana, area in November 2000. The reason for choosing Louisiana companies was the long-standing cooperation between the University of Innsbruck and the University of New Orleans. During the design phase of the case study research, the knowledge potential view was explored with the nine-dimension questionnaire. The case studies have the character of multiple real-life cases of how companies deal with knowledge management and measurement in-depth. The case study procedure follows the knowledge architecture design:

1. Feasibility Study: Knowledge-engineers conducted interviews with the chief executive officer (CEO) or president of each company (Appendix A).
2. Identification/Adaptation Process: The knowledge-engineers then conducted interviews with the knowledge workers named by the CEO or president (Appendix B).
3. Measurement Process: The collected data were analyzed to evaluate the knowledge potential measurement model. The uncertainty was calculated for knowledge momentum and knowledge position for each knowledge-engineer.
4. Implementation Process: Based on the results of the measurement, the CEO or president of each company received a final report with the key research findings.

The case study participants were informed about the interview procedure and about the intention of the interviews. The knowledge potential view was explained to the top management and participating knowledge workers in each company. The support of top management made questionnaire administration easier, and it created an open atmosphere during the interview sessions with the experts. Each participant agreed to the interviews and to their video taping in advance. The transcribed interviews with all participants are available on a CD-ROM [FiRK04] with a navigation system that leads one through all of the interviewer questions and videotapes.

6.1.2.1 CTL

CTL [FiRo03a; FiRK03] was founded as a Louisiana corporation to add Internet and Intranet capabilities to its mature and feature rich applications. CTL software is written in fourth generation and post fourth generation computer languages for relational databases, and it is designed for Internet and Intranet sites. CTL offers over a decade of experience in facility management and rapid analysis software, and it has developed data processing centers that respond immediately to data requests and report modifications. With a product emphasis that services the needs of local, regional, and state governments, courts, police departments, and every organization needing document management, CTL has earned industry designations as both a software house and an integrator, having designed and written dozens of complex custom applications and having integrated scores of third party software.

The CTL *mission statement* can be described follows: "At CTL our goal is to put our clients' information to work for them. We specialize in advanced database connectivity, deploying highly interactive networked applications, customizing and integrating third party products, and creating customized software to suit our clients' individual needs where 'shrink-wrapped solutions' just won't work. Whether the application is to run on the Internet, in a client-server environment, or on a mainframe, CTL can build an application to put the information where it's most needed ... *within your reach."*

In 1983, *Dr. Bob* founded CTL, and he directed its growth to its present state. He is responsible for long range planning, major sales, and oversight of the operations management executives. Under his guidance, the firm increased its staff by a factor of five and increased its gross revenue by a factor of eight. Bob has a Bachelor of Arts in Political Science from California State University Northridge, Master of Arts in Public Administration from the University of Nebraska, and a Ph.D. in Public Administration from the University of Oregon. Bob often participates in the design of systems subsequently developed by CTL staffers. Internationally, he has designed port authority systems for the countries of Somalia and Colombia. Domestically, the Departments of Justice, Labor and Transportation have retained him in a consulting and training capacity. CTL is located in recently opened (2000) Advanced Technology Center that anchors the University of New Orleans Research and Technology Park.

During the feasibility study, Bob named four knowledge workers in his company to be interviewed during the process of identification and adaptation. *Susan* is Vice President for Administration at CTL. She is involved with the management and oversight of all CTL employee activities. In this capacity, she works closely with CTL clients to insure that customer expectations were at a realistic level and that they were met in a timely manner by the CTL staff. To accomplish this, Susan personally reviews the daily activities and accomplishments of each CTL team member, tracks project progress, and remains in direct contact with CTL customers. In addition to her routine project and staff management duties,

Susan is involved at the proposal stage of most CTL projects. In this capacity, she has assessed needs and performed workflow analyses for a number of CTL clients.

Another knowledge worker named by Bob is *Matt*, who is the Technical Manager at CTL. Matt reviews, approves, and assumes ultimate responsibility for all technology related decisions made at CTL. This requires him to be current on new technology and in constant contact with all the CTL technical employees. His management responsibilities also require him to routinely assess the needs of all clients to insure they are being met on the technical level. He tracks projects, and he is involved with trouble shooting and problem solving. Matt is a key contributor in the development of all proposals produced by CTL. He knows several programming languages, including Visual Basic, Access, SQL Windows, VB Script, ASP, and Java Script.

Michael is a Software Engineer at CTL, and he is responsible for the design and coding of application software, project management, and the integration of third-party software packages, software documentation, and software research and development. For the City of New Orleans, Division of Housing and Neighborhood Development, Michael is developing an integrated system to streamline and automate functions associated with rehabilitation projects, eligibility standards, and local reporting requirements.

Sharon is the Senior Systems Analyst at CTL, and she designs, implements, integrates, and supports projects for the CTL client base. As one of the most experienced CTL system engineers, she oversees and directs many of the software development projects undertaken by the company. In addition, Sharon provides technical support to all CTL clients. She is an experienced systems integrator with a special interest in mainframe environments. Susan began working for CTL primarily as a software developer on the PICK mainframe system, providing technical support and project design and implementation. Recently she completed three major project installations simultaneously on schedule and within budget.

6.1.2.2 DataSolve

DataSolve [FiRo03b; FiRK03], founded in 1991, is one of the largest software development companies in New Orleans, Louisiana, and it is one of the fastest growing software companies in the Gulf South region of the United States. DataSolve focuses its service offerings on software development, web development, and web hosting. It realizes the need for streamlining business offerings and for becoming specialists in the areas that best serve their clients. All of its developers are required to earn industry standard certifications in their development area, certifications such as MCSE+I, MCSD, MCP+Site Building, or MCDBA. The mission statement of DatsSolve is: "If you can imagine it, we can create it." DataSolve moved into the Advanced Technology Center in November 2000.

One DataSolve partner is *Bellwether Technology Corporation*, a ComputerLand affiliate founded in 1980. Bellwether Technology is based in New Orleans, and it services the southeastern United States. Its strong management team and core commitment to customer satisfaction have facilitated its stability in an industry governed by change. With over 50 certified system engineers and technicians supporting value-added services, Bellwether Technology provides consulting, project management, and outsourcing to maximize its customer technology investments. Supporting business, government, and education markets, Bellwether Technology is a single source provider for networking, Internet services, training and programming. It is owned, operated, and staffed with local talent, making customer satisfaction and company success very personal for each employee.

The feasibility study interview was held with *Keith*, who is the Chief Operating Officer (COO) at DataSolve. He named Will as a knowledge worker representative who does a great deal of programming. *Will* is a graduate of the University of New Orleans, and he has a Bachelor of Science degree in Computer Science. He also is a Certified Microsoft Systems Engineer, meaning that he passed Microsoft Operating tests and that he is a Microsoft Certified Database Administrator. Chief Technologist at DataSolve, Keith maintains the internal network and decides whether to use new programming languages or to keep or upgrade them.

6.1.2.3 Resurgence™ Software

Resurgence™ Software [FiRo03c; FiRK03] specializes in the development of software solutions for the maritime industry. Its unique and innovative software is designed specifically to help ship owners and operators achieve greater profits through improvement in reliability, availability, and maintenance strategies. The software and services help owners and operators meet the business and management challenges of an increasingly high tech industry. The goal at Resurgence™ is to provide ship owners and operators with the best information management and analysis tools possible. Resurgence™ Software was formed in September 2000 for the specific purpose of commercializing software developed for the RAM/Shipnet project by the University of New Orleans Gulf Coast Region Maritime Technology Center (GCRMTC) and the Ship Operations Cooperative Program (SOCP). The software was awarded to Resurgence™ for commercial completion, support, and marketing through the University of New Orleans Technology Transfer Program. The Wave™ Software System is a software and information network for the maritime industry. It enables shipping companies to capture equipment performance data in a standard format and structure, to analyze this data using standard reliability and profitability protocols, and to make benchmark comparisons of performance internally between ships and externally against industry standards.

Resurgence™ Software is a new spin off company from DataSolve, and it was selected in a competitive bid process by the University of New Orleans Office of Technology Transfer to commercialize the RAM/Shipnet software. The interviews were conducted with the president of Resurgence™ Software, *Tom*, and his partner *Dave* (Customer Service Manager). Both worked at DataSolve prior to their founding of Resurgence™ Software in 2000, the period of time being five years for Dave. Resurgence™ Software also is located in the Advanced Technology Center. The knowledge workers selected were Tom and Dave because the company only was founded a few months before the interviews, and they were its only knowledge workers. The process of employing new knowledge workers was ongoing, and it had not finished during the interview time. Moreover, the company had yet to establish a mission statement.

6.1.3 Data Collection

Each case study is based on three different kinds of evidence:

1. Documents provided by each company, e.g., balance sheets, organizational diagrams, job descriptions, product/service brochures, and so on;
2. Interviews conducted by the knowledge-engineers [FiRo03a; FiRo03b; FiRo03c];

3. Interview videotapes that enable the verification of data and that facilitate the creation of the multi-media CD-ROM [FiRK04].

6.1.3.1 Expert Interviews

The interviews with the CEO or president and the knowledge workers were similar because they were conducted in a specially equipped conference room in each company. This room only was available for the interviews and videotaping. Professor Friedrich Roithmayr, Chair of the Department of Information Systems at the University of Innsbruck, and I were the knowledge-engineers who conducted the interviews. Both knowledge-engineers had extensive experience and special training in the conduct of knowledge management interviews. According to Gillham, several interview dimensions can be distinguished as illustrated in Figure "The Verbal Data Dimension" [Gill00, p. 60].

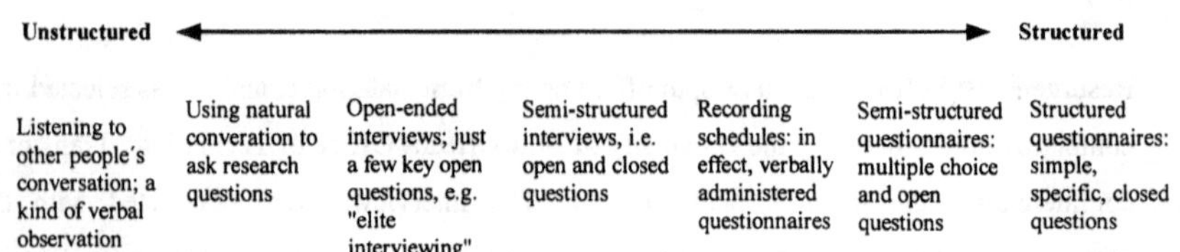
Unstructured
Structured
Listening to other people's conversation; a kind of verbal observation
Using natural converation to ask research questions
Open-ended interviews; just a few key open questions, e.g. "elite interviewing"
Semi-structured interviews, i.e. open and closed questions
Recording schedules: in effect, verbally administered questionnaires
Semi-structured questionnaires: multiple choice and open questions
Structured questionnaires: simple, specific, closed questions

Figure 29: The Verbal Data Dimension

All three case studies used what Gillham referred to as *"elite interviewing"*. This kind of interviewing is chosen to address someone in a special position or an expert. The CEO, the president, and all named knowledge workers are experts in their field of action. Gillham lists several characteristics of open-ended interviews [Gill00, p. 64]:

1. The respondents will know more about the topic and the setting than the interviewer. Sometimes they can even tell the interviewer what questions to ask.
2. By virtue of their authority and experience, they will have their own structuring of their knowledge. They will not allow an interview for which they have to answer a series of questions addressed at them.
3. The best thing the interviewer can hope for is a response to a topic raised.

4. The experts can be particularly informative about the location of documents, records, or other experts.
5. The experts will expect some control over the interviewer, and they also will demand a level of accountability and feedback.

These five characteristics of elite interviews also apply to the interview situation in the knowledge measurement process. Knowledge workers are highly experienced experts who want to articulate their knowledge in their own way. The questionnaires (Appendices A and B) are used as a guide for the knowledge-engineer to raise topics in each of the nine knowledge potential dimensions. In some cases, only a few questions had to be asked for the knowledge worker to continue talking about their special job, experiences, and future projects. Knowledge workers often gave many informative hints where to find other experts inside and outside the company. The face-to-face situation for the knowledge workers and knowledge-engineers enabled the knowledge-engineers to gather a great deal of knowledge about the experts necessary to accomplish the qualitative knowledge potential measurement process. At the conclusion of the interviews with all participants, the whole team - the CEO, president, knowledge-engineers, and knowledge workers - had a reflection session in which the key measurement results were presented, and even more importantly, discussed with each individual expert. The intention of the reflection process was to point out special knowledge strengths for each expert and to find solutions for knowledge dimensions on which the experts were weak. Finally, an action plan was developed for each expert in cooperation with the top management to reinforce the knowledge strengths and to improve weak rating scores on any of the nine dimensions.

The interview *transcription* took place right after the interview session was recorded on videotape. A native English speaker transcribed the recorded videotape in the first round. In the second round, the knowledge-engineers made corrections based on their specific knowledge and based on the videotapes made during the interviews.

The data were analyzed through *content analysis* [Hugl95] defined by Krippendorff [Krip80, p. 21] as "a research technique for making replicable and valid inferences from data to their context." Riffe et al. [RiLF98, p. 20] used a similar definition:

> *"Quantitative content analysis is the systematic and replicable examination of symbols of communication, which have been assigned numeric values according to valid measurement rules, and the analysis of relationships involving those values using statistical methods, in order to describe the communication, draw inferences about its meaning, or infer from the communication to its context, both of production and consumption."*

Hence, content analysis is a research tool used to determine the presence of certain words or concepts within texts or sets of texts. The combination of two *content forms* was used: (1) written communication in the form of the transcribed interviews; and (2) verbal communication in form of videotapes conducted by the knowledge-engineers with the knowledge workers during the interview sessions.

Riffe et al. [RiLF98, pp. 46] describe a general model for content analysis consisting of three processes:

1. *Conceptualization and purpose process* is concerned with the identification of the problem, the theory review, and the identification of specific research questions. For the knowledge measurement case studies, this stage focuses on the case selection process described in Chapter 6.1.2 and on the questionnaire design described in Chapter 5.3 and presented in Appendices A and B.
2. *The design process* is divided into several steps:
    a. *Definition of relevant content* is the issue concerned with the selection of relevant resources, in this case, videotapes [FiRK03], transcribed documents [FiRo03a; FiRo03b; FiRo03c], and other available material such job descriptions or organization diagrams.
    b. *Specification of formal design* refers to making the conceptualization process more specific and choosing the research settings and methods. The specification of the formal design, the knowledge potential measurement model, was achieved through the laboratory studies explained in Chapter 6.2.
    c. *Operationalization* is the process of moving from the conceptual level to the operational one by describing variables in terms of actual measurement procedures that coders can apply [RiLF98, pp. 50]. The content analysis

protocol or codebook is central because it explains how the variables in the study are to be measured and recorded on coding sheets or any other medium.

   d. *Pre-test process* is necessary for the correct formulation of the operational definitions and for training the coders in their use. Chapter 6.1.1 explains the pre-testing of the knowledge measurement framework and Chapter 6.2 explains the training of the students in the laboratory study.

3. *The data collection and analysis stages* cover the interview sessions conducted by knowledge-engineers. The data were collected by selected test groups of University of Innsbruck students who evaluated the knowledge potential measurement model in laboratory studies. Data analysis describes the case study research results examined in Chapter 6.2.

For every content analysis project, content must be reduced to measurement units [RiLF98, pp. 59]. There are two types of measurement units: (1) content units that are elements related to the meaning and production of content; and (2) study units that are elements of content selected and defined by the content analyst. Riffe et al. point out that content units and study units often are equivalent and that study units must be defined for every content analysis project. For the knowledge potential measurement case studies, sampling units are the three selected New Orleans companies; recording units are their knowledge workers; context units are the interview answers of knowledge workers for the nine measurement dimensions; and analysis units are the time periods needed by the knowledge-engineers for interview sessions and for videotaping each knowledge worker [FiRK04]. After the definition of units, numbers must be assigned [RiLF98, pp. 68] in the form of ordinal measurement scores [RiLF98, pp. 70]. Coding sheets allow knowledge-engineers (coders) to assign numbers to the content [Fink03]. The measurement process includes the identification of appropriate recording units, context units, analysis units, and the assignment of numbers to the content.

6.1.3.2 Videotaping

The interviewer sessions were characterized by a high degree of complex information because the knowledge workers communicated a lot of information about their personal experiences and skills. Each interview session was videotaped to accomplish a data analysis of high quality. The data collection by videotape enables the knowledge-engineers to evaluate each expert during the knowledge measurement process. For Summerfield [Summ83, pp. 7], videotaping in a controlled setting requires a special room prepared for that special purpose. The room should be quite, reflect little light, and free from confusing and intrusive visual details. In all three case studies conducted, a special room was assigned for the sole purpose of the knowledge interviews. All research subjects were shown the recording equipment before the session. The knowledge-engineers used a remote control to start, interrupt, and end the recording so they would not disturb the social setting. The videotaping had three applied purposes:

1. Help the knowledge-engineers in their knowledge measurement process for each named expert.
2. Design a multimedia CD-ROM [FiRK04] for the purpose of training students to evaluate knowledge workers and teaching them how to implement a knowledge organization.
3. Establishment of laboratory studies at the University of Innsbruck for an evaluation of the knowledge measurement model (see Chapter 6.2).

Maxwell and Pringle [MaPr83, pp. 33] point out that the use of videotaping has added a new dimension to the study of human behavior because of the considerable advantages of increased measurement reliability and validity. Through videotaping, the measurement is not limited to what is occurring in the real-time interview situation and to the number of observers. More importantly, measurement reliability can be increased through videotaping because the "ability to replay all or parts of a recorded [interview] makes it possible to develop scoring techniques that are highly reliable and to ensure that this is maintained throughout rating procedures" [MaPr83, p. 36]. Videotaping helped reduce the unreliability caused by knowledge-engineer fatigue during lengthy interview sessions. This source of unreliability also is the reason why the interviews always were conducted by two knowledge-engineers. During the pre-test, it became obvious that the interviews had to be conducted by two trained knowledge-engineers to ensure a standard interviewer session. Another source of unreliability is inexperience with the use of the technical equipment. Therefore, both knowledge-engineers were trained in advance in the use of video equipment and in the efficient and effective administration of the videotaping.

All interviews were recorded by the knowledge-engineers themselves without the support of a technician unfamiliar with the knowledge potential view. Analysis of the collected data was facilitated by the ability to replay the videotapes, the use of transcribed interviews, and the application of content analysis. Maxwell and Pringle [MaPr83, p. 43] note the benefit of videotaping as a research method for very complex situations with subtle behavior changes. With respect to the knowledge potential view, the situation is very complex for the knowledge-engineers and the experts. The quality of measurement for each knowledge worker by the knowledge-engineer is improved by videotaping because the ability to replay the interviews leads to a more accurate rating for each of the nine dimensions on the knowledge scale.

6.2 Data Analysis

"A little knowledge that acts is worth infinitely more than much knowledge that is idle."
(Khalil Gibran)

6.2.1 Evaluation of the Knowledge Measurement Model

Two experimental groups evaluated the nine-dimension measurement model [Fink03]. The role of the participants was analogous to that of knowledge-engineers. The objective of the evaluation process was to test the knowledge measurement model. The two groups were:

- **Experimental Group #1**: The participants in this group were Master of Business Administration students participating in the course, "Knowledge Management and Engineering," taught in the Department of Information Systems at the University of Innsbruck in the Spring (Summer) 2002 term, and Experimental Group #1 consisted of 12 students (N=12).
- **Experimental Group #2**: The participants in this group were Master of Business Administration students participating in the course, "Knowledge Management and Engineering," taught in the Department of Information Systems at the University of Innsbruck in the Fall (Winter) 2002 term, and Experimental Group #2 consisted of 16 students (N=16).

Those who participated in the evaluation process can be considered typical students who are familiar with knowledge management and measurement. The course instructors taught them the theoretical concepts, methodologies, and methods of knowledge measurement. It is a required course for students majoring in information systems. The course instructors, Friedrich Roithmayr and Kerstin Fink, trained the participants in the subject of knowledge measurement. Due to the complexity of knowledge management and its measurement methods, the instructors gave both experimental groups three full days of training in advance of the evaluation process. Furthermore, the instructors coordinated the evaluation studies. Consequently, the preparation provided the students with the same level of information about the knowledge measurement and its procedures.

Both experimental groups worked with identical instructional material in the same laboratory setting - the Department of Information Systems workshop room at the University of Innsbruck. The study was a workshop of five full days in which each expert was measured according to the knowledge measurement model. It took place in a controlled environment where both experimental groups had the same requirements and theoretical input. There was minimal confounding from external variables because of the controlled laboratory setting necessary to assess the validity of the knowledge measurement model. Both experimental groups were asked to measure each CTL, DataSolve, and Resurgence™ knowledge worker.

The collected data - videotapes and the transcribed documents [FiRo03a; FiRo03b; FiRo03c] - were given to each student on a Knowledge Measurement CD-ROM [FiRK04]. Each student also received an Excel-spreadsheet with the nine variables in rows and the knowledge workers (KW) in columns to record the measurement scores and a Word-document to record explanations for their scores. The tasks of the students (knowledge-engineers) were completing the spreadsheet and making detailed comments in the Word-document. The analysis method was content analysis. Table "CTL Measurement Results of Experimental Group #1" presents the measurement results for CTL by the members of Group #1; Table "CTL Measurement Results of Experimental Group #2" presents the results by members of Group #2.

Experimental Group #1						
KW	Excellent KW	Good KW	Undefined KW	Standard KW	Poor KW	
Bob	1	3	7	1	-	12
Matt	2	6	4	-	-	12
Michael	4	6	2	-	-	12
Sharon	-	1	3	6	2	12
Susan	3	5	4	-		12
Sum	10	21	20	7	2	60

KW	Excellent KW	Good KW	Undefined KW	Standard KW	Poor KW	
Bob	8.33%	25.00%	58.33%	8.33%	0.00%	100.00%
Matt	16.67%	50.00%	33.33%	0.00%	0.00%	100.00%
Michael	33.33%	50.00%	16.67%	0.00%	0.00%	100.00%
Sharon	0.00%	8.33%	25.00%	50.00%	16.67%	100.00%
Susan	25.00%	41.67%	33.33%	0.00%	0.00%	100.00%
Percentage	16.67%	35.00%	33.33%	11.67%	3.33%	100.00%

Table 21: CTL Measurement Results of Experimental Group #1

Experimental Group #2						
KW	Excellent KW	Good KW	Undefined KW	Standard KW	Poor KW	
Bob	-	5	7	4	-	16
Matt	3	8	5	-	-	16
Michael	5	6	5	-	-	16
Sharon	-	1	5	9	1	16
Susan	5	6	5	-	-	16
Sum	13	26	27	13	1	80

KW	Excellent KW	Good KW	Undefined KW	Standard KW	Poor KW	
Bob	0.00%	31.25%	43.75%	25.00%	0.00%	100.00%
Matt	18.75%	50.00%	31.25%	0.00%	0.00%	100.00%
Michael	31.25%	37.50%	31.25%	0.00%	0.00%	100.00%
Sharon	0.00%	6.25%	31.25%	56.25%	6.25%	100.00%
Susan	31.25%	37.50%	31.25%	0.00%	0.00%	100.00%
Percentage	16.25%	32.50%	33.75%	16.25%	1.25%	100.00%

Table 22: CTL Measurement Results of Experimental Group #2

From Tables “CTL Measurement Results of Experimental Group #1” and ““CTL Measurement Results of Experimental Group #2”, the results of the evaluation process of the knowledge measurement model differ slightly from Experimental Group #1 to Experimental Group #2. The evaluation of the same measurement object by different knowledge-engineers was only possible because of the laboratory study. The knowledge measurement model was verified as seen from the results presented in the evaluation tables ("CTL Measurement Results of Experimental Group #1" and "CTL Measurement Results of Experimental Group #2"). The same evaluation process was conducted for the DataSolve and Resurgence™ case studies. The DataSolve results were similar to those for CTL, showing only slight differences in the evaluation process (see Table "DataSolve Measurement Results of Experimental Group #1"; Table "DataSolve Measurement Results of Experimental Group #2"; Table "Resurgence™ Measurement Results of Experimental Group #1"; and Table "Resurgence™ Measurement Results of Experimental Group #2").

In the three case studies, both experimental groups came to near identical measurement results. The implications of these findings are that organizations can use the knowledge measurement model to measure the knowledge potential of each of their experts and to calculate the uncertainty of the knowledge-engineers, leading to a more objective measurement result. The laboratory study contributed to the following theoretical implication: the developed knowledge measurement model applied in the research setting could be used by different kinds of organizations in various industries to evaluate their employees, especially their knowledge workers. The measurement of the knowledge of their experts will become more and more important for organizations to improve decision making at both the individual and the organizational levels. The knowledge measurement model will enable organizations to achieve this goal because it can be applied to all kinds of knowledge processes. Moreover, the knowledge measurement model proved to be a useful approach for facilitating the evaluation of knowledge workers.

Experimental Group #1				
KW	**Excellent KW**	**Good KW**	**Undefined KW**	
Keith	2	8	2	12
Will	6	4	2	12
Sum	8	12	4	24

KW	Excellent KW	Good KW	Undefined KW	
Keith	16.67%	66.67%	16.67%	100.00%
Will	50.00%	33.33%	16.67%	100.00%
Percentage	33.33%	50.00%	16.67%	100.00%

Table 23: DataSolve Measurement Results of Experimental Group #1

Experimental Group #2				
KW	**Excellent KW**	**Good KW**	**Undefined KW**	
Keith	3	10	3	16
Will	7	7	2	16
Sum	10	17	5	32

KW	Excellent KW	Good KW	Undefined KW	
Keith	18.75%	62.50%	18.75%	100.00%
Will	43.75%	43.75%	12.50%	100.00%
Percentage	31.25%	53.13%	15.63%	100.00%

Table 24: DataSolve Measurement Results of Experimental Group #2

Experimental Group #1					
KW	**Excellent KW**	**Good KW**	**Undefined KW**	**Standard KW**	
Dave	1	7	2	2	12
Tom	3	5	4	-	12
Sum	4	12	6	2	24

KW	Excellent KW	Good KW	Undefined KW	Standard KW	
Dave	8.33%	58.33%	16.67%	16.67%	100.00%
Tom	25.00%	41.67%	33.33%	0.00%	100.00%
Percentage	16.67%	50.00%	25.00%	8.33%	100.00%

Table 25: Resurgence™ Measurement Results of Experimental Group #1

Experimental Group #2					
KW	**Excellent KW**	**Good KW**	**Undefined KW**	**Standard KW**	
Dave	1	11	2	2	16
Tom	4	7	5	-	16
Sum	5	18	7	2	32

KW	Excellent KW	Good KW	Undefined KW	Standard KW	
Dave	6.25%	68.75%	12.50%	12.50%	100.00%
Tom	25.00%	43.75%	31.25%	0.00%	100.00%
Percentage	15.63%	56.25%	21.88%	6.25%	100.00%

Table 26: Resurgence™ Measurement Results of Experimental Group #2

The laboratory setting was important because it facilitated a general evaluation of the knowledge measurement model. Without the case studies, it was not possible to test the knowledge potential view in real-life study situations. The findings of the laboratory study confirm the results obtained by the original knowledge-engineers, Roithmayr and Fink, who conducted the three case studies. Since both experimental groups arrived at nearly identical measurement results for each knowledge worker, one can conclude that the knowledge measurement model is appropriate for the measurement of experts.

A *second objective of the laboratory study* was the measurement of the knowledge momentum and the position uncertainty for each knowledge-engineer in each experimental group (see Table "Uncertainties of Knowledge-Engineers for Experimental Group #1 for CTL" and Table "Uncertainties of Knowledge-Engineers for Experimental Group #2 for CTL"). Each knowledge-engineer evaluated the knowledge workers, including the CEO and president, on the nine dimensions and on the velocity (quickness) of problem solving for each expert. This process enables one to measure the uncertainty for knowledge momentum and knowledge position for each knowledge-engineer. The original Uncertainty Principle from Heisenberg stated that the more precisely the position is determined, the less precisely the momentum is known and *vice versa*. The analysis of the uncertainty tables for the knowledge-engineers in each experimental group reveals that knowledge position uncertainty is higher if the knowledge momentum uncertainty is low and *vice versa*. However, there is the exception that both uncertainty factors do not vary significantly, for example KE1_1 has a knowledge momentum uncertainty of 0.64 and a knowledge position uncertainty of 0.61.

The laboratory study facilitated an exploration of the relationship between the knowledge momentum and the position uncertainty of the knowledge-engineers. This means that position uncertainty is significantly higher if the momentum uncertainty is low. The implication of this laboratory study can be reformulated into the following hypothesis concerning the uncertainty relationships:

> H1: The lower the knowledge momentum uncertainty calculation is for a knowledge-engineer, the higher the knowledge position uncertainty is for this specific knowledge-engineer, and *vice versa*.

For the DataSolve and Resurgence™ case studies, the uncertainties of momentum and position for each knowledge-engineer in each experimental group were calculated. The results reinforce the formulated hypothesis. Moreover, case studies were completed for

MLP Innsbruck [FiRo03d] and UBS Zurich [FiRo03e], and the measurement process is in the beginning stages. Its ultimate objective is to test the measurement model and the uncertainty hypothesis.

Experimental Group #1	Uncertainty	
Knowledge-Engineer	Knowledge Momentum	Knowledge Position
KE1_1	0.64	0.61
KE2_1	0.42	0.54
KE3_1	0.38	1.01
KE4_1	0.18	0.43
KE5_1	0.81	1.05
KE6_1	0.70	0.81
KE7_1	1.30	1.25
KE8_1	0.31	0.56
KE9_1	0.32	0.28
KE10_1	0.47	0.93
KE11_1	0.70	0.25
KE12_1	0.41	1.08

Table 27: Uncertainties of Knowledge-Engineers for Experimental Group #1 for CTL

Experimental Group #2	Uncertainty	
Knowledge-Engineer	Knowledge Momentum	Knowledge Position
KE1_2	0.55	0.46
KE2_2	0.14	0.26
KE3_2	0.82	0.36
KE4_2	0.48	0.54
KE5_2	0.34	0.45
KE6_2	0.56	0.63
KE7_2	0.59	0.45
KE8_2	0.70	0.64
KE9_2	0.83	0.54
KE10_2	1.03	0.43
KE11_2	0.67	0.45
KE12_2	0.71	1.17
KE13_2	0.34	0.95
KE14_2	0.82	0.54
KE15_2	0.93	1.43
KE16_2	0.98	0.91

Table 28: Uncertainties of Knowledge-Engineers for Experimental Group #2 for CTL

6.2.2 Evaluation Process of CTL

The last step in the knowledge measurement process is concerned with the evaluation of the experts and with the assignment of each knowledge worker to one of the five classifications on the knowledge rating scale. Table "Final Evaluation of CTL by Experimental Group #1" and Table "Final Evaluation of CTL by Experimental Group #2" summarize the survey results.

Knowledge Worker	Bob	Matt	Michael	Sharon	Susan
Median	8.12	6.14	5.88	10.50	7.14
Final Rating of KW	Undefined KW	Good KW	Good KW	Standard KW	Good KW

Table 29: Final Evaluation of CTL by Experimental Group #1

Knowledge Worker	Bob	Matt	Michael	Sharon	Susan
Median	8.13	6.38	7.02	10.58	6.46
Final Rating of KW	Undefined KW	Good KW	Good KW	Standard KW	Good KW

Table 30: Final Evaluation of CTL by Experimental Group #2

The statistical score of the *median* was selected to calculate the final knowledge potential value for each knowledge-worker including CTL CEO, Bob. The median [HoCr03, pp. 23] is the middle score of a set if they are organized from the smallest to the largest. Experimental Groups #1 and #2 came to the same results. Bob is evaluated as an undefined knowledge worker. The reasons for his weak rating are: median scores (3) for the four knowledge mass variables, e.g., for the "learning" dimension because CTL does not have sufficient training opportunities available for its employees or for the "networking" dimension because partnering with other companies was not common for CTL. Furthermore, bad (4) to very bad (5) scores were earned for the "culture" and "organizational structure" dimensions because CTL did not have a common understanding of the organizational culture and a well designed structure. Bob, the CTL owner or "big boss," did not tolerate any assistance, and he did not delegate management tasks to middle management, i.e., Susan and Matt. On the other hand, he had excellent (1) to good (2) scores for knowledge velocity and customer satisfaction.

Of the four named experts, 75 percent are good knowledge workers (Matt, Michael, and Susan), and Sharon is classified as a standard expert (25%). The knowledge potential value of 5.88 for Michael indicates that he can become an excellent knowledge worker. Susan's score of 7.14 is on the border for classifying her as an undefined knowledge worker. She has to improve her experience and value to CTL for her to retain good knowledge potential value. Figure "CTL Knowledge Worker Structure" symbolizes the CTL knowledge worker distribution (including the CEO Bob), and it shows that CTL is built on a large number of good knowledge workers who will increase the company's likelihood for solid future development.

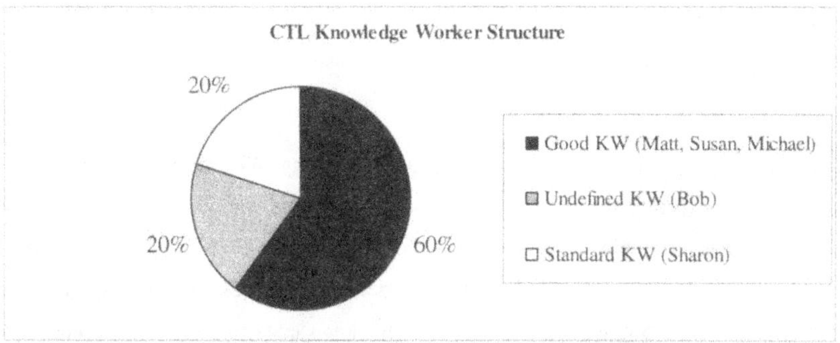

Figure 30: CTL Knowledge Worker Structure

The change process was based on the measurement results began in October 2002. CTL changed its name to Solutient to establish a new identity. For Bob, the new brand identity is enterprise collaboration, showing that Solutient is providing business solutions that enable internal and external people to share ideas, information, processes, and applications. Solutient primarily focuses on enterprise collaboration, including enterprise content management (ECM), enterprise application integration (EAI), business process management (BPM), and collaborate commerce. It also changed its organizational structure by investing in additional staff and by recruiting a Director of Business Development.

6.2.3 Evaluation Process of DataSolve

The same evaluation process described for CTL, was used for DataSolve. Each experimental group evaluated DataSolve knowledge workers according to the knowledge potential model. The Table "Final Evaluation of DataSolve by Experimental Group #1" and Table "Final Evaluation of DataSolve by Experimental Group #2" show the measurement results for each knowledge worker.

Knowledge Worker	Keith	Will
Median	6.11	5.86
Final Rating of KW	Good KW	Good KW

Table 31: Final Evaluation of DataSolve by Experimental Group #1

Knowledge Worker	Keith	Will
Median	6.08	5.90
Final Rating of KW	Good KW	Good KW

Table 32: Final Evaluation of DataSolve by Experimental Group #2

DataSolve CEO Keith has a good knowledge potential rating. Will, the representative of the programming experts also is classified as a good knowledge worker, and he can work on keeping or even improving his rating. Both knowledge workers had very good (1) to good (2) scores for knowledge mass and good (2) to medium (3) scores for knowledge velocity. This means, the person-dependent variables of the knowledge workers resulted in a good rating classification. Furthermore, the system-dependent variables showed primarily median scores (3) with the exception of the culture dimension that was rated as good (2). Learning, networking, organizational culture, and structure are important variables for DataSolve, and they also are communicated to employees who resemble its good knowledge classification. Also, for DataSolve, both experimental groups had nearly identical measurement results, an indication that the measurement model verification.

6.2.4 Evaluation Process of Resurgence™

The last case study was the DataSolve spin-off company, Resurgence™. The evaluation process was the same as it was for CTL and DataSolve. Table "Final Evaluation of Resurgence™ by Experimental Group #1" and Table "Final Evaluation of Resurgence™ by Experimental Group #2" display the knowledge worker measurement for Dave and Tom. The survey results show that both experimental groups came to the some evaluation classification for Dave and Tom.

Knowledge Worker	Dave	Tom
Median	6.88	7.10
Final Rating KW	Good KW	Good KW

Table 33: Final Evaluation of Resurgence™ by Experimental Group #1

Knowledge Worker	Dave	Tom
Median	6.83	7.38
Final Rating of KW	Good KW	Good KW

Table 34: Final Evaluation of Resurgence™ by Experimental Group #2

Both experts were classified with a good knowledge potential rating, but they have great potential for improving their rating and becoming excellent experts. Since the company was founded immediately before the interview sessions, most of the knowledge position variables have a lot of room for improvement, e.g., building partnerships, building networks, and implementing a knowledge management system. The evidence for good person-dependent scores is their special knowledge skills in the maritime sector, their excellent training, their deep understanding of the general business idea of Resurgence™, and their reliance on a good network structure with DataSolve programmers and with the knowledge competence of the University of New Orleans.

In the last two year, Resurgence™ focused primarily on the improvement *of the knowledge position variables*. On the culture dimension, Resurgence™ has formulated a mission statement: "At Resurgence™, we have dedicated ourselves to helping our customers increase their equipment reliability and operational safety while at the same time lowering costs and increasing profits. Our software and services are designed to provide maritime operators with the information they need for making critical equipment maintenance and procurement decisions." Therefore, the company is improving by communicating its mission statement not only to its own employees but also to its customers and partners. A further improvement is its organizational structure. The Resurgence™ Software Executive Team was founded, not only consisting of Tom as the President and Dave as the Vice-President for Customer Service, but also by the establishment of the positions of Chief Scientist, Vice-President for Business Development, and Vice-President for Product Development. Since Resurgence™ remains a growing company in a dynamic market, it is constantly searching for new skilled knowledge workers. The company has a strategy for increasing improvement on the system-dependent variables.

Additionally, the person-dependent variable, "networking," is a foundation for the constant improvement. Resurgence™ has instituted four partnership programs:

- Software Alliance Partnerships: this program is available to independent software vendors who wish to integrate their software with the Wave™ Software System.
- Strategic Alliance Partnerships: this program is reserved for maritime industry leaders who have a strong commitment to the success of their owner/operator customers. These partners are in a position to help its software users generate significant positive results.
- Certified Marketing Partnerships: this program is available for companies interested in reselling the Wave™ Software System.
- Certified Consulting Partnerships: this program is available for established reliable consulting companies interested in integrating Wave™ Software System expertise into their service offerings. Certified Consulting Partners are expected to help subscribers turn the equipment failure data gathered through the Wave™ Software System into a formal reliability program.

On January 1, 2003, Resurgence™ announced the formation of a software marketing agreement with Lloyd's Register which plans to make the New Orleans-based software vendor's Wave™ tool a key part of its risk and reliability offering to the marine industry. From the first measurement secession in 2000 until today, Resurgence™ constantly improved its measurement results for the person-dependent and for the system-dependent variables. This process is ongoing, and it will be extended in the future. The current measurement results for Tom and Dave show a tendency for excellent knowledge worker classifications.

The theoretical knowledge measurement model was evaluated through case studies. The results indicate that the theoretical measurement model is verified and that the classification of knowledge workers is possible. Furthermore, the uncertainty calculation for knowledge momentum and knowledge position enabled the formulation of a hypothesis that indicates relationships similar to those formulated in the Heisenberg Uncertainty Principle. The uncertainties for knowledge momentum and position make it possible to take interviewer biases into account in the classification of knowledge workers. The two uncertainties represent the individual and unique perspectives of raters compared to other knowledge-engineers.

7 Key Research Results and Future Research Fields

"They copied all that they could follow
but they could not copy my mind,
and I left 'em sweating and stealing
and a year and a half behind."
(Rudyard Kipling)

My objective in writing this book was the introduction of a different view of the development of a knowledge potential measurement system for organizations and their employees. The mere recognition of a new knowledge potential view is not enough. The key challenge is the transformation of traditional measurement systems into ones that focus on the skills of knowledge workers. A nine-dimension knowledge measurement system was offered for uncertainty factors. The future competitive advantage for knowledge organizations is more than the manifest experiences, skills, and attitudes of their respective experts. The knowledge potential view identifies the knowledge of an organization and determines its knowledge variables which are a combination of person-dependent and system-dependent variables. Factors that either prohibit or promote future knowledge growth or transfer can be identified and linked to an effective and improved knowledge strategy. Situations characterized by high levels of expert knowledge and by high levels of knowledge uncertainty demand a measurement system that provides information about its current knowledge potential and about its future knowledge potential development (see Figure "Research Area" in Chapter 1).

The *case studies* described earlier show the value of the knowledge potential measurement model. The calculated knowledge momentum and knowledge position uncertainties resemble the bias of the individual knowledge-engineer in interview sessions. Therefore, once the uncertainties are calculated, the experienced knowledge-engineer can function autonomously as a knowledge interviewer. Their uncertainties are taken into consideration during each measurement process, and they do not have to be determined every time a measurement process is ongoing. Knowledge uncertainties have advantages (e.g., for consulting companies) because they can be taken into consideration for each consulting project once the interviewer biases are known, and the output can be corrected by the uncertainty factors.

Furthermore, the experienced knowledge-engineer can train new inexperienced knowledge-engineers by showing them how the nine-dimension knowledge measurement process affects knowledge workers. The importance of interviewer training is that it guarantees respondent answers of a higher level of quality, and they translate into a higher level of the quality for the knowledge measurement process. The calculation of interviewer errors (uncertainties) is necessary to control the knowledge measurement process. The ideal design has a minimum of *two knowledge-engineers* to conduct interviews with the knowledge workers. The case studies, moreover, revealed that the presence of two knowledge-engineers had a great impact on the quality of the interviewer sessions and on the answers of the experts because of the reduction of interviewer biases such as fatigue during a long interview, the reformulation of questions, and the use of the video and technical equipment.

Alternatively, a company must balance the additional cost of using two knowledge-engineers instead of one and the advantage of a more precise and higher quality measurement result. A team of two knowledge-engineers can accomplish two goals simultaneously: the establishment of a comfortable communication relationship between the interviewers and respondents and the reduction in the time necessary for reporting and accurately recording interview responses by defining specific tasks for each knowledge-engineer. The effect of interviewer style on knowledge workers minimizes interviewer error.

Additionally, the presence of two knowledge-engineers enables them to use Schön's *reflection theory* [Schö82]. Schön distinguishes two reflection processes: (1) *reflection-in-action* which concerns reflection about actions during the process, i.e., spontaneous actions, recognitions, and judgments; and (2) *reflection-on-action* which concerns reflection about actions which already took place. In the context of knowledge measurement, it means that the two knowledge-engineers reflect-in-action at the time of the interviewer sessions with the knowledge workers. The two knowledge-engineers reflect-on-action when they communicate their views about rating knowledge momentum and knowledge position after the interview sessions. The discussion results in an agreement on a rating score on the nine knowledge variables. Moreover, the final rating of each knowledge worker is discussed with top company management to develop an action plan for the improvement and reenforcement of the nine knowledge variables. With respect to the laboratory studies, the instructors took the role of company top management, and they reflected-on-action with their students about the action programs developed for CTL, DataSolve, and Resurgence™.

The knowledge potential measurement system permits the evaluation and classification of knowledge workers and the calculation of uncertainty factors. Building on the case study results, *one practical implication* is the use of a knowledge-engineer team to improve the decision making process for the knowledge potential view. A *second practical implication* is the use of multimedia technologies to enhance the quality of the knowledge measurement process. The face-to-face communication with knowledge workers coupled with the audio-visual based communication improves the ability for decision making and the quality of the measurement results.

The knowledge measurement model enables the calculation of a single knowledge potential value for a knowledge worker. Future case studies need to develop and test knowledge potential measurement model *aggregation*, e.g.

- Aggregation on the team level;
- Aggregation on the department level; and
- Aggregation on the organization level.

Knowledge potential measurement is not limited to a single knowledge worker. Rather, it can be applied to more complex organizational structures. The knowledge potential measurement model is characterized by a high level of *flexibility*, and it can be applied to different industries (e.g., the government sector, consulting companies, or banks) and to different organizational structures (e.g., teams, departments, and so on).

Another future research field is the assignment of *monetary values* to the knowledge potential of knowledge workers, teams, departments, and a company. The key question is formulated as follows: What is the knowledge potential of an organization and its corresponding monetary value? The proper measurement of the knowledge potential of a knowledge organization can contribute to a competitive advantage through information about the knowledge value of the organization. This information can be useful for *merger and acquisition* deals because each organization can compare its monetary value with the other one in making buy or sell decisions. Organizations must transform knowledge into value to remain competitive. For example, the value of the creative skills used in research and development departments can be determined by transforming the output of the knowledge potential measurement model into a monetary value.

The knowledge potential measurement model attempts to quantify, measure, and describe human knowledge quanta in organizations and to give managers a tool to recognize the strengths and weaknesses of business processes and areas. This process leads to improvement in knowledge quanta and to constant learning loops to acquire new knowledge (Figure "Knowledge Potential Value Spiral"). If organizations are serious about making knowledge measurement a priority objective, they have to consider and analyze the balance between traditional financial measures and new human-resource based measures. The organization will gain competitive advantages only by changing the interaction between both measurement systems.

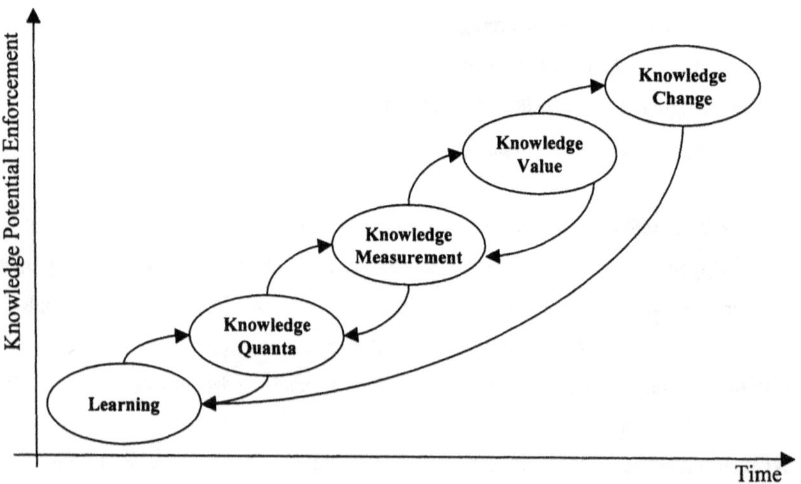

Figure 31: Knowledge Potential Value Spiral

A third question worth pursuing is the impact of *weight factors* on the quality of the knowledge measurement model. One extension of the knowledge potential measurement model is through the introduction of *weight factors for each knowledge variable.* This process leads to a specification of the nine-dimension measurement model because each company can assign weight factors to each knowledge variable, depending on the importance of each variable to the company. This measurement refinement has the advantage of taking company specific factors into consideration, e.g., knowledge worker networking skills are more important than cultural influences or the impact of competitors has more weight than the impact of customers. Another extension of the knowledge potential measurement model is the use of *weight factors for knowledge mass, knowledge velocity, knowledge momentum, and knowledge position*. To distinguish it from the first refinement, the summed values for the four variables are weighted instead of the nine single values.

Future research also should examine *reliability tests*. McClave and Sincich [McSi03, p. 8] define reliability as "a statement (usually quantified) about the degree of uncertainty associated with a statistical inference". Thus, theories of test reliability estimate the effect of inconsistency on the accuracy of psychological measurement. For Murphy and Davidshofer [MuDa01, pp. 111], the objectives of reliability theory are the estimation of measurement error and the improvement in error minimization. This means that future research should focus on reliability tests to accomplish better knowledge measurement error estimation. The hypothesis test formulated in Chapter 6.2.1 is done through the use of additional case studies like those done for MLP Innsbruck [FiRo03d] and UBS Zurich [FiRo03e].

An additional area for future research is the development of a *software tool* that supports the knowledge architecture, the knowledge potential measurement model, and the uncertainty calculation for knowledge-engineers. Content analysis of the interviews conducted is a highly complex task. Therefore, the *knowledge-based systems* research field provides sources for support of the knowledge potential measurement model. The knowledge-engineers can be aided with an expert system that helps reduce the complexity of content analysis and the data analysis process. Also, memory and natural language processing (NLP) research deals with the need for knowledge representation [IwSh00] and the development of semantic networks. Negnevitsky [Negn02, p. 257], for example, emphasizes the need for hybrid intelligent systems that combine different intelligent technologies [SaAN02] such as probabilistic reasoning, fuzzy logic, neural networks, and evolutionary computation. The combination of a *neural network* with *fuzzy systems* results in a neural-fuzzy system [Negn02, pp. 266] which could be used for the knowledge potential measurement model because the combination enables parallel computation and learning abilities of neural networks with the human-like representation and the explanation abilities of fuzzy systems. The field of computational intelligence (see Chapter 2.1.5) offers a variety of research areas that can be taken into consideration for knowledge potential and uncertainty measurement, especially expert, neural, and fuzzy systems that handle the uncertainty and ambiguity of human knowledge.

In the knowledge society era where the power of an organization and of a nation lies primarily in the skills and competencies of knowledge workers, intelligent systems are required to capture the expertise of knowledgeable persons and to reason under uncertain conditions similar to those of humans. The transformation of the individual knowledge of experts into measurable knowledge quanta can be supported by intelligent systems, thus improving the knowledge potential measurement process for the knowledge-engineers. Intelligent technologies such as expert, neural, fuzzy systems, or intelligent agents re-enforce and support the knowledge potential measurement process and its quality.

Appendices

Appendix A: Questionnaire for the Head of the Company

A1: Content

1. What is your **personal understanding of knowledge**? What is the difference between the term knowledge and information?
2. What are essential skills a knowledge worker **must** have? What are the skills a knowledge worker **should** have?
3. What is the importance of social competence, methodical competence, and professional competence?
4. What are the **consequences** for the company if the mentioned knowledge/skills are not available?

A2: Culture

5. What is the **mission** statement of the company?
6. Do you have written **guiding principles** of the department/company? Can you give them to us?
7. Are your knowledge workers **open-minded** to new ideas or do they stick to the traditional working processes?

A3: Networking

8. Do you have a **strategic knowledge network** with other partners, like suppliers, the government, environmental groups, lobby groups, the community, or the university? (What kind of relationships with partners outside the company are relevant?)
9. Do you have an overview of the **knowledge flow inside the department or company**? This is, do you know which knowledge worker communicates with another knowledge worker? Could you draw a **map of the communication** of your department? Do these communication processes differ depending on the problem?
10. How is a problem being solved? Do you work in **teams** or does everybody work individually?
11. Is team work **skill-based** or tasked-based?

A4: Organizational Structure

12. Can you identify and describe the **present knowledge areas/processes** of the department/company? (Which are the key processes for serving the customer?)
13. Can you specify the **future knowledge** areas/processes of the department/company?
14. What kind of **organizational structure** do you have (hierarchical, process oriented, or top down co-ordination)?
15. Are you organized by **functional** departments or by customer opportunity teams?
16. Over the last 10 years, was the **organization stable**? Did you have constantly changing organizational structures?

A5: Skills of Knowledge Worker

17. Can you give me a **definition of a knowledge** worker?
18. What **characteristics** must a knowledge worker have?
19. Could you **name the knowledge workers** for your department/company?
20. As the head of the department, could you generally **describe the individual knowledge** of the named knowledge workers? Can you identify the three most important skills?
21. We have prepared a portfolio for you. Can you position the knowledge workers in the **portfolio**?
22. What is your company doing to **keep the knowledge worker** from changing jobs? Do you have any idea of the knowledge worker fluctuation rate?
23. You also need **supportive staff** in the department. Could you name them and do they have any possibility for future personal development? What is the ratio knowledge worker to supportive staff?
24. In the future, what kind of workers would you prefer: The **multi-skilled** workers or the single skilled workers? Is it more important to train the staff for solving general problems or specific problems (Generalization or Specification)?
25. Do you have a **description** of job skills? Do you have a **knowledge profile** stating requirements for each position?
26. To accomplish your future work/processes/projects what kind of **future** knowledge worker do you need?
27. What **knowledge** is required from the future knowledge workers?

A6: Learning and Experience

28. How do you **motivate** appropriately skilled and knowledgeable staff?
29. Is the **competence** of these knowledge workers constantly **growing**? Are they taking part in training programs?
30. Do you have special **training** programs for knowledge workers?
31. Do you also give the **"supportive staff"** training possibilities in order to improve their internal position?

A7: Competitors

32. Let's look at the **market position** of the department/company. What is the direction of development? Are there any problems? Do you plan future mergers and acquisitions?
33. What are the **key competitors**? Can you name them, and the knowledge area that is affecting your business?
34. What are **your future competitors**?
35. Are you **benchmarking** your company?

A8: Customers

36. How would you characterize the **products** you sell? Are they knowledge intensive?
37. Are there any plans for **new future products/services**? Do your customers have individual ideas about future knowledge areas/processes?
38. Who/what are your **key customers**?
39. Do you have any internal indicators to **measure** the impact of your business on the customer's business, e.g., cost deduction, faster delivery, image improvement?
40. Do you attract **new customers** in new markets or in existing markets?

A9: I&CT and Knowledge Management Systems (KMS)

41. Is your company already implementing **knowledge management tools** or are there any plans to do so? If yes, what is your experience with the knowledge management tools? Did you buy a standard knowledge management tool or did you implement an

individual knowledge management tool? How does knowledge management play a part in the performance of a solution?

42. Do you have a **database** where all information about the skills of knowledge workers is monitored and where you can see the knowledge transfer processes?
43. Are there any platforms for **knowledge sharing**, e.g., chat rooms, information document systems, retrieval systems, and regular meetings?

Appendix B: Questionnaire for the Knowledge Workers

B1: Content (Knowledge)

1. What is your personal understanding of **knowledge** and information? (Is there a difference?)
2. What is a special **strength** of the company?
3. If we are talking about strengths, do you also see **weaknesses**? Are you able to describe any weakness? Is it affecting your working process?
4. What are **opportunities** for the company?
5. What are **threats** for the company?

B2: Culture

8. Do you know the **guiding principles** of the department/company? Do they reflect your understanding of work?
9. For doing your job, is it necessary to be **open-minded** to new ideas?
10. Could you describe the **department culture** from your personal point of view?

B3: Networking

11. What kind of **organizational structure** do you have (hierarchical, process oriented, top down coordination)?
12. Are communication processes **two-way** or **one-way** (top-down vs. bottom up)?
13. Are you encouraged to **share knowledge** and teamwork, or are your focused on individual performance and rewards? Does the organizational structure facilitate knowledge sharing throughout the company? Do you work in teams or do you focus on individual department goals and assignments?
14. Are you **rewarded** for **teamwork**, or does the company/department use individual performance metrics?
15. Is teamwork **skill-based** or tasked-based?
16. Are you cooperating **across** organizational lines? Do you use cross-functional teams? Are you organized by functional departments or by teams oriented to solve customer problems?

17. Can you draw us a **map** of your personal communication (e.g., Internet, e-mail, telephone, fax, face-to-face communication)? What is the **content** of the communication?
18. Can you name us **persons** you are mostly communicating with?
19. How does knowledge flow **inside** the organization?
20. If we look closer at these persons, what **kind of knowledge** do they have? Can you give us a description? Can you name five key knowledge areas for these experts?
21. Can you make your **own decisions** or do you have to talk to your manager first?
22. Do you communicate with **partners**? What kind of partners (internal or external)? Are the major partners treated as trusted partners?
23. Do you have regular **meetings** in your department?
24. How would you **describe your work**? Are you asked to think, to work **creatively**? In general, is your work creative or more standard?

B4: Organizational Structure

25. Can you identify the **present** knowledge areas/processes of the department/company?
26. Can you specify **future** knowledge areas?
27. From your point of view, are your skills and knowledge be treated as **assets**, or is asset management only focused on equipment/machinery?
28. In the past, did you have many **reengineering** processes?
29. What kind of **social skills** are most needed to fulfil your daily job?

B5: Skills of Knowledge Worker

30. Can you give us some information about your **educational background**?
31. What is your actual **position** at the department? Can you describe your working processes?
32. For doing your job, must you be a **multi-skilled** worker or the specialist?
33. Can you give me a **definition of a knowledge** worker?
34. What **characteristics** do you have as a knowledge worker?
35. What are your **key** professional **skills**?
36. Could you **name other knowledge workers** in your department/company?

37. What is **the individual knowledge** of the named knowledge worker?
38. We have prepared a portfolio for you. Can you position the knowledge workers in the **portfolio**?
39. What is your company doing to keep you from **changing jobs**?
40. You also need "**supportive staff**" in the department. Could you name them and do they have any possibilities for future personal development?
41. Do you have a **description** of your personal job skills? Does a personal **knowledge profile** exist?
42. In order to accomplish your future work/processes/projects, what kind of **future** skills do you need?

B6: Experience and Learning

43. Are your encouraged to take part in **training** programs?
44. Can you explain us how you **personally** develop/keep/care about your knowledge?
45. What are your personal **career ideas**?
46. What are your ideas about your **future** personal **training programs**?
47. What are you doing to **renew** your knowledge?
48. When was your **last time** you took part in a training program?

B7: Competitors

49. What are the **key competitors**? Can you name them and knowledge area in which they are affecting your business?
50. What are **your future competitors**?

B8: Customers

51. Do you have any internal indicators to **measure** the impact of your business on the customer's business, e.g., cost deduction, faster delivery, and image improvement?
52. How would you characterize the **products** you sell? Are they knowledge intensive?
53. What are your **key customers**?

B9: I&CS and Knowledge Management Systems (KMS)

54. Do you use any **knowledge management tools**?
55. Do you have any **plans** for using knowledge management tools?
56. Do you have a **database** where all information about the skills of knowledge workers is monitored and where you can see the knowledge transfer processes?
57. Are there any **platforms** for knowledge sharing, e.g., chat rooms, information document systems, retrieval systems, regular meetings and so on?

Appendix C: Heisenberg's derivation of the Uncertainty Relation

[http://www.aip.org/history/heisenberg/p08a.htm, Date 2003-01-12; Reference: Zeitschrift für Physik 43 (1927), pp. 172-198]

180 W. Heisenberg,

ermöglichen, als es der Gleichung (1) entspricht, so wäre die Quantenmechanik unmöglich. Diese Ungenauigkeit, die durch Gleichung (1) festgelegt ist, schafft also erst Raum für die Gültigkeit der Beziehungen, die in den quantenmechanischen Vertauschungsrelationen

$$pq - qp = \frac{h}{2\pi i}$$

ihren prägnanten Ausdruck finden; sie ermöglicht diese Gleichung, ohne daß der physikalische Sinn der Größen p und q geändert werden mußte.

Für diejenigen physikalischen Phänomene, deren quantentheoretische Formulierung noch unbekannt ist (z. B. die Elektrodynamik), bedeutet Gleichung (1) eine Forderung, die zum Auffinden der neuen Gesetze nützlich sein mag. Für die Quantenmechanik läßt sich Gleichung (1) durch eine geringfügige Verallgemeinerung aus der Dirac-Jordanschen Formulierung herleiten. Wenn wir für den bestimmten Wert η irgend eines Parameters den Ort q des Elektrons zu q' bestimmen mit einer Genauigkeit q_1, so können wir dieses Faktum durch eine Wahrscheinlichkeitsamplitude $S(\eta, q)$ zum Ausdruck bringen, die nur in einem Gebiet der ungefähren Größe q_1 um q' von Null merklich verschieden ist. Insbesondere kann man z. B. setzen

$$S(\eta, q) \text{ prop } e^{-\frac{(q-q')^2}{2q_1^2} - \frac{2\pi i}{h} p'(q-q')}, \text{ also } S\bar{S} \text{ prop } e^{-\frac{(q-q')^2}{q_1^2}}. \qquad (3)$$

Dann gilt für die zu p gehörige Wahrscheinlichkeitsamplitude

$$S(\eta, p) = \int S(\eta, q) S(q, p)\, dq. \qquad (4)$$

Für $S(q, p)$ kann nach Jordan gesetzt werden

$$S(q, p) = e^{\frac{2\pi i p q}{h}}. \qquad (5)$$

Dann wird nach (4) $S(\eta, p)$ nur für Werte von p, für welche $\frac{2\pi(p-p')q_1}{h}$ nicht wesentlich größer als 1 ist, merklich von Null verschieden sein. Insbesondere gilt im Falle (3):

$$S(\eta, p) \text{ prop } \int e^{\frac{2\pi i (p-p') q}{h} - \frac{(q'-q)^2}{2q_1^2}}\, dq,$$

d. h.

$$S(\eta, p) \text{ prop } e^{-\frac{(p-p')^2}{2p_1^2} + \frac{2\pi i}{h} q'(p-p')}, \text{ also } S\bar{S} \text{ prop } e^{-\frac{(p-p')^2}{p_1^2}},$$

wo

$$p_1 q_1 = \frac{h}{2\pi}. \qquad (6)$$

References

[Abel00] Abell, A.: Skills for Knowledge Environments. In: The Information Management Journal. July 2000, pp. 33-41.

[AfSe99] Afriat, A., Selleri, F.: The Einstein, Podolsky, and Rosen Paradox in Atomic, Nuclear, and Particle Physics. Plenum Press, New York/London 1999.

[AlNe99] Albright, T., Neville, H.: Neurosciences. In: Wilson, R., Keil, F. (Eds.): The MIT Encyclopedia of the Cognitive Sciences. The MIT Press, Cambridge, Massachusetts/London 1999, pp. li-lxxii.

[Alst98] Alston, W.: Empiricism. In: Craig, E. (Ed.): Routledge Encyclopedia of Philosophy. Volume 3, Routledge, London/New York 1998.

[Amar02] Amar, A. D.: Managing Knowledge Workers. Unleashing Innovation and Productivity. Quorum Books, Westport, Connecticut/London 2002.

[Anas76] Anastasi, A.: Psychological Testing. Fourth Edition, Macmillan Publishing, New York 1976.

[Ande93] Anderson, J.: Rules of the Mind. Lawrence Erlbaum Associates, Hillsdale, New Jersey 1993.

[APQC99] American Productivity and Quality Center: Benchmarking: Leveraging Best-Practice Strategies. APQC White Paper for Senior Management. http://www.apqc.org/free/whitepapers, Date 2002-10-23.

[Arno84] Arnold, M.: Memory and the Brain. Lawrence Erlbaum Associates, Hillsdale, New Jersey/London 1984.

[Bach00] Bach, V.: Business Knowledge Management: Wertschöpfung durch Wissensportale. In: Bach, V., Österle, H., Vogler, P.: Business Knowledge Management in der Praxis. Prozessorientierte Lösungen zwischen Knowledge Portal und Kompetenzmanagement. Springer Verlag, Berlin et al. 2000, pp. 51-119.

[Bada96] Badaracco, J.: Knowledge Links. In: Myers, P.: Knowledge Management and Organizational Design. Butterworth-Heinemann, Boston et al. 1996, pp. 133-149.

[Band81] Band, W.: Quantum Theory of Measurement. In: Lerner, R., Trigg, G. (Eds.): Encyclopedia of Physics. Addison-Wesley Publishing, London et al. 1981, pp. 823-826.

[Barn92] Barnes, J.: Aristoteles. Eine Einführung. Philipp Reclam jun., Stuttgart 1992.

[Barr99] Barrett, J.: The Quantum Mechanics of Minds and Worlds. Oxford University Press, Oxford 1999.

[BeJa02] Bean, L., Jarnagin, B.: New Cost Priorities: Using a Balanced Scorecard Approach in Financial Reports. In: The Journal of Corporate Accounting & Finance. March/April 2002, pp. 55-62.

[Berr00] Berry, J.: Culture. In: Kazdin, A. (Ed.): Encyclopedia of Psychology. Volume 2, Oxford University Press, Oxford 2000.

[BiCK92] Bialynicki-Birula, I., Cieplak, M., Kaminski, J.: Theory of Quanta. Oxford University Press, New York/Oxford 1992.

[Blos00] Blosch, M.: Customer Knowledge. In: Knowledge and Process Management. Volume 7, Number 4, 2000, pp. 265-268.

[Bols89] Bol'shev, L.: Theory of Errors. In: Encyclopedia of Mathematics. Volume 3, Kluwer Academic Publishers, Dordrecht et al. 1989, pp. 416-417.

[Bont00] Bontis, N.: Assessing Knowledge Assets: A Review of the Models Used to Measure Intellectual Capital. Framework Paper. Queen's University at Kinston, April 2000.

[Bont01] Bontis, N.: CKO Wanted - Evangelical Skills Necessary: A Review of the Chief Knowledge Officer Position. In: Knowledge and Process Management. Volume 8, Number 1, 2001, pp. 29-38.

[Bont96] Bontis, N.: There's a price on your Head: Managing Intellectual Capital Strategically. In: Business Quarterly, Summer 1996, pp. 40-47.

[BoPa98] Borghoff, U., Pareschi, R. (Eds.): Information Technology for Knowledge Management. Springer Verlag, Berlin/Heidelberg 1998.

[Born98] Bornemann, M.: Empirical Analysis of the Intellectual Potential of Value Systems in Austria According to the VAIC™ Method. February 1998. http://www.measuring-ip.at, Date 2003-02-28.

[Boro67] Borowitz, S.: Fundamentals of Quantum Mechanics. Benjamin, New York/Amsterdam 1967.

[Broc96] Brockington, R.: Accounting for Intangible Assets. A New Perspective on the True and Fair View. Addison-Wesley, Wokingham, England et al. 1996.

[Buff02] Buff, R.: Uncertain Volatility Models - Theory and Application. Springer Verlag, Berlin/Heidelberg 2002.

[BuWi00] Bukowitz, W., Williams, R.: The Knowledge Management Fieldbook. Prentice Hall, London et al. 2000.

[Came82] Cameron, J. M.: Error Analysis. In: Kotz, S., Johnson, N. (Eds.): Encyclopedia of Statistical Sciences. Volume 2, John Wiley & Sons, New York et al. 1982, pp. 545-551.

[Carl00] Carlson, N.: Neuron. In: Kazdin, A. (Ed.): Encyclopedia of Psychology. Volume 5, Oxford University Press, Oxford et al. 2000.

[Chie99] Chierchia, G.: Linguistics and Language. In: Wilson, R., Keil, F. (Eds.): The MIT Encyclopedia of the Cognitive Sciences. The MIT Press, Cambridge Massachusetts/London 1999, pp. xci-cix.

[Chom75] Chomsky, N.: Reflections on Language. Pantheon Books, New York 1975.

[Chom98] Chomsky, N.: On Language. The New Press, New York 1998.

[Chur86] Churchland, P.: Neurophilosophy. Towards a Unified Science of the Mind-Brain. The MIT Press, Cambridge, Massachusetts/London 1986.

[Clif96] Cliff, N.: Ordinal Methods for Behavioral Data Analysis. Lawrence Erlbaum Associates, Mahwah, New Jersey 1996.

[Cohe96] Cohen, B.: Explaining Psychological Statistics. Brooks/Cole Publishing Company, Pacific Grove, California et al. 1996.

[CoKV99] Courtney, H., Kirkland, J., Viguerie, P.: Strategy Under Uncertainty. In: Harvard Business Review on Managing Uncertainty. A Harvard Business Review Paperback, Boston 1999.

[Cole95] Coleman, D.: Emotional Intelligence. Why it can matter more than IQ. Bantam Books, New York et al. 1995.

[Colm01] Colman, A.: A Dictionary of Psychology. Oxford University Press, New York, 2001.

[Cong97] Congdon, P.: Bayesian Statistical Modelling. John Wiley & Sons, Chichester et al. 1997.

[Cont01] Contractor, F.: Intangible Assets and Principles for Their Valuation. In: Contractor, F.: Valuation of Intangible Assets in Global Operations. Quorum Books, Westport, Connecticut/London 2001, pp.1-24.

[Core01] Coren, S.: Neuropsychological Development. In: The Corsini Encyclopedia of Psychology and Behavioral Science. Third Edition. Volume 3, John Wiley & Sons, New York et al. 2001.

[Crai98] Craig, E. (Ed.): Routledge Encyclopedia of Philosophy. Routledge, London/New York 1998.

[DaMa92] Davidow, W., Malone, M.: The Virtual Corporation. Structuring and Revitalizing the Corporation for the 21st Century. Harper Business, New York 1992.

[DaMe86] Das, A., Melissinos, A.: Quantum Mechanics. A Modern Introduction. Gordon and Breach Science Publishers, New York et al. 1986.

[DaPr98] Davenport, T., Prusak, L.: Working Knowledge. How Organizations Manage What They Know. Harvard Business School Press, Boston 1998.

[DeCh00] Despres, C., Chauvel, D. (Eds.): Knowledge Horizons. The Present and the Promise of Knowledge Management. Butterworth-Heinemann, Boston et al. 2000.

[Dein00] Deininger, W.: Aristotle. In: Roth, J., Moose, C., Wildin, R. (Eds.): World Philosophers and Their Works. Volume I, Salem Press, Pasadena, California/Hackensack, New Jersey 2000.

[DoCo92] Downing, D., Covington, M. (Eds.): Dictionary Of Computer Terms. Third Edition. Barron's Educational Series, New York 1992.

[DoRT98] Dowling, C., Roberts, F., Theuns, P.: Recent Progress in Mathematical Psychology. Psychophysics, Knowledge, Representation, Cognition, and Measurement. Lawrence Erlbaum Associates, Mahwah, New Jersey/London 1998.

[DrDr87] Dreyfus, H., Dreyfus S.: Künstliche Intelligenz. Von den Grenzen der Denkmaschine und dem Wert der Intuition. rororo computer, Reinbek bei Hamburg 1987.

[DrDr97] Dreyfus, H., Dreyfus, S.: Why Computers May Never Think Like People. In: Ruggles, R. (Ed.): Knowledge Management Tools. Butterworth-Heinemann, Boston et al. 1997, pp. 31-50.

[Drey02] Dreyfus, H.: Intelligence Without Representation. http://www.hfac.uh.edu/cogsci/dreyfus.html, Date 2003-02-02.

[Druc92] Drucker, P.: The New Society of Organizations. In: Harvard Business Review. September-October 1992, pp. 95-104.

[Duff00] Duffy, J.: Knowledge Management: What Every Information Professional Should Know. In: The Information Management Journal, July 2000, pp. 10-16.

[Dunn83] Dunn-Rankin, P.: Scaling Methods. Lawrence Erlbaum Associates, Hillsdale, New Jersey 1983.

[Dych02] Dyché, J.: The CRM Handbook. A Business Guide to Customer Relationship Management. Addison-Wesley, Boston et al. 2002.

[Earl96] Earl, M.: Knowledge Strategies: Propositions From Two Contrasting Industries. In: Earl, M. (Ed.): Information Management. Oxford University Press, Oxford et al. 1996, pp. 1-15.

[EdMa97] Edvinsson, L., Malone, M.: Intellectual Capital. Realizing your Company's True Value by Finding its Hidden Brainpower. HarperBusiness, New York 1997.

[EiPR35] Einstein, A., Podolsky, B., Rosen, N.: Can Quantum-Mechanical Description of Physical Reality Be Considered Complete. In: Wheeler, J., Zurek, W. (Eds.): Quantum Theory and Measurement. Princeton University Press, Princeton, New Jersey 1983, p.138-141.

[EiRe85] Eisberg, R., Resnick, R.: Quantum Physics of Atoms, Molecules, Solids, Nuclei, and Particles. Second Edition. John Wiley & Sons, New York et al. 1985.

[Enzy92] Enzyklopädie der Philosophie. Weltbild Verlag, Augsburg 1992.

[Este91] Estes, W.: Statistical Models in Behavioral Research. Lawrence Erlbaum Associates, Hillsdale, New Jersey et al. 1991.

[Eyse90] Eysenck, M. (Ed.): The Blackwell Dictionary of Cognitive Psychology. Blackwell Reference, Oxford 1990.

[Faur00] Faurot, J.: René Descartes. In: Roth, J., Moose, C., Wildin, R. (Eds.): World Philosophers and Their Works. Volume I, Salem Press, Pasadena, California 2000.

[Fife95] Fife-Schaw, C.: Questionnaire Design. In: Breackwell, G., Hammond, S., Fife-Schaw, C. (Eds.): Research Methods in Psychology. Sage Publications, London et al. 1995, pp. 174-192.

[Fine97] Finerty, T.: Integrating Learning and Knowledge Infrastructure. In: Journal of Knowledge Management. Volume 1, Number 2, December 1997, pp. 98-104.

[Fink00a] Fink, K.: Know-how-Management. Oldenbourg Verlag, München/Wien 2000.

[Fink00b] Fink, K.: Architektur für Know-how-Prozesse. In: Blum, U., Cleven, H., Esswein, W., Greipl, E., Müller, S. (Eds.): Kundenbindung bei veränderten Wettbewerbsbedingungen. Dresdner Beiträge zu Wettbewerb und Unternehmensführung. B. G. Teubner, Stuttgart et al. 2000, pp. 123-155.

[Fink03] Fink, K.: Knowledge Potential Measurement Results. Department of Information Systems. University of Innsbruck. Internal Paper, Draft 2003.

[FiRK04] Fink, K., Roithmayr, F., Kofler, G.: Knowledge Management Case Studies. The Multimedia CD-ROM is available at the Department of Value Process Management/Information Systems, University of Innsbruck, CD-ROM 2004.

[FiRo02] Fink, K., Roithmayr, F.: Evaluation Model for Real and Virtual Learning Environments: Theoretical Concept and Empirical Results. In: Khosrow-Pour, M. (Ed.): Issues and Trends of Information Technology Management in Contemporary Organizations. Volume 1, Idea Group Publishing, Hershey et al. 2002, pp. 219-222.

[FiRo03a] Fink, K., Roithmayr, F.: CTL Knowledge Management Case Study. Part A-D. Department of Value Process Management/Information Systems, University of Innsbruck 2003.

[FiRo03b] Fink, K., Roithmayr, F.: DataSolve Knowledge Management Case Study. Part A-D. Department of Value Process Management/Information Systems, University of Innsbruck 2003.

[FiRo03c] Fink, K., Roithmayr, F.: Resurgence™ Knowledge Management Case Study. Part A-D. Department of Value Process Management/Information Systems, University of Innsbruck 2003.

[FiRo03d] Fink, K., Roithmayr, F.: MLP Innsbruck Knowledge Management Case Study. Part A-D. Department of Value Process Management/Information Systems, University of Innsbruck. Draft 2003.

[FiRo03e] Fink, K., Roithmayr, F.: USB Zurich Knowledge Management Case Study. Part A-D. Department of Value Process Management/Information Systems, University of Innsbruck. Draft 2003.

[Fowl91] Fowler, F.: Reducing Interviewer-Related Error Through Interviewer Training, Supervision, and other Means. In: Biemer, P., Groves, R., Lyberg, L., Mathiowetz, N., Sudman, S. (Eds.): Measurement Error in Surveys. John Wiley & Sons, New York et al. 1991.

[Fraa91] Fraassen, B.: Quantum Mechanics: An Empiricist View. Clarendon Press, Oxford 1991.

[FrRo83] Fromkin, V., Rodman, R.: An Introduction to Language. Third Edition. Holt, Rinehart and Wilson, New York et al. 1983.

[FrSm97] French, S., Smith, J.: The Practice of Bayesian Analysis. Arnold Publishers, London 1997.

[Gall01] Gallupe, B.: Knowledge Management Systems: Surveying the Landscape. In: International Journal of Management Reviews. Volume 3, Issue 1, March 2001, pp. 61-77.

[GeGa87] Geschwind, N., Galaburda, A.: Cerebral Lateralization. Biological Mechanisms, Associations, and Pathology. The MIT Press, Cambridge 1987.

[Gent89] Gentner, D.: The Mechanisms of Analogical Learning. In. Vosniadou, S., Ortony, A.: Similarity and Analogical Reasoning. Cambridge University Press, Cambridge et al. 1989.

[Gent99] Gentner, D.: Analogy. In: Wilson, R., Keil, F. (Eds.): The MIT Encyclopedia of the Cognitive Sciences. The MIT Press, Cambridge, Massachusetts/London 1999, pp. 17-20.

[Gerj93] Gerjuoy, E.: Uncertainty Principle. In: Parker S. (Ed.): McGraw-Hill Encyclopedia of Physics. Second Edition. McGraw-Hill, New York et al. 1993, pp. 1490-1491.

[GeSt83] Gentner, D., Stevens, A.: Mental Models. Lawrence Erlbaum Associates, Hillsdale, New Jersey 1983.

[GiKr00] Gibbert, M., Krause, H.: Practice Exchange in a Best Practice Marketplace. In: Davenport, T., Probst, G. (Eds.): Knowledge Management Case Book. Best Practices. MCD Verlag/John Wiley & Sons, Erlangen et al. 2000, pp. 68-84.

[Gill00] Gillham, B.: Case Study Research Methods. Continuum, London/New York 2000.

[Gran97] Grant, J.: Foundations of Economic Value Added. Frank J. Fabozzi Associates, New Hope, Pennsylvania 1997.

[Gree00] Green, H.: Information Theory and Quantum Physics. Physical Foundations for Understanding the Conscious Process. Springer Verlag, Berlin et al. 2000.

[Grib84] Gribbin, J.: In Search of Schrödinger's Cat. Quantum Physics and Reality. Bantam Books, New York et al. 1984.

[Grib95] Gribbin, J.: Schrödinger's Kittens and the Search for Reality. Solving the Quantum Mysteries. Back Bay Books/Little, Brown and Company, Boston et al. 1995.

[Grib99] Gribbin, J.: Q is for Quantum. An Encyclopedia of Particle Physics. A Touchstone Book, New York 1999.

[GrMa93] Graf, P., Masson, M.: Implicit Memory. New Directions in Cognition, Development, and Neuropsychology. Lawrence Erlbaum Associates, Hillsdale, New Jersey et al. 1993.

[GrRo99] Grib, A., Rodrigues, W.: Nonlocality in Quantum Physics. Kluwer Academic/Plenum Publishers, New York 1999.

[Gupt00] Gupta, U.: Information Systems. Success in the 21st Century. Prentice Hall, Upper Saddle River, New Jersey 2000.

[Gupt92] Gupta, M.: Intelligence, Uncertainty and Information. In: Ayyub, B., Gupta, M., Kanal, L. (Eds.): Analysis and Management of Uncertainty: Theory and Applications. North-Holland, Amsterdam et al. 1992.

[HaJT01] Hall, B., Jaffe, A., Trajtenberg , M.: Market Value and Patent Citations: A First Look. University of California, Berkeley, Economics Department. Working Paper No. E01-304. August 2001. http://repositories.cdlib.org/iber/econ/E01-304, Date 2002-07-27.

[HaSu00] Harrison, S., Sullivan, P.: Profiting from Intellectual Capital. Learning from Leading Companies. In: Journal of Intellectual Capital. Volume 1, No. 1, 2000, pp. 33-46.

[Hein94] Heinrich, L. J.: Systemplanung. Planung und Realisierung von Informatik-Projekten. Band 2. 5. vollständig überarbeitete und ergänzte Auflage. Oldenbourg Verlag, München/Wien 1994.

[Hein96] Heinrich, L. J.: Systemplanung. Planung und Realisierung von Informatik-Projekten. Band 1. 7., korrigierte Auflage. Oldenbourg Verlag, München/Wien 1996.

[Hein99] Heinrich, L. J.: Informationsmanagement. 6. Auflage. Oldenbourg Verlag, München/Wien 1999.

[Henr99] Henrion, M.: Uncertainty. In: Wilson, R., Keil, F. (Eds.): The MIT Encyclopedia of the Cognitive Sciences. The MIT Press, Cambridge, Massachusetts/London 1999, pp. 853-855.

[HeHR04] Heinrich, L. J., Heinzl, A., Roithmayr, F.: Wirtschaftsinformatik-Lexikon. 7., vollständig überarbeitete und erweiterte Auflage. Oldenbourg Verlag, München/Wien 2004.

[HeVe01] Henderson, L., Vedral, V.: Center for Quantum Computation: Quantum Entanglement. http://www.qubit.org/intros/entang/, Date 2001-07-05.

[HeVo01] Heisig, P., Vorbeck, J.: Cultural Change Triggers Best Practice Sharing - British Aerospace. In: Mertins, K., Heisig, P., Vorbeck, J. (Eds.): Knowledge Management. Best Practice in Europe. Springer Verlag, Berlin et al. 2001, pp. 138-147.

[Hint96] Hinterhuber, H.: Strategische Unternehmensführung. Band 1. Strategisches Denken. 6. Auflage. Walter de Gruyter, Berlin/New York 1996.

[HoBe01] Housel, T., Bell, A.: Measuring and Managing Knowledge. McGraw-Hill/Irvin, Boston et al. 2001.

[HoCr03] Howitt, D., Cramer, D.: An Introduction to Statistics in Psychology. Revised 2nd Edition. Prentice Hall, Harlow, England et al. 2003.

[HöEd98] Högberg, C., Edvinsson, L.: A Design for Futurizing Knowledge Networking. In: Journal of Knowledge Management. Volume 2, Number 2, December 1998, pp. 81-92.

[Hofe81] Hofer, M.: The Roots of Human Behavior. W. H. Freeman and Company, San Francisco 1981.

[Hoff01] Hoffmann, I.: Knowledge Management Tools. In: Mertins, K., Heisig, P., Vorbeck, J. (Eds.): Knowledge Management. Best Practice in Europe. Springer, Berlin et al. 2001, pp. 74-94.

[HoKP87] Honig, W., Kraft, D., Panarella, E.: Quantum Uncertainties. Recent and Future Experiments and Interpretations. NATO ASI Series. Plenum Press, New York/London 1987.

[Hold02] Holden, N.: Cross-Cultural Management. A Knowledge Perspective. Prentice Hall, Harlow, England 2002.

[Holy99] Holyoak, K.: Psychology. In: Wilson, R., Keil, F. (Eds.): The MIT Encyclopedia of the Cognitive Sciences. The MIT Press, Cambridge, Massachusetts/London 1999, pp. xxxviv-xlix.

[Hugh89] Hughes, R.: The Structure and Interpretation of Quantum Mechanics. Harvard University Press, Cambridge 1989.

[Hugl95] Hugel, U.: Qualitative Inhaltsanalyse und Mind-Mapping. Ein neuer Ansatz für Datenauswertung und Organisationsdiagnose. Gabler Verlag, Wiesbaden 1995.

[Isha95] Isham, C.: Lectures on Quantum Theory. Mathematical and Structural Foundations. Imperial College Press, Singapore 1995.

[IwSh00] Iwańska, Ł., Shapiro, S. (Eds.): Natural Language Processing and Knowledge Representation. Language for Knowledge and Knowledge for Language. AAAI Press/The MIT Press, Menlo Park, California et al. 2000.

[Jamm74] Jammer, M.: The Philosophy of Quantum Mechanics. The Interpretations of Quantum Mechanics in Historical Perspective. John Wiley & Sons, New York et al. 1974.

[John99] Johnson-Laird, P.: Mental Models. In: Wilson, R., Keil, F. (Eds.): The MIT Encyclopedia of the Cognitive Sciences. The MIT Press, Cambridge, Massachusetts/London 1999, pp. 525-527.

[JoRu99] Jordan, M., Russel, S.: Computational Intelligence. In: Wilson, R., Keil, F. (Eds.): The MIT Encyclopedia of the Cognitive Sciences. The MIT Press, Cambridge, Massachusetts/London 1999, pp. lxxiii-xc.

[Jose93] Joseph, R.: The Naked Neuron. Evolution and the Languages of Body and Brain. Plenum Press, New York/London 1993.

[KaKK01] Kakabadse, N., Kouzmin, A., Kakabadse, A.: From Tacit Knowledge to Knowledge Management: Leveraging Invisible Assets. In: Knowledge and Process Management, Volume 8, Number 3, 2001, pp. 137-154.

[KaNo01] Kaplan, R., Norton, D.: The Strategy-Focused Organization. How Balanced Scorecard Companies Thrive in the New Business Environment. Harvard Business School Press, Boston, Massachusetts 2001.

[KaNo92] Kaplan, R., Norton, D.: The Balanced Scorecard. In: Harvard Business Review, Volume 70, Issue 1, January/February 1992, pp. 71-80.

[KaNo96] Kaplan, R., Norton, D.: The Balanced Scorecard. Translating Strategy into Action. Harvard Business School Press, Boston, Massachusetts 1996.

[KaTe01] Karagiannis, D., Telesko, R.: Wissensmanagement. Konzepte der Künstlichen Intelligenz und des Softcomputing. Oldenbourg Verlag, München/Wien 2001.

[Kean88] Keane, M.: Analogical Problem Solving. Ellis Horwood Limited, Chichester 1988.

[KeCa93] Kelley, R., Caplan, J.: How Bell Labs create Star Performers. In: Harvard Business Review, July-August 1993, pp. 128-139.

[Keda88] Kedar-Capelli, S.: Analogy - From a Unified Perspective. In: Helman, D. (Ed.): Analogical Reasoning. Perspectives of Artificial Intelligence, Cognitive Science, and Philosophy. Kluwer Academic Publishers, Dordrecht et al. 1988, pp. 65-103.

[Kess92] Kess, J.: Psycholinguistics. Psychology, Linguistics, and the Study of Natural Language. John Benjamins Publishing Company, Amsterdam/ Philadelphia 1992.

[Khou02] Khoury, S.: Valuing Intellectual Properties - The Technology Factor Method. http://www.inavisis.com/articles/valuingip.pdf, Date 2002-09-13.

[KiFr00] Kitchin, R., Freundschuh, S.: Cognitive Mapping. In: Kitchin, R., Freundschuh, S. (Eds.): Cognitive Mapping. Past, Present and Future. Routledge, London/New York 2000.

[Kilm01] Kilmann, R.: Quantum Organizations. A New Paradigm for Achieving Organizational Success and Personal Meaning. Davies-Black Publishing, Palo Alto, California 2001.

[KlSL01] Kluge, J., Stein, W., Licht, T.: Knowledge Unplugged. The McKinsey & Company Global Survey on Knowledge Management. Palgrave, Houndmills 2001.

[Kmuc00] Kmuche, W.: Stragischer Erfolgsfaktor Wissen. Content Management: Der Weg zum erfolgreichen Informationsmanagement. Deutscher Wirtschaftsdienst, Köln 2000.

[KoFr00] Koulopoulos, T., Frappaolo, C.: Why Do a Knowledge Audit. In: Cortada, J., Woods, J. (Eds.): The Knowledge Management Yearbook 2000-2001. Butterworth-Heinemann, Boston et al. 2000.

[KoJO01] Koop, H., Jäckel, K., van Offern, A. (Eds.): Erfolgsfaktor Content Management. Vom Web Content bis zum Knowledge Management. Vieweg & Sohn Verlagsgesellschaft, Braunschweig/Wiesbaden 2001.

[Krec74] Krech, D.: Elements of Psychology. Alfred Knopf, New York 1974.

[KrIN00] Krogh, G., Ichijo, K., Nonaka, I.: Enabling Knowledge Creation. How to Unlock the Mystery of Tacit Knowledge and Release the Power of Innovation. Oxford University Press, Oxford et al. 2000.

[Krip80] Krippendorff, K.: Content Analysis. An Introduction to its Methodology. Volume 5, Sage Publications, Beverly Hills/London 1980.

[Kroe94] Kroemer, H.: Quantum Mechanics. For Engineering, Materials Science, and Applied Physics. Prentice Hall, Englewood Cliffs, New Jersey 1994.

[LaLa00] Laudon, K., Laudon J.: Management Information Systems. Organization and Technology in the Networked Enterprise. Sixth Edition, Prentice Hall, Upper Saddle River, New Jersey 2000.

[LaLi77] Landau, L., Lifshitz, E.: Quantum Mechanics. Non-Relativistic Theory. Volume 3, Pergamon Press, Oxford et al. 1977.

[Land98] Landsman, N. P.: Mathematical Topics Between Classical and Quantum Mechanics. Springer Verlag, New York 1998.

[Lee97] Lee, P.: Bayesian Statistics. An Introduction. Arnold Publishers, London et al. 1997.

[Leon95] Leonhard-Barton, D.: Wellsprings of Knowledge. Building and Sustaining the Sources of Innovation. Harvard Business School Press, Boston, Massachusetts 1995.

[Lev01] Lev, B.: Intangibles. Management, Measurement, and Reporting. Brookings Institution Press, Washington, D. C. 2001.

[Levi99] Levinson, S.: Language and Culture. In: Wilson, R., Keil, F. (Eds.): The MIT Encyclopedia of the Cognitive Sciences. The MIT Press, Cambridge, Massachusetts/London 1999, pp. 441-442.

[Libo80] Liboff, R.: Introductory Quantum Mechanics. Holden-Day, San Francisco 1980.

[LiSt97] Lipnack, J., Stamps, J.: Virtual Teams. Reaching Across Space, Time, and Organizations with Technology. John Wiley & Sons, New York et al. 1997.

[LuJa00] Lundquist, L., Jarvella, R.: Language, Text, and Knowledge. Mental Models of Expert Communication. Mouton de Gruyter, Berlin/New York 2000.

[LuSt89] Luger, G., Stubblefield, W.: Artificial Intelligence and the Design of Expert Systems. The Benjamin/Cummings Publishing Company, Redwood City, California et al. 1989.

[Luth98] Luthy, D.: Intellectual Capital and its Measurement. College of Business. Utah State University, Logan 1998.

[LyKa91] Lyberg, L., Kasprzyk, D.: Data Collection Methods and Measurement Error: An Overview. In: Biemer, P., Groves, R., Lyberg, L., Mathiowetz, N., Sudman, S. (Eds.): Measurement Errors in Surveys. John Wiley & Sons, New York et al. 1991, pp. 237-257.

[Malh00] Malhortra, Y.: Knowledge Management and Virtual Organizations. Idea Group Publishing, Hershey/London 2000.

[MaPr83] Maxwell, G., Pringle, J.: The Analysis of Video Records. In: Dowrick, P., Biggs, S. (Eds.): Using Video. Psychological and Social Applications. John Wiley & Sons, Chichester et al. 1983, pp. 33-44.

[Mark98] Markie, P.: Rationalism. In: Craig, E. (Ed.): Routledge Encyclopedia of Philosophy. Volume 8, Routledge, London/New York 1998.

[Mart89] Martin, J.: Information Engineering. Book I: Introduction. Prentice-Hall, London et al. 1989.

[Mart90a] Martin, J.: Information Engineering. Book II: Planning & Analysis. Prentice-Hall, London et al. 1990.

[Mart90b] Martin, J.: Information Engineering. Book III: Design & Construction. Prentice-Hall, London et al. 1990.

[McIn68] McInerny, R.: Studies in Analogy. The Hague, Martinus Nijhoff, Netherlands 1968.

[McSi03] McClave, J., Sincich, T.: Statistics. Ninth Edition. Prentice Hall, Upper Saddle River, New Jersey 2003.

[MeAY01] Mentzas, G., Apostolou, D., Young, R., Abecker, A.: Knowledge Networking: a Holistic Solution for Leveraging Corporate Knowledge. In: Journal of Knowledge Management. Volume 5, Number 1, 2001, pp. 94-106.

[MeRa73] Mendenhall, W., Ramey, M.: Statistics for Psychology. Duxburg Press, North Scituate, Massachusetts 1973.

[MeRe00] Mehra, J., Rechenberg, H.: The Historical Development of Quantum Theory. Volume 6, Part 1, Springer Verlag, New York et al. 2000.

[MeRe82a] Mehra, J., Rechenberg, H.: The Historical Development of Quantum Theory. Volume 1, Part 1, Springer Verlag, New York et al. 1982.

[MeRe82b] Mehra, J., Rechenberg, H.: The Historical Development of Quantum Theory. Volume 1, Part 2, Springer Verlag, New York et al. 1982.

[MeRe82c] Mehra, J., Rechenberg, H.: The Historical Development of Quantum Theory. Volume 2, Springer Verlag, New York et al. 1982.

[MeRe82d] Mehra, J., Rechenberg, H.: The Historical Development of Quantum Theory. Volume 3, Springer Verlag, New York et al. 1982.

[MeRe82e] Mehra, J., Rechenberg, H.: The Historical Development of Quantum Theory. Volume 4, Part 1 and Part 2, Springer Verlag, New York et al. 1982.

[MeRe87a] Mehra, J., Rechenberg, H.: The Historical Development of Quantum Theory. Volume 5, Part 1, Springer Verlag, New York et al. 1987.

[MeRe87b] Mehra, J., Rechenberg, H.: The Historical Development of Quantum Theory. Volume 5, Part 2, Springer Verlag, New York et al. 1987.

[Mese99] Meseroll, T.: Instantaneous Data Transfer over Temporal Boundaries: A Method for Communicating with the Past and Future. Hughes Space and Communication Company. El Segundo, California 1999. http://www-ssc.igpp.ucla.edu/~meseroll/Quantum_Entanglement.html, Date 2003-02-17.

[Mich99] Michell, J.: Measurement in Psychology. Critical History of a Methodological Concept. Cambridge University Press, Cambridge 1999.

[Mill90] Miller, A.: Sixty-Two Years of Uncertainty. Historical, Philosophical, and Physical Inquiries into the Foundations of Quantum Mechanics. Proceedings of a NATO Advanced Study Institute. Plenum Press, New York/London 1990.

[MoCN97] Morris, S., Cork, D., Neapolitan, R.: The Cognitive Processing of Causal Knowledge. In: Geiger, D., Shenoy, P. (Eds.): Uncertainty in Artificial Intelligence. Proceedings of the Thirteenth Conference. Morgan Kaufman Publishers, San Francisco 1997.

[MoDo02] Mockler, R., Dologite, D.: Strategically-Focused Enterprise Knowledge Management. In. White, D. (Ed.): Knowledge Mapping & Management. IRM Press, Hershey/London 2002, pp. 14-22.

[MoSe88] Molfese, D., Segalowitz, S.: Brain Lateralization in Children. Developmental Implications. The Guilford Press, New York/London 1988.

[MuDa01] Murphy, K., Davidshofer, C.: Psychological Testing. Principles and Applications. Fifth Edition. Prentice Hall, Upper Saddle River, New Jersey 2001.

[NaKa99] Nadeau, R., Kafatos, M.: The Non-Local Universe. The New Physics and Matters of the Mind. Oxford University Press, Oxford et al. 1999.

[Nakr00] Nakra, P.: Knowledge Management: The Magic is in the Culture. In: Competitive Intelligence Review. Volume 11 (2) 2000, pp. 53-60.

[NaKr01] Najda, L., Krcmar, H.: IKT-gestütztes Wissensmanagement in der Unternehmensberatung – ein kooperationsorientierter Ansatz. In: WIRTSCHAFTSINFORMATIK 43 (2001) 5, pp. 445-455.

[Nede93] Nedelsky, L.: Mass. In: Parker, S. (Ed.): McGraw-Hill Encyclopedia of Physics. Second Edition. McGraw-Hill, New York et al. 1993.

[Neef98] Neef, D.: The Knowledge Economy. Butterworth-Heinemann, Boston et al. 1998.

[Negn02] Negnevitsky, M.: Artificial Intelligence. A Guide to Intelligent Systems. Addison-Wesley, Harlow, England et al. 2002.

[Nils98] Nilsson, N.: Artificial Intelligence. A New Synthesis. Morgan Kaufmannn Publishers, San Francisco, California 1998.

[NoKT01] Nonaka, I., Konno, N., Toyama, R.: Emergence of "Ba". A Conceptual Framework for the Continuous and Self-transcending Process of Knowledge Creation. In: Nonaka, I., Nishiguchi, T. (Eds.): Knowledge Emergence. Social, Technical, and Evolutionary Dimensions of Knowledge Creation. Oxford University Press, Oxford et al. 2001, pp. 13-29.

[Nona92] Nonaka, I.: Wie japanische Konzerne Wissen erzeugen. In: HARVARD manager. 2/1992, pp. 95-103.

[NoRe00] Nonaka, I., Reinmoeller, P.: Dynamic Business Systems for Knowledge Creation and Utilization. In: Despres, C., Chauvel, D. (Eds.): Knowledge Horizons. The Present and the Promise of Knowledge Management. Butterworth-Heinemann, Boston et al. 2000, pp. 89-112.

[Norm83] Norman, D.: Some Observations on Mental Models. In: Gentner, D., Stevens, A. (Eds.): Mental Models. Lawrence Erlbaum Associates, Hillsdale, New Jersey/London 1983.

[Nort98] North, K.: Wissensorientierte Unternehmensführung. Wertschöpfung durch Wissen. Gabler Verlag, Wiesbaden 1998.

[NoRu70] Norman, D., Rumelhart, D.: A System for Perception and Memory. In: Norman, D. (Ed.): Models of Human Memory. Academic Press, New York/ London 1970.

[NoTa95] Nonaka, I., Takeuchi, H.: The Knowledge Creating Company. How Japanese Companies Create the Dynamics of Innovation. Oxford University Press, New York/Oxford 1995.

[OECD00] OECD: Knowledge Management in the Learning Society. Education and Skills. OECD Publications, France 2000.

[OECD96] OECD. The Knowledge-Based Economy. OCDE/GD(96)102.

[Omnè94] Omnès, R.: The Interpretation of Quantum Mechanics. Princeton University Press, Princeton 1994.

[OrCa91] Ornstein, R., Carstensen, L.: Psychology. The Study of Human Experience. Third Edition. Harcourt Brace Jovanovich Publishers, San Diego et al. 1991.

[ÖsFA00] Österle, H., Fleisch, E., Alt, R.: Business Networking. Shaping Enterprise Relationships on the Internet. Springer Verlag, Berlin et al. 2000.

[Öste00] Österle, H.: Business Model of the Information Age. In: Bach, V., Österle, H., Vogler, P. (Eds.): Business Knowledge Management in der Praxis. Prozessorientierte Lösungen zwischen Knowledge Portal und Kompetenzmanagement. Springer Verlag, Berlin et al. 2000, pp. 11-50.

[Pars01] Parsons, S., Qualitative Methods for Reasoning under Uncertainty. The MIT Press, Cambridge, Massachusetts/London 2001.

[Pear00] Pearson, T.: Measurements and the Knowledge Revolution. In: Cortada, J., Woods, J. (Eds.): The Knowledge Management Yearbook 2000-2001. Butterworth-Heinemann, Boston et al. 2000.

[Pear90] Pearl, J.: Bayesian Decision Methods. In: Shafer, G., Pearl, J. (Eds.): Readings in Uncertain Reasoning. Morgan Kaufman Publishers, San Mateo, California 1990, pp. 345-352.

[Pear99] Pearl, J.: Bayesian Networks. In: Wilson, R., Keil, F. (Eds.): The MIT Encyclopedia of the Cognitive Sciences. The MIT Press, Cambridge, Massachusetts/London 1999, pp. 72-74.

[PfSc99] Pfeifer, R., Scheier, C.: Understanding Intelligence. The MIT Press, Cambridge, Massachusetts/London 1999.

[PiCh77] Price, W., Chissick, S.: The Uncertainty Principle and Foundations of Quantum Mechanics. A Fifty Years' Survey. John Wiley & Sons, London et al. 1977.

[Pink97] Pinker, S.: How the Mind Works. W. W. Norton & Company, New York/ London 1997.

[Pola85] Polanyi, M.: Implizites Wissen. 1. Auflage. Suhrkamp Verlag, Frankfurt am Main 1985.

[Pola97] Polanyi, M.: Tacit Knowledge. In: Prusak, L. (Ed.): Knowledge in Organizations. Butterworth-Heinemann, Boston et al. 1997, pp. 135-146.

[Polk84] Polkinghorne, J.C.: The Quantum World. Longman, London/New York 1984.

[Pric95] Price, M.: The Everett FAQ. February 1995. http://www.hedweb.com/ manworld.htm, Date 2003-02-17.

[PrRR97] Probst, G., Raub, S., Romhardt, K.: Wissen managen. Wie Unternehmen ihre wertvollste Ressource optimal nutzen. Gabler Verlag, Wiesbaden 1997.

[Prus97] Prusak, L.: Knowledge in Organizations. Butterworth-Heinemann, Boston et al. 1997.

[Puci96] Pucik, V.: Strategic Alliances, Organizational Learning, and Competitive Advantage: The HRM Agenda. In: Myers, P. (Ed.): Knowledge Management and Organizational Design. Butterworth-Heinemann, Boston et al. 1996, pp. 151-166.

[Puli00] Pulic, A.: VAIC™ - An Accounting Tool for IC Management. January 2000. http://www.measuring-ip.at, Date 2002-08-27.

[Puli97] Pulic, A.: The Physical and Intellectual Capital of Austrian Banks. February 1997. http://www.mint.mcmaster.ca, Date 2003-02-27.

[Rabi99] Rabiner, L.: Speech Recognition in Machines. In: Wilson, R., Keil, F. (Eds.): The MIT Encyclopedia of the Cognitive Sciences. The MIT Press, Cambridge, Massachusetts/London 1999, pp. 790-792.

[Rae92] Rae, A.: Quantum Mechanics. Third Edition, Institute of Physics Publishing, Bristol/Philadelphia 1992.

[RaEs00] Rattoni, F., Escobar, M.: Neurobiology of Learning. In: Pawlik, K., Rosenzweig, M. (Eds.): International Handbook of Psychology. Sage Publications, London et al. 2000, pp. 136-149.

[RaRa85] Ray, W., Ravizza, R.: Methods Toward a Science of Behavior and Experience. Second Edition. Wadsworth Publishing Company, Belmont, California 1985.

[RaRi93] Ray, M., Rinzler, A. (Eds.): The New Paradigm in Business. Emerging Strategies for Leadership and Organizational Change. G. P. Putnam's Sons, New York 1993.

[Reis99] Reisberg, D.: Learning. In: Wilson, R., Keil, F. (Eds.): The MIT Encyclopedia of the Cognitive Sciences. The MIT Press, Cambridge, Massachusetts/London 1999, pp. 460-461.

[ReKr96] Rehäuser, J., Krcmar, H.: Wissensmanagement im Unternehmen. In: Schreyögg, G., Conrad, P. (Eds.): Managementforschung 6. Wissensmanagement. Walter de Gruyter, Berlin/New York 1996, pp. 1-40.

[ReSc99] Reilly, R., Schweihs, R.: Valuing Intangible Assets. McGraw-Hill, New York et al. 1999.

[RiLF98] Riffe, D., Lacy, S., Fico, F.: Analyzing Media Messages. Using Quantitative Content Analysis in Research. Lawrence Erlbaum Associates, Mahwah, New Jersey/London 1998.

[RiSi99] Rickheit, G., Sichelschmidt, L.: Mental Models: Some Answers, Some Questions, Some Suggestions. In: Rickheit, G., Habel, C. (Eds.): Mental Models in Discourse Processing and Reasoning. Elsevier, Amsterdam et al. 1999.

[Robi97] Robinett, R.: Quantum Mechanics. Classical Results, Modern Systems, and Visualized Examples. Oxford University Press, New York/Oxford 1997.

[Rock75] Rock, I.: An Introduction to Perception. Macmillan Publishing, New York 1975.

[RoFi02] Roithmayr, F., Fink, K.: The Knowledge Organization. Presentation at SAP Business School Vienna, September 2002.

[RoFi97] Roithmayr, F., Fink, K.: Know-how-Unternehmen. In: WIRTSCHAFTS-INFORMATIK 39 (1997) 5, pp. 503-506.

[RoFi98] Roithmayr, F., Fink, K.: Information and Communication Systems for Know-how-Collaboration in a Global Market Place. Know-how-Collaboration is more than the Exchange of Information. In: China International Business Symposium. Shanghai 1998, pp. 476-483.

[RoFi99a] Roithmayr, F., Fink, K.: Case Study "M". Department Value Process Management/Information Systems, University of Innsbruck. Part A, 1999.

[RoFi99b] Roithmayr, F., Fink, K.: Case Study "M". Department Value Process Management/Information Systems, University of Innsbruck. Part B, 1999.

[RoFi99c] Roithmayr, F., Fink, K.: Case Study "M". Department Value Process Management/Information Systems, University of Innsbruck. Part C, 1999.

[Rone88] Ronen, Y.: The Role of Uncertainties. In: Ronen, Y. (Ed.): Uncertainty Analysis. CRC Press, Boca Raton 1988, pp. 2-39.

[Rowl00] Rowley, J.: From Learning Organization to Knowledge Entrepreneur. In: Journal of Knowledge Management. Volume 4, Number 1, 2000, pp. 7-15.

[RuBP98] Ruspini, E., Bonissone, P., Pedrycz, W. (Eds.): Handbook of Fuzzy Computation. Institute of Physics Publishing, Bristol/Philadelphia 1998.

[Rugg97] Ruggels, R.: Knowledge Management Tools. Butterworth-Heinemann, Boston et al. 1997.

[RuNo95] Russell, S., Norvig, P.: Artificial Intelligence. A Modern Approach. Prentice Hall, Upper Saddle River, New Jersey 1995.

[Rusk93a] Rusk, R.: Velocity. In: Parker S. (Ed.): McGraw-Hill Encyclopedia of Physics. Second Edition. McGraw-Hill, New York et al. 1993, pp. 1501-1502.

[Rusk93b] Rusk, R.: Speed. In: Parker S. (Ed.): McGraw-Hill Encyclopedia of Physics. Second Edition. McGraw-Hill, New York et al. 1993, p. 1327.

[SaAN02] Sarker, R., Abbass, H., Newton, C.: Heuristics & Optimization for Knowledge Discovery. Idea Group Publishing, Hershey et al. 2002.

[SaSZ97] Sanchez, E., Shibata, T., Zadeh, L.: Genetic Algorithms and Fuzzy Logic Systems. Soft Computing Perspectives. World Scientific, Singapore et al. 1997.

[ScAA00] Schreiber, G., Akkermans, H., Anjewierden, A., de Hoog, R., Shadbolt, N., Van de Velde, W., Wielinga, B.: Knowledge Engineering and Management. The CommonKADS Methodology. The MIT Press, Cambridge, Massachusetts/London 2000.

[Scha99] Schacter, D.: Implicit vs. Explicit Memory. In: Wilson, R., Keil, F. (Eds.): The MIT Encyclopedia of the Cognitive Sciences. The MIT Press, Cambridge, Massachusetts/London 1999, pp. 394-395.

[Sche01] Scheibeler, A.: Balanced Scorecard for KMU. Kennzahlenermittlung mit ISO 9001:2000 leicht gemacht. Springer Verlag, Berlin/Heidelberg 2001.

[Schm93] Schmidt, P.: Momentum. In: Parker, S. (Ed.): McGraw-Hill Encyclopedia of Physics. Second Edition, McGraw-Hill, New York et al. 1993, p. 812.

[Schö82] Schön, D.: The Reflective Practitioner. How Professionals Think in Action. Basic Books, New York 1982.

[Scho89] Schommers, W. (Ed.): Quantum Theory and Pictures of Reality. Springer Verlag, Berlin et al. 1989.

[Schr83] Schrödinger, E.: The Present Situation in Quantum Mechanics: A Translation of Schrödinger's "Cat Paradox" Paper. In: Wheeler, J., Zurek, W. (Eds.): Quantum Theory and Measurement. Princeton University Press, Princeton, New Jersey 1983, pp. 152-167.

[ScIn71] Schoeninger, D., Insko, C.: Introductory Statistics for the Behavioral Sciences. Allyn and Bacon, Boston 1971.

[SeBl85] Sekuler, R., Blake, R.: Perception. Alfred A. Knopf, New York 1985.

[Seng90] Senge, P.: The Fifth Discipline. The Art & Practice of The Learning Organization. Currency Doubleday, New York et al. 1990.

[SiKa89] Simon, H., Kaplan, C.: Foundations of Cognitive Science. In: Posner, M. (Ed.): Foundations of Cognitive Science. The MIT Press, Cambridge, Massachusetts 1989.

[Simo99] Simon, H.: Problem Solving. In: Wilson, R., Keil, F. (Eds.): The MIT Encyclopedia of the Cognitive Sciences. The MIT Press, Cambridge, Massachusetts/London 1999, pp. 674-676.

[Sing97] Singh, J.: Quantum Mechanics. Fundamentals and Applications to Technology. John Wiley & Sons, New York et al. 1997.

[Skyr00] Skyrme, D.: New Metrics: Does it all Add up? In: Despres, C., Chauvel, D. (Eds.): Knowledge Horizons. The Present and the Promise of Knowledge Management. Butterworth-Heinemann, Boston et al. 2000, pp. 307-323.

[Skyr98] Skyrme, D.: Measuring the Value of Knowledge. Metrics for the Knowledge-Based Business. Business Intelligence, London 1998.

[Skyr99] Skyrme, D.: Knowledge Networking. Creating the Collaborative Enterprise. Butterworth-Heinemann, Oxford et al. 1999.

[Smit95] Smith, W.: The Quantum Enigma. Finding the Hidden Key. Sherwood Sugden & Company, Peru, Illinois 1995.

[SpHi99] Sperber, D., Hischfeld, L.: Culture, Cognition and Evolution. In: Wilson, R., Keil, F. (Eds.): The MIT Encyclopedia of the Cognitive Sciences. The MIT Press, Cambridge, Massachusetts/London 1999, cxi-cxxxii.

[Star97] Starbuck, W.: Learning by Knowledge-Intensive Firms. In: Prusak, L. (Ed.): Knowledge in Organizations. Butterworth-Heinemann, Boston et al. 1997, pp. 147-175.

[StBe02] Standing, C., Benson, S.: An Issues Framework for the Role of Organisational Culture and Climate in Knowledge Management. In: Khosrow-Pour, M. (Ed.): Issues and Trends of Information Technology Management in Contemporary Organizations. Volume 1, Idea Group Publishing, Hershey et al. 2002, pp. 647-651.

[Stew97] Stewart, T.: Intellectual Capital. The New Wealth of Organizations. Doubleday Currency, New York et al. 1997.

[StRi00] Steane, A., Rieffel, E.: Beyond Bits: The Future of Quantum Information Processing. In: Computer, January 2000, pp. 38-45.

[StSR01] Stern, J., Shiely, J., Ross, I.: The EVA Challenge. Implementing Value-Added Change in an Organization. John Wiley & Sons, New York et al. 2001.

[Sull00] Sullivan, P.: Value-Driven Intellectual Capital. How to Convert Intangible Corporate Assets into Market Value. John Wiley & Sons, New York et al. 2000.

[Summ83] Summerfield, A.: Recording Social Interaction. In: Dowrick, P., Biggs, S. (Eds.): Using Video. Psychological and Social Applications. John Wiley & Sons, Chichester et al. 1983, pp. 3-11.

[Svei02a] Sveiby, K.: Methods for Measuring Intangible Assets. http://www.sveiby.com/articles/IntangibleMethods.htm, Date 2002-11-29.

[Svei02b] Sveiby, K.: The Balanced Scorecard (BSC) and the Intangible Asset Monitor - A Comparison. http://www.sveiby.com/articles/BSCandIAM.html, Date 2002-09-11.

[Svei97] Sveiby, K.: The New Organizational Wealth. Managing and Measuring Knowledge-Based Assets. Berrett-Koehler Publishers, San Francisco 1997.

[Thag88] Thagard, P.: Dimensions of Analogy. In: Helman, D. (Ed.): Analogical Reasoning. Perspectives of Artificial Intelligence, Cognitive Science, and Philosophy. Kluwer Academic Publishers, Dordrecht et al. 1988, pp. 105-124.

[TiAD00] Tissen, R., Andriessen, D., Deprez, F.: The Knowledge Dividend. Creating High-Performance Companies through Value-Based Knowledge Management. Prentice Hall, London et al. 2000.

[Tiwa00] Tiwana, A.: The Knowledge Management Toolkit. Practical Techniques for Building Knowledge Management System. Prentice Hall, Upper Saddle River, New Jersey 2000.

[Tiwa01] Tiwana, A.: The Essential Guide to Knowledge Management. E-Business and CRM Applications. Prentice Hall, Upper Saddle River, New Jersey 2001.

[Tobi71] Tobin, J.: Essays in Economics. Volume 1: Macroeconomics. North-Holland Publishing Company, Amsterdam et al. 1971.

[Tobi75] Tobin, J.: Essays in Economics. Volume 2: Consumption and Econometrics. North-Holland Publishing Company, Amsterdam et al. 1975.

[Toma99] Tomasello, M.: The Cultural Origins of Human Cognition. Harvard University Press, Cambridge, Massachusetts/London 1999.

[Torg58] Torgerson, W.: Theory and Methods of Scaling. John Wiley & Sons, New York 1958.

[TrCo00] Transnational College of LEX: What is Quantum Mechanics? A Physics Adventure. Language Research Foundation, Boston 2000.

[TrHa98] Trompenaars, F., Hampden-Turner, C.: Riding the Waves of Culture. Understanding Diversity in Global Business. Second Edition. McGraw-Hill, New York et al. 1998.

[TvKa86] Tversky, A., Kahneman, D.: Judgment Under Uncertainty: Heuristics and Biases. In: Arkes, H., Hammond, K. (Eds.): Judgment and Decision Making: An Interdisciplinary Reader. Cambridge University Press, Cambridge et al. 1986, pp. 38-55.

[Vier87] Viertl, R.: Probability and Bayesian Statistics. Plenum Press, New York/ London 1987.

[WaMa01] Walker, G., MacDonald, R.: Designing and Implementing an HR Scorecard. In: Human Resource Management. Volume 40, No. 4, Winter 2001, pp. 365-377.

[WaPl02] Wang, F., Plaskoff, J.: An integrated Development Model for KM. In: Bellaver, R., Lusa, J. (Eds.): Knowledge Management Strategy and Technology. Artech House, Boston/London 2002, pp. 113-134.

[Weil93] Weil, J.: Units of Measurement. In: Parker S. (Ed.): McGraw-Hill Encyclopedia of Physics. Second Edition. McGraw-Hill, New York et al. 1993, pp. 1493-1499.

[Wert99] Wertsch, J.: Vygotsky, Lev Semenovich. In: Wilson, R., Keil, F. (Eds.): The MIT Encyclopedia of the Cognitive Sciences. The MIT Press, Cambridge, Massachusetts/London 1999, pp. 878-879.

[WeWW01] Welty, J., Wicks, C., Wilson, R., Rorrer, G.: Fundamentals of Momentum, Heat, and Mass Transfer. Fourth Edition. John Wiley & Sons, New York et al. 2001.

[Whit02] White, D.: Knowledge Mapping & Management. IRM Press, Hershey et al. 2002.

[Whit68] Whitla, D.: Handbook of Measurement and Assessment in Behavioral Sciences. Addison-Wesley, Reading, Massachusetts et al. 1968.

[WiCi94] Whishaw, B., Cioe, J.: Brain. In: Ramachandran, V. (Ed.): Encyclopedia of Human Behavior. Volume 4, Academic Press, San Diego et al. 1994, pp. 425-434.

[Wick95] Wick, D.: The Infamous Boundary: Seven Decades of Controversy in Quantum Physics. Birkhäuser, Boston 1995.

[Wiig00] Wiig, K.: Knowledge Management: An Emerging Discipline Rooted in a Long History. In: Despres, C., Chauvel, D. (Eds.): Knowledge Horizons. The Present and the Promise of Knowledge Management. Butterworth-Heinemann, Boston et al. 2000, pp. 3-26.

[WiKe99] Wilson, R., Keil, F.: The MIT Encyclopedia of the Cognitive Sciences. The MIT Press, Cambridge, Massachusetts/London 1999.

[Wils99a] Wilson, R.: Philosophy. In: Wilson, R., Keil, F. (Eds.): The MIT Encyclopedia of the Cognitive Sciences. The MIT Press, Cambridge, Massachusetts/London 1999, pp. xv-xxxvii.

[Wils99b] Wilson, M.: Descartes René. In: Wilson, R., Keil, F. (Eds.): The MIT Encyclopedia of the Cognitive Sciences. The MIT Press, Cambridge, Massachusetts/London 1999, pp. 229-230.

[Wu86] Wu, T.: Quantum Mechanics. World Scientific, Singapore 1986.

[Zade99] Zadeh, L.: Fuzzy Logic. In: Wilson, R., Keil, F. (Eds.): The MIT Encyclopedia of the Cognitive Sciences. The MIT Press, Cambridge, Massachusetts/London 1999, pp. 335-336.

[ZaWh00] Zairi, M., Whymark, J.: The Transfer of Best Practices: How to Build a Culture of Benchmarking and Continuous Learning - Part 1. In: Benchmarking: An International Journal. Volume 7, No. 1, 2000, pp. 62-78.

[Zoha97] Zohar, D.: Rewiring the Corporate Brain. Using the New Science to Rethink How We Structure and Lead Organizations. Berrett-Koehler, San Francisco 1997.

Index

L

M

T

U

V

W

GPSR Compliance
The European Union's (EU) General Product Safety Regulation (GPSR) is a set of rules that requires consumer products to be safe and our obligations to ensure this.

If you have any concerns about our products, you can contact us on

ProductSafety@springernature.com

In case Publisher is established outside the EU, the EU authorized representative is:

Springer Nature Customer Service Center GmbH
Europaplatz 3
69115 Heidelberg, Germany

www.ingramcontent.com/pod-product-compliance
Lightning Source LLC
Chambersburg PA
CBHW071410050326
40689CB00010B/1816

* 9 7 8 3 8 2 4 4 2 1 8 3 1 *